The Anatomy of Jazz

Leroy Ostransky

THE ANATOMY OF JAZZ

GREENWOOD PRESS, PUBLISHERS
WESTPORT, CONNECTICUT

781.5
O85a

Library of Congress Cataloging in Publication Data

Ostransky, Leroy.
   The anatomy of jazz.

   Reprint of the ed. published by University of
Washington Press, Seattle.
   Bibliography: p.
   1. Jazz music. I. Title.
[ML3561.J309 1973]   781.5'7   73-11857
ISBN 0-8371-7092-3

To Natalie

PREFACE

T<small>HIS BOOK IS AN ATTEMPT,</small> first, to present jazz in its proper perspective to those whose primary interest is in "serious" or classical music, and to relate jazz theory to music theory in general; second, to introduce those whose primary interest is in jazz to the problems of nonjazz composers and performers by relating jazz to the history of music in general. Finally, I have tried to indicate to jazzmen what I believe to be their present position in music, as well as their musical responsibility to the future.

As is often the case when setting out to conciliate opposing forces, the would-be conciliator finds that, instead of being met with good will, he is himself belabored by both camps, and he learns to his dismay that apparently very few want, or see the need for, conciliation. When his explanations are intended for one side they are sure to seem elementary and redundant to the other, especially when each side heeds carefully only what is being addressed to the other side. What he considers the main strength of each side is often interpreted (by the opposing side) as its main weakness, and his seemingly endless parleying, however honorably intentioned, only serves to emphasize what must seem like irreconcilable differences. This is, of course, the chance he takes. All he can hope is that after the two sides have finished dealing with him and return to their primary targets—each other—some small points overlooked earlier will seem to need further clarification and reconsideration; he can hope that something he implied or suggested or stated openly will result in new lines of questioning.

Mainly, this book is an introduction, and I have not attempted to be exhaustive. It is quite likely, however, that I have emphasized certain aspects of jazz and classical music to the prejudice of other, perhaps important, aspects. I have tried to cover a lot of ground, and I can recall running sometimes, walking other times, and occasionally crawling, and readers will no doubt find areas that seem untraversed. Books have been written, and will continue to be written, on subjects to which I have devoted a chapter, or even only a few paragraphs. John Mehegan, for example, has recently completed the first volume of a two-volume work on improvisation, and Paul Oliver has a book on the blues in preparation. Perhaps Oliver's book will explore the many aspects of jazz singing, a subject I have not touched upon. Jazz singing of course has not developed and advanced in the same sense instrumental jazz has; and in the past twenty years—since the death of the incomparable Bessie Smith—there has been no development of jazz singing. For this reason I believe the subject of jazz singing will eventually, and properly, come under the classification of folk music studies. The position of ragtime has also been a point of concern; like jazz singing, it has had no development, the work of pianists like Wally Rose and Ralph Sutton notwithstanding. I believe ragtime is a music that flourished alongside jazz, and that while on occasion it served the same function as jazz—and was even performed by major jazz figures—it is nonetheless a musical phenomenon distinct from jazz and deserves the high degree of exclusive care and attention it has received from Rudi Blesh and Harriet Janis.

This may also be the proper place to suggest that Dixieland is not so much a special style of jazz, or technique of playing jazz, as it is a spirit of performance. Dixieland rooters often refer to their music as "happy" music, and rightly so. Probably its main quality is its brisk, often effervescent exuberance; exuberance, however, is not a technical quality. This is not to say that Dixieland has not been a force in jazz; it has. I believe that I have stated clearly, in the chapters on New Orleans style and preswing, the way that Dixieland has contributed to the development of jazz. Followers of the happy music will perhaps feel that I have not given it its proper due. I do not question its popularity or the enthusiasm of its devotees. If I do not dwell on Dixieland in this book it is because this book is, in many ways, a technical book, and the technique of Dixieland—"old and new," as some put it—is most easily observed in New Orleans style and, later, in swing. As a final note to the problem of distinguishing between Dixieland as a musical style and Dixieland style as a spirit of performance, I refer the reader to what may well be the nadir of the Dixieland influence: the recent recording "Lawrence Welk Plays Dixieland," (Coral).

If I mention Art Tatum at this point it is only because I wish to forestall someone's saying that this is a book on jazz that mentions Lawrence Welk but neglects Art Tatum, Fats Waller, Fate Marable, Larry Marable, and Chano Pozo, not to mention the Lunceford band of 1935. Tatum is one of the most distinguished jazz pianists of all time, and the Lunceford band of 1935 helped make history. I must, however, take an author's refuge behind the book's introductory nature.

I wish to express acknowledgment and thanks to the publishers who have granted permission to quote excerpts, as follows:

Bregman, Vocco and Conn, Inc., from the song "It's Sand, Man"; The Citadel Press, from *Jazz: A People's Music* by Sidney Finkelstein, copyright 1948; for excerpts from an article reprinted from "That Old Gang of Mine" by Richard Gehman, a chapter in *Eddie Condon's Treasury of Jazz*, copyright 1956 by Eddie Condon and Richard Gehman, and used with the permission of the publishers, The Dial Press; E. P. Dutton and Co., Inc., from *Jazz: Hot and Hybrid* by Winthrop Sargeant, copyright 1946;

Grove Press, Inc., from *Jazz: Its Evolution and Essence* by Andre Hodeir; excerpts from the song "Tight Like This" by A. Curl, copyright MCMXXIX, MCMXLVII by Leeds Music Corporation, 322 West 48th Street, New York, N.Y., reprinted by permission, all rights reserved; W. W. Norton and Company, Inc., from *American Jazz Music* by Wilder Hobson; Oxford University Press, Inc., from *Hungarian Folk Music* by Béla Bartók, and *The Story of Jazz* by Marshall Stearns; Rinehart and Company, Inc., from *Hear Me Talkin' to Ya* by Nat Shapiro and Nat Hentoff, and from *The Jazz Makers* by the same authors; Silhouette Music Corp., from the song "Tour de Force" in *Dizzy Gillespie World Statesman;* The Stackpole Company, from *The Kingdom of Swing* by Benny Goodman and Irving Kolodin; and The Viking Press, Inc., from *A History of Jazz in America* by Barry Ulanov.

I am indebted to Mr. Murray Morgan for a critical reading of early chapters of the manuscript, for his encouragement, and for his many helpful suggestions.

I wish to thank Mr. Edmund C. Barnard for the use of his early Duke Ellington records; Mr. Leo Herzog for his help in locating record information; Mr. Allan L. Overland for the use of his Count Basie records; Mr. Richard Weeks and Radio Station KTAC for the use of their collection of New Orleans records; and Miss Edith Anderson, of the Record Shop, for the general use of her jazz record collection.

I wish to express my appreciation to Sheldon Harris and

the Institute of Jazz Studies, Inc., for help in checking references in out-of-print periodicals.

I owe a particular debt to Mr. Warren Perry, librarian at the University of Puget Sound, and his staff for their special efforts in locating out-of-print materials. I am further indebted to the staff of the Tacoma Public Library for the special use of their jazz book collection.

Finally, I wish to thank Mr. and Mrs. Allen Petrich for the use of their house on Fox Island, Washington, where most of this book was written.

LEROY OSTRANSKY

November, 1959
University of Puget Sound
Tacoma, Washington

CONTENTS

1	*Some Early Difficulties*	*3*
2	*Toward a Definition of Jazz*	*23*
3	*Understanding Improvisation*	*46*
4	*The Musical Elements of Jazz*	*85*
5	*Understanding Style*	*122*
6	*New Orleans Style*	*148*
7	*Preswing*	*185*
8	*Swing*	*223*
9	*The Modern Era*	*254*
10	*Toward the Future*	*305*
	Notes	*333*
	A Selected Jazz Bibliography	*345*
	Index	*357*

The Anatomy of Jazz

It is . . . our responsibility to help the students see the music of any given period in the light of its own social, political and cultural climate; to understand that the esthetic laws and technical considerations of one period cannot be superimposed upon another; to make known to the student the varying convictions of leading musicians, both past and present, in order to help him make his own judgments; to learn that art is not concerned with conformity; to equip the student to deal with the novel without ridicule or fear of its strangeness, yet without being impressed by sheer novelty, and with the ability to probe the depths of the unfamiliar.

The Juilliard Report on Teaching
the Literature and Materials of
Music, 1953

chapter 1

SOME EARLY
DIFFICULTIES

As RECENTLY AS TEN YEARS ago, technical jazz analysis had been given little serious or systematic thought. The prime reason for this lack of thoughtful analysis may be found in the analyses and evaluations made by jazz writers who apparently had difficulty in making themselves understood. The language of jazz was coined, for the most part, by jazz musicians with little regard for the written word, or by well-meaning writers with little technical knowledge of music in general, or—and worst of all—by a small but influential school of semiliterate enthusiasts whose main interest seemed to lie not in furthering jazz itself, but in merchandising the adjuncts of jazz: records, horns, bop berets, and tired stock arrangements. Aimed at adolescents and jungle intellects, the language of this last group jangled with nouns and verbs that carried little meaning and adjectives that, while scarcely descriptive, were on the whole redundant. Unable to make even an attempt at straightforward musical analysis (or, for that matter, to write a straightforward sentence), they adopted a gibbering prose calculated to hide the thinness of their analysis and evaluation.

With the establishment in 1934 of *Down Beat*, a jazz magazine, there was hope for serious discussion of the subject, a hope soon betrayed, for the editors aimed their publication at adolescent jazz fans and conceived their function to be that of serving the jazz industry as movie magazines served Hollywood. Until the swing era, there was little mention of jazz in popular magazines of national circulation, and whatever notice jazz received in the daily press was—its scantiness notwithstanding—pejorative and a little absurd. Jazz buffs therefore welcomed the new publication sight unseen, only to find its critical writing a disappointment. Serious jazz students, who had little to choose from among the writing on jazz before *Down Beat*, soon learned not to expect much of *Down Beat* either. Nat Hentoff, a former associate editor of *Down Beat*, summed up the magazine's twenty-five years of publication when he said:

> *Down Beat* is especially shallow and is apparently geared for less advanced high school sophomores.
> . . . Critical and historical jazz writing does appear to be slowly improving, but fervid amateurism is apt to be predominant for some time, because the fan-writer is well entrenched. As long as *Down Beat* remains the "bible" of the field, the writing will be of a caliber more appropriate to revealed religion than to responsible criticism.[1]

4

Some Early Difficulties

Because of their inability to write on jazz as music, writers for most of the popular jazz journals turned their hands to grinding out deadline record reviews and uncovering sensational biographical data that were then translated into trite but shocking headlines; or they concocted diffuse, sophomoric think-pieces intended to show why the jazz musician is a nice guy or a bad guy or simply a misunderstood guy who never got the breaks until the writer discovered him in a tired but happy moment.

The language problem is one thing, but wrong-headed intolerance is another. For some time now there has been a tendency among jazz writers to look down upon anyone who doesn't "dig" jazz. Their attitude toward the uninitiated layman has often been one of indifference. But their attitude toward classical musicians has been one of intolerance—not just a passive intolerance, but an active one. In its most primitive form, this intolerance manifests itself in simple name-calling; in a somewhat higher form it appears in the condescension apparent in the following items. The first compares the musical intelligence of the classical musician to that of the jazzman.

CAT ON KEYS

New York—Drummer Osie Johnson was telling of the time a group of classical musicians were gathered in a jazzman's home, and the latter put some Charlie Parker records on the phonograph.

After a few seconds, one of the classical men protested: "Come on now, fix the machine. That motor's obviously going too fast. Nobody can play that many notes so fast." The jazzman took great and obvious delight in proving that there was nothing at all wrong with the machine.[2]

The second is a three-column headline of an article on recording studios which reminds its readers: "Classics Recorders Just Discovering Something Jazz Fans Found Out Early." [3]

Square or classical musicians, finding themselves patronized by the self-appointed defenders of jazz, were unlikely to seek to overcome their feeling of alienation from jazz. The tone of *Down Beat* helped cement many of the squares into four-square blocks of antagonism toward all jazz. It is a happy circumstance that many serious musicians are able to disregard the rather obvious insinuations of petty jazz writers who, to retaliate for fancied snubs, attack with their fists flying in the name of defending jazz. There are many first-rate musicians who believe it is possible, and even desirable, to study, understand, and enjoy the work of Armstrong as well as the work of Bach; the work of Mozart as well as the work of Thelonious Monk. Such musicians (and it would seem that jazz has need of many) may be amused at the ineptness of undistinguished jazz reporters, but they are less likely to be amused when a critic of André Hodeir's reputation and sensitivity asks a question such as this: "Isn't it true that those who prefer the Beethoven work [*Ninth Symphony*] confess implicitly their inability to understand Stravinsky's masterpiece [*Le Sacre du Printemps*]?" [4]

If Hodeir means to imply by his question that there are musicians who prefer Beethoven to Stravinsky, or that there are musicians who believe there is something unnatural about any music that is not German, then he should say so. No one will question this. If, however, his question is to be taken at face value, it seems to indicate an inability on Hodeir's part to recognize the distinctions between comprehension, appreciation, and enjoyment. A respectable number of classical musicians understand fully the nature of Stravinsky's work, but nevertheless prefer Beethoven's *Ninth Symphony* to Stravinsky's *Le Sacre*—and if not Beethoven's *Ninth*, then a Bach suite perhaps, or a Mozart divertimento, a Schubert song, a Chopin étude. Moreover, there can be no doubt that many musicians, and laymen as well, not only do not prefer *Le Sacre*, but do not understand it; neither is there any doubt, in my mind at least, that there are a good many who prefer Beethoven's *Ninth* and don't understand *it*, either. The fact remains that it is not necessary to understand a work in order to like it; or, to put it another way: a musician may have a comprehensive understanding and appreciation of a work—jazz or otherwise—without liking it. The failure to understand this principle—perhaps the guiding principle in critical evaluation—is part of the reason for the apparent schism between some well-known jazz critics and contemporary classical musicians who evince an interest in jazz.

Jazz has reached an important stage in its growth. In the past decade it has finally attracted a number of men of literary taste and musical perception, and this favorable climate must be maintained. Jazz needs the aid and interest of historians, theorists, composers, estheticians—anyone willing to lend his support, knowledge, and experience to the task of establishing jazz as a significant part of music. Jazz is an important branch of music, of American music especially; as such, it must be allowed to flourish, cultivated by respectful consideration and intensive study. Much has been done in the past ten years toward this goal: the inauguration of jazz study groups and institutes, for example, and the recognition of jazz as a subject for study in institutions of higher learning. Of the highest significance, also, is the probing look backward by men of appropriate intellectual habits, men who feel the compulsion to take the study of jazz out of the shadows of semiliterateness and anti-intellectualism and place it in the light of serious and searching study.

Jazz has at last become respectable. But in order to understand the origins of its present-day problems—semantic and otherwise—it is necessary to survey, however briefly, early jazz criticism. As long ago as 1946, Winthrop Sargeant wrote: "There has been a great deal of dubious and highly confusing writing around the subject of jazz. Probably no musical movement in history has been made the subject of more leaky speculation. . . ." [5] Many critics have since echoed, in more or less detail, Sargeant's view. In order to show the scope of the work still to be done, I have listed the following representative statements, which, I believe, pose the most important problems faced by present-day jazz writers and theorists. Morroe Berger, a Columbia University fellow in sociology, wrote in 1946:

Some Early Difficulties

The origins of jazz and the story of its spread, as well as the careers of its players, are all subjects about which there is still considerable question. The importance of these matters is, in addition, not limited to music itself, or to the interest of collectors or to the reputation of musicians; they are significant, also, for the problems of the origins and diffusion of culture, and racial interaction, which involve other arts as well as some sciences.[6]

In 1955 Keepnews and Grauer commented on the growing importance and complexities of jazz in America:

Perhaps the truest measure of the validity of jazz is that it can be all things to all men: a mild form of amusement; an emotional or an intellectual stimulant; an art form; a social commentary; a cult; something to like, love, or even hate for a wide variety of esthetic, emotional or social reasons. Thus jazz is both simple (no more than the combinations of notes you hear) and incredibly complex (as complex as human beings and as the world we inhabit). And thus it is a fit subject for all the analysis, history, biography, criticism, and written what-have-you that has been built up alongside it.[7]

In 1956 Jacques Barzun emphasized the difficulty we are concerned with:

It [jazz] ranks with sports and philately as the realm of the self-made expert and of the controversialist as well, for musicology has not yet settled all the historical, stylistic, and biographical problems that have been raised about it.[8]

In 1957 Shapiro and Hentoff summed up the question: "Since jazz musicians are notoriously inarticulate verbally, a good deal of analytical and creative writing about jazz during the past three decades has been speculative, fanciful, romantic and wrong." [9]

9

Shapiro and Hentoff's statement brings us back to the semantic problem. It is sometimes easy for us to forget how new the language of jazz is, and quite frequently how subjective the meanings are of even its most established terms. "One of the difficulties of describing an elusive music like jazz," Whitney Balliett has said, "is a made-at-home terminology that includes such aimless and largely inscrutable brand names as 'swing,' 'bebop,' and 'Dixieland.' " [10]

To say nothing of "jazz." Although the word "jazz" was undoubtedly in use for a good many years before 1914, it was not until then, according to Nick La Rocca, founder of the Original Dixieland Jazz Band, that "jazz" appeared in an advertisement. "The Original Dixieland Jazz Band," he wrote to Nicolas Slonimsky, "was the first band in the world to be called a Jazz Band. Our first billing was in the year of 1914, month of March, place Boosters Club, Chicago, Illinois, Manager Harry James." Two years later *Variety* wrote, "Chicago has added another innovation to its list of discoveries in the so-called 'Jazz Bands.' " According to Slonimsky, this may be the first mention of the word "jazz" in print. A year after the *Variety* item appeared, the Victor Company issued their first jazz record (March, 1917), and in 1918 the Columbia Phonograph Company issued its first jazz record, "Darktown Strutters Ball" and "Indiana," played by the Original Dixieland Jass Band.[11]

Conjecture on the derivation of the word "jazz" (or "jass") has ranged widely. The term has been variously considered as a corruption of "Charles" by way of "Chas," "jass," "jazz"; a diminution of *"jaser,"* that is, to exhilarate; and some linguistic scholars claim to have traced its origins to West Africa. In the early days of jazz writing, it may have seemed more profitable to seek the linguistic origins of jazz than to try to define it. Once it was out of its infancy, however, little could be said of its linguistic origins that had not been said before, and critics—the apt and inept alike—set about defining, or not defining, jazz.

Many of those attempting to define jazz took advantage of the elusiveness of the term by using jazz as a springboard for sociological, psychological, and anthropological speculations, without once recognizing that jazz is music; nevertheless, many of these critics have made some contribution to the understanding of jazz. Before we attempt to search out the musical aspects of jazz, it might be well to acknowledge the work of those social critics who had a hand in creating the image of jazz still dominant in the minds of many people. These are the critics who have, in the main, produced the miasmatic atmosphere in which jazzmen often have had to perform. These are the critics who have stamped their opinions and attitudes upon the jazz-uninformed reading public and have made it difficult, and sometimes impossible, to convince the uninitiated of the worth of jazz, or to persuade them to accept the analysis of jazz as a serious and worthy enterprise.

For the social critics of jazz and the people they have influenced, the years between 1920 and 1929 were the cru-

11

cial years, the years when all good men strode onto the field of Armageddon, pen in hand, to conquer the evil forces of jazz. It is therefore natural to search for the corpus of social criticism of jazz in the writings of Jazz Age critics—not because its critics were unmusical (or, in some cases, not even American), but because their criticism reflects the literate viewpoint of sincere writers and jazz-innocent readers at the time when first impressions of jazz were being formed.

In 1920 Harold Spender, a representative critic of American mores and author of *A Briton in America,* was led to believe that many of the jazz tunes he had heard were African in origin. This caused him painful concern. If we were not careful, American musical tradition might be "submerged by the aboriginal music of the negro," and, if we insisted on stomping along such "semibarbaric paths," heaven knows where we would end up.[12] But Harold Spender, the Englishman, was a mild fellow indeed compared with a critic whom I shall call "The Amazing American." That author, who preferred to remain nameless, wrote a provocative study ingeniously entitled "The Amazing American," in which—and his lack of comprehension did not deter him a bit—he spoke of jazz, among other evils. The place of America in the future spiritual scheme of things was, he opined, assured. Any nation capable of producing the "nigger minstrel, rag-time music and the tango dance," was close to the top. His indictment of jazz, however, is spiritless compared to his brilliantly indiscriminating castigation of American culture in general. In 1925 he wrote:

> In deathless page, in song, in art, America has contributed but little to the world's treasury. If that land were to cease to be to-morrow, its most flattering epitaph would be the sign of the dollar chiselled in the stone. . . . It is a land of flesh-pots, with no great national aim speaking through a national art. . . . The general attitude of the American mind is in deadly opposition to culture.[13]

Outbursts of this sort were not uncommon even among authors who signed their work. At about the same time, the distinguished writer Aldous Huxley had a go at us. He said much the same thing as the others, but with more style. Here, in jazz prose, is a sample from his book, *Jesting Pilate: An Intellectual Holiday:*

> Jazz it up, jazz it up. Keep moving. Step on the gas. Say it with dancing. The Charleston, the Baptists. Radios and Revivals. Uplift and Gilda Gray. The pipe organ, the nigger with the saxophone, the Giant Marimbaphone. Hymns and the movies and Irving Berlin. Petting Parties and the First Free United Episcopal Methodist Church. Jazz it up! [14]

If laid end to end, all the jazz-inspired, pointed-finger, stream-of-licentiousness pieces of the twenties on the debilitating effects of wine, women, and jazz would span the distance from New Orleans to New York—by way of Memphis, Kansas City, and Chicago—and back again. Jazz, for critics in the twenties, was a social manifestation, not a musical one. For anyone interested in jazz as music, the critical climate promised little sunshine.

13

The slow progress in jazz analysis is probably due chiefly to the confusion of jazz with commercial popular music. It is scarcely credible nowadays that certain writers of the Jazz Age were unable to recognize that jazz is a manner of performance rather than a collection of Tin Pan Alley tunes. Nevertheless, such was the case, and this confusion resulted in establishing men like Paul Whiteman, George Gershwin, and Irving Berlin at the top of the jazz hierarchy. By now, of course, their place in jazz is clear; their place in popular music even clearer. But in the twenties the confusion—even in the minds of otherwise acute writers— enabled Whiteman to attain the unchallenged position of King of Jazz. For the general public the songs of Berlin and Gershwin, as played by the Whiteman band, had enough characteristics in common with whatever fragments of jazz they knew to seem to be much the same thing. Those who heard genuine jazz occasionally—the music of Armstrong, say, or Fletcher Henderson—heard these men and their groups play tunes with the same titles used by Whiteman, and they naturally assumed they were hearing a poor version of Whiteman's music. To their conditioned ears, Whiteman's "jazz" was smoother, richer, cleaner, and more civilized. In 1926, at the height of the confusion, Henry O. Osgood wrote *So This Is Jazz*, a book Whitney Balliett has happily described as "a triumphant and fascinating failure." In this work Osgood showed how it was possible to write a book on jazz without actually considering the Negro's position in jazz. Here is the premise on which Osgood's book was based:

Some Early Difficulties

Nowhere have I gone into detail about negro jazz bands. There are so many good ones, it would be hard to pick out a few for special mention. None of them, however, are as good as the best white bands, and very rarely are their best players as good as the best white virtuosos. Their playing makes up for what it may lack in smoothness and finish by abandon, dash, spirit and warmth. There are fewer trained musicians, consequently more of the improvisations and variations which characterized early jazz.[15]

Osgood was not alone in his beliefs; other, more astute writers than he made the same mistakes. In 1923, Gilbert Seldes, then a brilliant young critic with unrestrained interests and perpetually *au courant,* set about answering another critic who believed that jazz was on the way out. "Jazz, for me," Seldes wrote, in *Dial,* August, 1923, "isn't a last feverish excitement, a spasm of energy before death. It is the normal development of our resources, the expected, and wonderful, arrival of America at a point of creative intensity."

Now, that was an enthusiastic, patriotic, moving, even poetic statement, except for one thing: Seldes had little notion of what jazz was in 1923. He made the fashionable mistake of thinking that certain pieces of sheet music were jazz—good or bad—and others were not; that certain songwriters were better jazz composers than other songwriters; and that the notated melodic, harmonic, and rhythmic structure of a piece of music determined its jazz quality. Seldes is a good man to have on your side in any literary battle, but in 1923 he was not writing about jazz; he was writing about popular music. He was not yet aware that the jazz quality of a piece is determined by the manner in which it is played. Jazz is not a piece called "Tiger Rag," "St. Louis Blues," "Wang Wang Blues," or "Yes We Have No Bananas." The title determines nothing; Whiteman's recording of "Wang Wang Blues" had about as much to do with jazz as his performances of "Song of India," "By the Waters of the Minnetonka," or "Oh Katherina," with its "Ach Du lieber Augustin" introduction. Seldes, apparently unaware of this, made an extraordinary effort to show that Irving Berlin was a great jazz composer. "Mr. Berlin's masterpieces . . . in jazz," he wrote in the same article, "are *Everybody Step* and *Pack Up Your Sins*." Other of Seldes' favorites were "I'm Gonna Pin My Medal on the Girl I Left Behind" and "Someone Else May Be There While I'm Gone"; he admired these tunes because they were equally good played slow or fast. "Berlin's work," he added, "is musically interesting, and that means it has a chance to survive. I have no such confidence in *Dardanella* or *Chicago*."

Seldes then went on to distinguish between white jazz and colored jazz, and it is here that he missed the riverboat entirely. About the future of American music, he wrote, "I say the negro is not our salvation because with all my feelings for his desirable indifference to our set of conventions about emotional decency, I am on the side of civilization." Words like these from a man of Seldes' unquestionable intellect and sensitivity helped delay the unprejudiced, thoroughgoing analysis of jazz a good many years. As long as critics of Seldes' caliber and reputation continued to write about "emotional decency" and whatever it is that is not "on the side of civilization," jazz continued to seek its laurels along skid road.

In 1929, or shortly before the release of Ellington's "Wall Street Wail," P. F. Laubenstein, a serious music critic, made an attempt to present the prevailing position of jazz in an essay in the *Musical Quarterly*. Trying manfully to be objective—but not always succeeding—Laubenstein was not especially sympathetic to jazz. His essay did, however, summarize certain significant aspects of jazz and recognized certain problems of the future at a time when many hoped that jazz had no future. Here, from "Jazz—Debit and Credit," is Laubenstein's summation:

> The musical historian of the future will doubtless find his *bête noire* in this inescapable task of evaluating jazz. Indeed, many of its contemporaries there be who execrate the "stuff" as inebriate, doggerel, degenerate, ghoulish, vulturine, etc. *ad infinitum*—music, or as not music at all, bearing inherent frailties which spell its own ephemerality. Its enthusiastic devotees see in its local generation and popular cultivation the very best attestation of its truly representative American character, and from its study would derive invaluable leadings as to the direction which a national music should take. Those holding a middle ground discover in it some elements of permanent value and certain developments which must be counted as real contributions toward the progress of music.[16]

Critical onslaughts in books, journals, and magazines were, of course, the bulk of jazz criticism. In addition, the daily press, acting as if it were woefully certain that jazz would flourish under any circumstances, offered little sympathy or understanding. Until recently, jazz news consisted mostly of unfavorable criticisms by names in the news and self-styled watch and ward societies. The subject of jazz, with its popular connotations, could usually be counted on to make provocative and lively news copy. What the general reader read in the newspapers about jazz was what he wanted to believe; and what the press published reflected his opinion. He knew nothing about jazz as music, but he had a firm opinion that the men and women of jazz were degenerate and unwholesome. The average reader received (and still receives) great comfort in believing that there were people to whom he could feel superior. And much feature writing was intended to reinforce the reader's opinions. With few exceptions, it is not an easy task to find a news item of the twenties on jazz that does not speak of jazz with tongue in cheek, as a kind of drollery always good for a chuckle, if not a laugh. Overseas items, from France particularly, were always welcome and in the twenties were usually offered with heavy-handed merriment. The following headlines from the *New York Times* reflect the general public's attitude toward jazz in the Jazz Age:

Fails to Stop Jazz, Is Arrested Later [July 7, 1922]
French Police Stop Jazz Band Burial; Dead Man Wanted It in Procession, but the Mourners were Foxtrotting [October 18, 1923]
France Orders Our Jazz Players Expelled [May 31, 1924]
Isadora Duncan Plans Greek Temple for Nice; She is Reported to Have Bought the Theatre Promenade des Anglais to Fight Jazz [May 1, 1925]
Ford Wars on Jazz; Gives Party for Old Time Dances, Seeking to Revive Their Popularity [July 12, 1925]

Some Early Difficulties

American Dancer Jazzing the "Marseillaise" Angers Friendly
  Audience in Paris Music Hall [January 31, 1926]
Church Jazz Wedding Utilizes Saxophone [November 14,
  1926]
Damrosch Assails Jazz [April 17, 1928]
French Find Our Jazz Too Soul-disturbing [February 3,
  1929]

From these headlines, it would seem that nobody in the
twenties dared say a kind word for jazz. By the thirties,
however, the jazz initiate could sense that some changes
would be made. The Roosevelt administration's early efforts to lift the nation out of the Big Depression looked as
if they would work, and everything, jazz included, sud-
denly seemed brighter and more useful. Many intellectuals
sought, and found, rewards in studying America's popular
culture, and folk songs and jazz came in for a good share
of the spotlight. In 1933, the repeal of Prohibition and the
subsequent opening of many night clubs and dance halls
led to the employment of more jazz musicians and to a
wider audience for jazz. It is possible also that the general
unrest caused by events in Europe helped create a small
musical nationalism, much of which may well have been
fostered by the reports in the daily press of various actions
and pronouncements against jazz in European countries.
On March 15, 1933, the National Socialist head of the
Berlin Rundfunk forbade the broadcasting of "Negro
jazz," and on January 7, 1934, a headline in the *New York
Times* read: "Ban against Jazz Sought in Ireland." (A week
before, an Irish antijazz group had paraded in Mohall,
Ireland, with banners and posters bearing the slogan

19

"Down with Jazz and Paganism." The unruly antijazzists had been aroused by the actions of their finance minister, Sean MacEntee, who had stood by while jazz bands broadcast their wares over the state broadcasting system.) On October 12, 1935, Eugen Hadamowski, director of the German broadcasting system, issued an order banning broadcasts of jazz in order, as he put it, "to do away with the last remnants of the culture-Bolshevistic Jew." [17]

By the time these items appeared in the press, the swing era was under way, and swing—or jazz—was beginning to enjoy unprecedented popularity in the United States, and Hadamowski was no longer talking about the music of a handful of people, but the music of millions. Americans, generally speaking, were not particularly curious about their own culture. As long as they regarded jazz as something they were permitted to take or leave alone, they left it alone—it seemed socially more prudent to do so.

However, once swing as a popular movement surged forward, and they learned that other nations saw jazz as a threat to their way of life, many Americans began to see in jazz a symbol of their own freedom, and foreign pronouncements condemning jazz became something to ridicule and defy. There were no great public refutations or demonstrations, of course (unless one so considers the crowds flocking to the New York Paramount Theater, Randall's Island, and Carnegie Hall swing concerts), and the thought that jazz was a symbol of anything was for the most part left unsaid. Altogether, though, there was increasing public support for jazz as something American. And this was all to the good. Pronouncements like those issued by the Nazis may not have sent anyone into a fit of righteous rage, but perhaps such items made it possible for people—some of them public figures—to feel less queasy about defending jazz, in whatever aspect.

In the late thirties, swing burst forth and reached all parts of the nation. Radio and admen—agencies responsible for much of its growth—were becoming powerful and influential; a shrewd promotion of swing, big white bands in particular (with Benny Goodman's name leading the rest), resulted in making swing a suitable, if controversial, topic for conversation however genteel. Since respected figures occasionally spoke up for swing, tongue-in-cheek press notices diminished (to increase again after World War II, with Dizzy Gillespie and his early high jinks) and became serious, objective, and sometimes even sympathetic reports. And on May 5, 1937, the *New York Times* reported that "Dr. Carleton Sprague Smith, head of the Music Division of the N.Y. Public Library, championed 'swing' music tonight, terming it an 'appropriate' musical expression which must receive serious consideration."

During this same period, however, the opposite point of view continued to be expressed with varying degrees of violence. The president of the Dancing Teachers Business Association, for example, in a talk to his associates reported by the *New York Times* on July 7, 1938, said that swing music was a "degenerated form of jazz," and its devotees were "unfortunate victims of economic instability." He went on to predict hopefully that "the popularity

of swing will fade with the return of economic stability."
Furthermore, if people wished to dance, there were plenty
of suitable and proper tangos, rumbas, and waltzes. On
May 22, 1938, an exhibition of "degenerate music" opened
in Düsseldorf. Nazi Germany wished to prevent the spread
of jazz and atonal music—"the microbes of musical decom-
position"—and to wipe out all music that showed "Marxist,
Bolshevistic, Jewish, or any other un-German tenden-
cies." [18] And, finally, Dr. Harry D. Gideonse, then head of
the economics and social science department of Barnard
College, stated in the *New York Times* of November 2,
1938, "Swing is musical Hitlerism."

Altogether, it is not difficult to understand why so little
serious work on jazz was accomplished in the twenties and
thirties. Add the confusions, misunderstandings, disagreements, and misconceptions of those sincerely interested in
jazz to the rantings and bitterness of those opposed to jazz,
and you have the main reason why jazz analysis was de-
layed until we were well into the swing era. By the middle
forties, serious attempts to analyze jazz as music became
more frequent. Most critics began to recognize the need
for emphasizing proper jazz analysis and evaluation and
de-emphasizing the social import of jazz and attempts to
tie jazz in with sociology became less and less rewarding.
Freed of its social shackles, jazz in the forties finally became a fit subject for serious study, and students of jazz
were now able to ask, "What is jazz?"

chapter **2**

TOWARD
A DEFINITION
OF JAZZ

DESPITE SEMANTIC DIFFICUL-
ties and the hostile social atmosphere, there were many
serious, if unfruitful, attempts at formulating a definition
of jazz, especially after the swing era. Critics, historians,
theorists, composers, and performers took a crack at it.
Some began by saying that jazz was something indefinable
and then went on to attempt a definition; others offered
short, all-encompassing definitions of jazz that upon examination turned out to be just as valid for much of the
classical music of the eighteenth and nineteenth centuries.
Still others have maintained that the truth about jazz is to
be found in defining what jazz does, rather than by defining what it is. Finally, there have been critical examinations of jazz by those who believe jazz to be an important
aspect of twentieth-century music, deserving its own definition in musical terms.

The discussion that follows does not include all the definitions of jazz or swing, or even the greater part of them, but those given are representative of the various kinds of definitions that have been given in the past. In the process of evolving a satisfactory definition of jazz, writers seem to have agreed only that jazz is music; but there are among them writers who, while they believe that jazz is music, see it not as one aspect of all music, but rather as a separate and distinct art—despite its musical content. Nevertheless, as will appear, most writers have been able to find certain broad areas of agreement.

(Before we go on to examine the various definitions of jazz, it is necessary to recognize the important influence of the swing era on all subsequent jazz criticism and explication. From the beginning of the swing era, the question "What is swing?" was asked over and over by a public determined to keep asking the question regardless of the number or quality of the answers it got. When the questions and answers finally subsided, it became apparent that the question "What is swing?" could not be answered properly without first defining jazz. It was soon plain to almost everyone concerned that "swing" is another word for "jazz," and thereafter many critics used the terms "swing" and "jazz" practically interchangeably. Except where it is stated otherwise, this holds true for all subsequent quotations.)

When Sidney Finkelstein wrote, "Jazz is a flow of motion in music guided by the most conscious skill, taste, artistry and intelligence," [1] he was stating, however felicitously,

that jazz is created the same way as other music. His statement is as true of Tchaikovsky's *Pathetique* as it is of Ellington's "Mood Indigo," leading one to ask: Doesn't jazz
have any *special* qualities? André Hodeir pointed out that
jazz is "perhaps essentially the Negro interpretation of
elements borrowed from other music." [2] It is difficult to
argue with "perhaps" and "essentially." Nevertheless, it
seems necessary to ask whether jazz may suffer certain non-
Negro "interpretations."

Definition by metaphor is a delight to read and frequently illuminates a dark corner. Charles Ives, writing
about ragtime in 1920, said it "is something like wearing
a derby hat on the back of the head, a shuffling lilt of a
happy soul just out of a Baptist Church in old Alabama."
(In answer to those who believed that jazz was America's
ruination, he went on to say: "Ragtime has its possibilities. But it does not 'represent the American nation' any
more than some fine old senators represent it.") During
World War I, Erik Satie said, "What I love about jazz is
that it's 'blue' and you don't care." [3] Since then, Satie's and
Ives's definitions have been, in effect, repeated countless
times. Definitions by metaphor, while not particularly ex-
plicative, do help reveal the spirit of jazz and, to some,
its mystery. Definitions by metaphor are, of course, esthetic
ones. They are more usually made by the relatively inarticulate jazz performer than by the more articulate composer. Esthetic definitions of jazz by jazzmen may be found
in most books on jazz, and they are all trying to say what
Chick Webb said: "It's like lovin' a gal, and havin' a fight,

25

and then seein' her again." [4] Jazzmen and composers alike will continue making esthetic definitions. The elusiveness of jazz invites emotionally conceived definitions, and composers—even those accustomed to handling the musical materials of jazz—may surely be permitted a colorful phrase or two. André Hodeir, the composer, and currently one of the most respected of jazz analysts (we shall come to his definitions presently), explains why definitions by metaphor will continue to be with us:

> On the surface there is disorder and conflict in jazz. No common definition of this music has been reached. It resists dictionary definition, and its musicians splutter nervously and take refuge in the colorful ambiguities of its argot. Nonetheless, its beauty can be proved; its badness can be separated from its boldness. . . .

And, a few pages later:

> From an examination of jazz musicians' own words, it is possible to glean the subtle, unruly, and almost mystical concept of the jazz spirit or feeling, or thinking—it is all these things and is so understood by the jazz musician himself. . . . [5]

George Gershwin, in a definition neither colorful nor profound, said, "Jazz is music; it uses the same notes Bach used." [6] Apparently this definition was intended to be a defense of jazz, or of Gershwin's personal position in jazz. (Although few serious jazz critics credit Gershwin with any contribution to jazz, to the general public—the European public particularly—he is *the* jazz composer. In any case, I do not believe it would be improper to say that jazz did more for Gershwin than Gershwin did for jazz.) Although the fashion of coupling Bach's name with jazz has long since become a commonplace for certain jazz intellectuals, Gershwin's statement has no intellectual overtones. He would have been just as happy to say that jazz used the same notes Josquin des Près used. His statement was intended to show only that jazz can be notated. In 1933, when Gershwin made his statement, the question of "improvised" jazz versus "notated" jazz was being explored, and the answer to this question was important to Gershwin's reputation as a composer of jazz. A few years later, with the coming of the swing era, the gist of Gershwin's statement was to have many defenders.

In the late thirties, defining jazz became more difficult for some and easier for others. Those who had never attempted to define jazz now found it easy and convenient to say, "Jazz is swing." This was also true of many who had previously had difficulty defining jazz. For one group, swing became a branch or at least an offshoot of jazz; for another, swing had roots of its own. The fact is, neither the word "swing" itself, nor the controversy it initiated, was new. The swing public (and happily the general public) carefully and solemnly listened to jazz sinners and evangelists alike. Paul Whiteman said, "Swing is, after all, nothing more than good old jazz," and Cootie Williams said, "There is no difference between jazz and swing."

For Fletcher Henderson (whose swing arrangements had much to do with launching the swing era) there was, as he put it, "a certain difference in the technical significance; swing means premeditation and jazz means spontaneity, but they still use the same musical material and are fundamentally the same idiom." [7] Hodeir, too, apparently had some difficulty distinguishing between the two.

> It took me years [he wrote in 1957] to realize that what I thought was "swing" was really only the "hot" aspect of a performance and that swing was intimately connected with getting the notes perfectly in place rhythmically. Since then, I have met hundreds of fans who have yet to grasp this essential point; nearly always, I have found it impossible to get it across to them. [8]

For Hodeir, then, swing is a fundamental quality of jazz, if not jazz itself. Wilder Hobson in his early study, *American Jazz Music*, presented another aspect of the problem confronting Hodeir:

> "Swing" has often been spoken of as if it were an absolute quality—either a band swings or it does not, etc. But "swing" will be present to some degree wherever a momentum is built up in suspended rhythms. In other words, it is not confined to jazz. It may, for instance, be in ragtime, Schumann's syncopations, Astaire's tappings. [9]

For those who believe that swing *is* jazz, the disagreement between Hobson and Hodeir is superficial. There were, however, deeper disagreements. One point of view implied that swing was not only different from jazz, but was somehow better. In the *New Republic* of January 29, 1936, Frank Norris said, "Swing is to jazz what the poetic quality is to verse"; another journalist, Gama Gilbert, in a piece entitled "Swing: What Is It?" in the *New York Times* of September 5, 1937, said, "Unlike ordinary jazz, it [swing] is a creative process necessarily engendered in a state of highest emotional excitement." And Virgil Thomson interposed the power of his reputation into the general debate by presenting "swing-music" with a definition all its own. "Swing-music," he wrote, "is a form of two-step in which the rhythm is expressed quantitatively by instruments of no fixed intonation, the melodic, harmonic and purely percussive elements being freed thereby to improvise in free polyphonic style." [10]

The foregoing remarks, by critics with amateur jazz standing, received little attention from the forces who considered themselves the true jazz polemicists. These embattled few managed to create an air of hostility that has not yet been dissipated. On one side stood the traditionalists: the defenders of true jazz (also variously known as real jazz, hot jazz, old-time jazz, genuine jazz, and of course traditional jazz). Opposing the traditionalists were the modernists or, as they have been called, the progressives. In any event, the engagement that followed only intensified the confusion and disagreement and led bewilderingly to an impasse not yet unblocked. The crux of this disagreement—perhaps the most profound of all disagreements among the critics of jazz—is made clear by Barry Ulanov. In *A History of Jazz in America*, he said:

> Confusion surrounded the use of the two terms "swing" and "jazz" as soon as swing became popularly accepted. There was one school of thought, of which critic Robert Goffin was the most rabid exponent, that believed "swing" denoted the commercialization and prostitution of real jazz, that it had partly supplanted jazz, and that it consisted only of written arrange-

ments played by big bands, whereas jazz consisted only of improvised music played by small bands. . . .[11]

Although they were hard pressed to define jazz, the Goffinites stood for "pure" jazz. They might have disagreed among themselves on a definition of jazz, but it was nevertheless obvious to them that swing was not true jazz. Such a controversy could not be resolved satisfactorily for all concerned as long as the arguments of both sides continued to be delivered with inflammatory words. For the "mechanized orchestration" and "prefabricated phrases" of swing, the Goffinites offered "collective improvisation," "a general trance," and "spontaneous fancy." They refused to accept the "artificial dynamism" of swing as a substitute for the "spirit of pure jazz." All in all, they saw swing as an enfeebling influence, an intellectually contrived music that debased the emotionally conceived true jazz; they therefore stood opposed to swing, or anything else inclined to diminish the pure, real, hot, traditional jazz. They were not opposed to swing as such, but the idea that swing could pass itself off as jazz was quite another thing. Goffin, himself, stated their final position:

> Jazz has passed from the state of pure improvisation into that of swing, which might be called an intellectual construction assisted by solos. Some prefer one format, some the other; those who are sufficiently objective can like both kinds, taking into full consideration the respective differences of evolution and atmosphere.[12]

In recent years, the great majority of writers have agreed that swing is jazz. My own position (stated more fully in

Toward a Definition of Jazz

the chapter on swing) is that jazz is a generic term, swing a specific term; in short, swing is a style of jazz whose characteristics were formed mainly between 1935 and 1945. This leads us back to the persistent question: What is jazz?

Until a few years ago, those who attempted jazz definitions were too often subjectively involved in controversy and were more concerned with proving the validity of their position than with fashioning a definition of jazz suitable for all. Prescience is not often a trait of the traditionalists' makeup, and they saw little need to look for the future directions of jazz. In any case, of those who attempted definitions early in jazz history (and in seeking jazz definitions the thirties may be considered early history), too many afterward felt compelled to view the jazz scene in the light of their own definitions. By starting with meager historic and stylistic data, they inadvertently maneuvered themselves into a position of trying to justify their sincere but inadequate definitions; by cutting corners sharply, they were able to measure the contemporary jazz scene to their satisfaction—but with a yardstick short of standard. The fact is that in order to formulate proper standards in jazz—or, for that matter, in any art—one must have the benefit of historical and stylistic perspective; that is, one must be able to see the parts in relation to each other.

Although relatively little time has passed since the early attempts at defining jazz, the wide dissemination and proliferation of jazz since the thirties make those early efforts seem quite remote in time. Therefore, definitions of jazz

31

by critics who are flexible enough to keep up with the changing scene and to accept the jazz of *all* periods as worthy of study, and who believe jazz has a future as well as a past, seem to have greater validity (and certainly a wider application) than the limited definitions of the jazz pioneers. For an inclusive definition of jazz, therefore, we must look to the work of those writers who have the advantage of historical hindsight as well as literary and musical perception.

For this reason, I have selected for detailed analysis various definitions and qualifying remarks put forward by Paul Eduard Miller, Barry Ulanov, Marshall Stearns, and André Hodeir. It has also seemed necessary to include Hodeir's statement on the conditions for the production of swing because he considers swing to be an indispensable element in all jazz. There are, of course, other definitions and remarks worthy of inclusion in this group; I believe, however, that the subsequent analyses and resulting concordances will encompass the sense—if not the words—of those omitted. Here, then, are the opening arguments.

Paul Eduard Miller:

> Primarily, and above everything else, jazz is music. Now, if jazz deserves the term "music," then, inevitably, jazz must be approached as music, and not as a *type* of music distinct from all others and completely out of the sphere of the aesthetic criteria of the classical realm. . . .
>
> To be sure, there exists a qualitative difference, technically, between jazz and classic. Briefly, classical music is a procedure of writing and playing according to academically recognized standards (as taught in books, schools). Jazz differs from classic

in the following characteristics: (1) *Rhythm*. A rigid 4/4 beat (occasionally 2/4 or 8/8) combined with polyrhythms, or cross-rhythms more commonly known as syncopation, and the use of free rubato. (2) *Harmony*. The blues triad (dominant, sub-dominant, tonic), which has been intermixed with harmonies stemming from European traditions, including polyphony and polytonality. (3) *Figurations*. Refers chiefly to suspensions, afterbeats, passing tones and melodic intervals. Since the use of figurations results in a mixture of concords and discords, this accounts for the disregard of the so-called pure tone and the subsequent utilization of what has come to be known as jazz intonation.

Swing contains all the elements of jazz, plus unresolved rhythm, i.e., the melodic tone commences or ends on the off beat. These are the simplest possible technical definitions. They do not tell us everything. These other things (non-technical) comprise the substance of articulate appreciation.[13]

Barry Ulanov:

This, then, is how one might define jazz: it is a new music of a certain distinct rhythmic and melodic character, one that constantly involves improvisation—of a minor sort in adjusting accents and phrases of the tune at hand, of a major sort in creating music extemporaneously, on the spot. In the course of creating jazz, a melody or its underlying chords may be altered. The rhythmic valuations of notes may be lengthened or shortened according to a regular scheme, syncopated or not, or there may be no consistent pattern of rhythmic variations so long as a steady beat remains implicit or explicit. The beat is usually four quarter-notes to the bar, serving as a solid rhythmic base for the improvisation of soloists or groups playing eight or twelve measures, or some multiple or dividend thereof.[14]

Marshall Stearns:

. . . jazz is a separate and distinct art that should be judged by separate and distinct standards. Like any other dynamic art, however, the special qualities of jazz cannot be described in a few words. The history of jazz may be told, its technical characteristics may be grasped, and the response it evokes in various individuals may be analyzed. But a definition of jazz in the most complete sense—how and why it communicates satisfying human emotions—can never be fully formulated.

. . . we may define jazz tentatively as a *semi-improvisational American music distinguished by an immediacy of communication, an expressiveness characteristic of the free use of the human voice, and a complex flowing rhythm; it is the result of a three hundred years' blending in the United States of the European and West African musical traditions; and its predominant components are European harmony, Euro-African melody, and African rhythm.*[15]

André Hodeir:

There would seem to be five optimal conditions for the production of swing. (I couldn't deny the theoretical possibility of swing's resulting from others, though I have never seen this happen.) They are:
1. the right infrastructure;
2. the right superstructure;
3. getting the notes and accents in the right places;
4. relaxation;
5. vital drive.

The first three are technical in nature and can be understood rationally; the last two, which are psychophysical, must be grasped intuitively. Only the second (and, to a lesser degree, the first) has to do with what is properly referred to as musical conception. . . .[16]

We may start by considering the moot points. Miller sees jazz as music, as a musical style containing primarily the same definable elements that are found in art music of the past. Ulanov's "new music" falls into a somewhat narrower category because it is not clear whether he means "new music" to serve as a synonym for "modern music," or perhaps "contemporary music," or whether "new music" is simply being used loosely to distinguish it from "old music." (The newest "new music," for most music historians, started around 1900 as a reaction against German romanticism, or, at least, as a reaction against *some* earlier music. This is a small point, of course, and is one of terminology. If one is not aware that "new music" has a special technical meaning, there is no confusion. Even so, if the theory of jazz is to grow, the technical language of all jazz writers will have to be rooted in the same meanings. Only by exposing and scrutinizing the meaning of those words and phrases that are persistent troublemakers can we hope some day to arrive at a standard terminology.)

Stearns sees jazz as a separate and distinct art. It seems to me that Stearns's definition implies he is more concerned with having jazz *judged* by separate and distinct standards than he is in building up a case for jazz as a separate and distinct art. If the implication exists only in my mind, the question must be raised: What is jazz to be separate and distinct *from?* Stearns's statement that the how and why of jazz communication can never be fully formulated is an important one, as is his concern with "expressiveness"; but in these, his position is no different from Miller's when Miller says that technical definitions "do not tell us everything"; or from Hodeir's when he tells us that the last two of his conditions for swing—"relaxation and vital drive"

35

—are psychophysical and "must be grasped intuitively."

The question of improvisation will be discussed more fully in the chapter on improvisation. For the present, it is sufficient to say that Miller does not believe improvisation to be "an essential and distinctive characteristic of jazz." [17] He believes that improvisation, properly executed, may affect the relative excellence of a jazz work, but not its essential jazz nature. Stearns's term, "semi-improvisation," is apparently an effort to find a term to settle the difference between "free" improvisation and big-band jazz, and perhaps concede something to "head arrangements." On the place of improvisation in jazz, Stearns disagrees with Miller. To Stearns, but not to Miller, improvisation is a basic characteristic of jazz and the essence of creativity in jazz; it is the primary basis for judging excellence because, as Stearns puts it, "it is utterly impossible to conceal the *quality* of your improvisation in jazz, where you are judged on the spot by your peers." [18]

Hodeir is inclined to agree with Stearns; he believes free improvisation to be synonymous with creative performance. There is, however, conscious or subconscious thought controlling the improvisation, and the quality of improvisation depends on the performer's depth of thought. When a performer's fingers simply " 'recite' a lesson they have learned . . . there is no reason to talk about creation." [19] It is not unlikely that Miller, Stearns, and Hodeir would all accept Ulanov's "improvisation of a minor sort" and "of a major sort" without necessarily accepting his qualifying remarks. In any case, it is reasonably certain that all four would agree that first-rate jazz has usually contained an abundance of first-rate improvisation—major or minor, creative or derivative.

The question of rhythm is an unruly one. Miller apparently regards as the *sine qua non* a maintenance of a rigid duple meter, simple or compound, against which are heard syncopation and "free" rubato. (Unless by "free" rubato Miller means the "full" rubato of classical composers—a rubato degenerating into a tempo without metrical pulse, and practically unknown in jazz except in the last two or three measures of a piece—then "free" appears to be redundant.) Miller makes a further qualification for swing, what he calls "unresolved rhythm"—a term apparently intended to mean a rhythmic disagreement with the meter (strong melodic rhythms that fall in metrically weak places, and the other way around). Miller's "rigid beat" becomes Ulanov's "steady beat"; and for Ulanov the beat may be implicit—an important distinction for understanding present-day jazz, the Jimmy Giuffre trio, for example. Ulanov's conception of duple meter, however ("four quarter notes to the bar"), is somewhat narrower than Miller's. Stearns, by requiring a "complex flowing rhythm," not only takes in Miller's and Ulanov's requirements, but indicates, it seems to me, a tolerance of future rhythmic possibilities in jazz; his "African rhythm" as a predominant jazz component seems, however, to extol rhythmic characteristics belonging not to jazz in general but to several specific styles of jazz.

Hodeir's "right infrastructure" is, in brief, the same

simple and compound duple meter required by Miller and Ulanov, but in a "right" tempo. "Tempos at which swing is possible," Hodeir claims, "range from about 54 quarter notes a minute to about 360." [20] He believes that a medium tempo—168 quarter notes a minute—is properly called the "swing tempo," and that a certain balanced relationship is necessary between theme and tempo. His "right superstructure" is essentially the favorable employment of Miller's "unresolved rhythm," the rhythmic disagreement or dislocation of the melodic rhythm with the metrical accents. Hodeir's third requirement—"getting the notes and accents in the right places"—deals first with the question of the proper placement of syncopated notes, and then with the necessity, in ensemble playing, for the subordination of the individual to the group. On this latter point, there seems little need for discussion; on the question of where to place syncopated notes, however, I believe Hodeir has fallen into error as a result of failing to distinguish between the general characteristics of jazz and specific characteristics of certain styles.

In music, theory follows practice. It is not the analyst's job to point out, as Hodeir does, what he considers to be faulty syncopations in the work of Johnny Dodds and Kid Ory. "One of the oldtimers' most common weaknesses," he writes, "results from their playing syncopated notes prematurely, in moderate tempos, on the second third of the beat. This 'corny' syncopation is a carry-over from the polka-style. Rhythmically, the effect is deplorable. . . ." [21] Now, whether Hodeir considers the effect to be deplorable or not is a matter of taste, not of analysis, and I am not taking issue with Hodeir's taste. I simply contend that the proper analysis needs first to be centered on style. For the theorist, music is seldom judged as good or bad, right or wrong; either a piece of music is stylistically consistent or it is not. The musical style of a period is created by the composers and performers of the period, and when a theorist says that something is deplorable he, in effect, chastens the creators of the music for not doing in their time what the theorist believes they should have done. (A related example of this practice by theorists is strikingly evident in the case of Willi Apel who, knowing that baroque composers used the terms "chaconne" and "passacaglia" interchangeably and indiscriminately, nevertheless classified certain chaconnes as passacaglias and vice versa, implying that baroque composers would have done the same if they had known better.)

On the question of harmony in jazz, Miller, Ulanov, Stearns, and Hodeir all agree that its basis is in European harmony. Miller talks of the "blues triad" but goes on to show that the primary triads have grown into chords of larger proportions and have themselves merged with a greater harmonic complex. Ulanov seems to imply, by omission, that he believes the harmonic language of jazz in general is not substantially different from that of music in general. Hodeir tells us what the harmonic language of jazz was in 1957, when he wrote his book. "To sum up," he writes, "jazz musicians have no special reason for taking pride in an harmonic language that, besides being

39

easily acquired, does not really belong to them but rather to a 'light harmony' that North America borrowed from decadent Debussyism." [22]

Turning to the question of melody, I must assume that Miller's "figurations" refer, generally, to melodic tones and, specifically, to their harmonic or nonharmonic functions. (Certain of Miller's terms are endowed with a fuzzy quality that makes his intention difficult to determine. Figuration, for example, usually has a straightforward meaning for theorists: it refers to the employment and repetition of stereotyped figures; and in this sense one may reasonably speak of certain kinds of florid riffs, say, as being figural. Miller's grouping together of the nonharmonic tones, the suspension and passing tone, in the same breath, so to speak, with "afterbeat"—a term that is common to rhythm, not melody—is particularly confusing. It is possible that he is referring to an unresolved nonharmonic tone that falls on an unaccented beat, or part of a beat. In any event, it is perplexing language to deal with.) When Miller talks of the difference between jazz and classical music, he seems to include as "classical music" all art music of the past; if this is the sense in which he uses it, then his reference to "figurations" does not show any disparity between the "figurations" of jazz and those of classical music.

Ulanov speaks of "a certain distinct rhythmic and melodic character," which seems inclusive enough. Stearns's "Euro-African melody," however, is more inclusive. There is no question that the unaccompanied melodies in which jazz has its roots had *their* roots in African melody; the move away from unaccompanied melody to accompanied melody resulted (in art music as well as in jazz) in the harmonically conceived melody, and this type of melody is European. It is Hodeir, however, who offers the all-inclusive definition when he quotes Evelyne Reuter, who said that melody is "a succession of sounds that describe, by their varying musical pitches, a musical curve." [23]

Improvisation, rhythm, harmony, melody—these are the ingredients of jazz that serious jazz writers have treated at great length. These elements of jazz have been considered the basic ones. But in recent years, on a broader base of criticism, jazz has been increasingly referred to certain other aspects of art music—intonation, form, style, tension and release, for example—and it is with these that we are presently concerned. Miller, Ulanov, Stearns, Hodeir, all have dealt with one or more of these aspects of jazz (with certain ones more thoroughly than others, of course), and it seems proper to explore these views, however briefly, before going on to the final summation.

Ulanov evidently felt the need to include a word on form in his definition. His "eight or twelve measures, or some multiple or dividend thereof" has certainly been a structural unit in jazz forms—the twelve measures for blues, and the eight measures for most other tunes. Stearns believes that jazz form is restricted by the requirements of improvisation. "As long as improvisation is a vital element in jazz," he writes, "the blues will probably be the prime form for its expression." [24] When Hodeir says, "The only structure in jazz is the theme and variations, which is the simplest of all and the one best adapted to improvisation," [25] one hopes that he is talking not about the theme and variations as a form (despite the strong implication) but about the technique of variation. The theme and variations, as well as the passacaglia, chaconne, and others, are individual structures in a category known as variation form. The technique of variation is essentially the basis for much of the art music composed in the past five centuries—jazz included. If Hodeir insists that the theme and variations (one specific architectural idea) is the *only* structure in jazz, it would at once disallow the contrapuntal forms currently engaging the attention of many first-rate jazzmen, the Modern Jazz Quartet, for example. At any rate, both Stearns and Hodeir base their statements on the significance of improvisation, and we have come full circle again—improvisation being the key word. We return to improvisation in chapter 3; for the present, however, we must go on.

Miller's statement, "Since the use of figurations results in a mixture of concords and discords, this accounts for the disregard of the so-called pure tone and the subsequent utilization of what has come to be known as jazz intonation," deserves further exploration. First, the use of figurations (suspensions, "afterbeats," and passing tones) does *not* result in a mixture of concords and discords. The use of nonharmonic tones results only in discord—to use Miller's term. To put it technically, the use of nonharmonic tones results in harmonic dissonance. The terms "concord" and "discord" have more currency with estheticians than with analysts; concord and discord have connotations of pleasantness and unpleasantness, whereas consonance and dissonance mean resolved and unresolved. Furthermore, if Miller's figurations *did* result in a mixture, there is no reason to believe that this would account for the "disregard of the so-called pure tone." Approached from any angle, the logic is faulty.

Then again, it is not clear whether by "pure tone" Miller refers to pitch or to tone quality. On the outside chance that he is speaking of tone quality, it would seem that the question is not one of disregard of pure tone, but rather one of special regard for a distinctive tone. No jazz performer, to my knowledge, has been penalized for trying to play with a "pure tone"—provided he was playing good jazz. Bix Beiderbecke's tone has been described as "beautiful," and Benny Goodman's as "legitimate." Surely the position of these two jazz performers (doubtless there are others) has not suffered because of their enduring success in producing beautiful, legitimate tones. Their greatness is in the jazz that flowed out of their horns and not in any arbitrary regard or disregard for tone. Although the future position in jazz of men like Pee Wee Russell, Dizzy Gillespie, Tony Scott, Stan Getz, Paul Desmond, and others is still not fully determined, their ultimate position will depend not upon the degree of their disregard for pure tone, but upon the jazz they will have created. The search for distinctive tone and "new" sounds—while necessary to the growth and development of jazz—is an inadequate substitute for rhythmic, melodic, and harmonic creativity. Unusual musical sounds and textures are fertile ground, and worth exploring, but they are not uniquely the province of jazz. No performer's ultimate position in jazz is delimited by the quality of his tone.

Much more important to the future of jazz theory is Hodeir's preliminary discussion of tension and release ("jazz consists essentially of *an inseparable but extremely variable mixture of relaxation and tension*").[26] This is an aspect of jazz theory that needs to be studied to gain insight not only into the creation of jazz, but also into the admittedly subjective process of evaluating it. For Hodeir, relaxation is as indispensable to swing as swing is to jazz. However, one feels the need for an expansion of the subject of tension and release in jazz; rhythmic tension and release should be studied in conjunction with melodic, harmonic, coloristic, textural, structural, and directional tension and release. It is only by such studies that a theory of jazz can be properly formulated; and jazzmen and critics will need to recognize that these problems exist before they can set about solving them. Exposing some of the theoretical problems of jazz has been one of the primary purposes of this chapter.

In this chapter, along with what I hope has been a partial disentangling of terminology, I have attempted to clarify what I believe needed clarifying. It would not be strange if, for some, I have beclouded what at first sight seemed clear enough. The language of jazz, like jazz itself, grows rapidly. Whitney Balliett said, "Because of its nature and the speed with which the music has developed, writing about jazz is, of course, somewhat like trying to photograph a jet plane with a Brownie." To photograph jazz on the run requires, first, a technical and linguistic ability to make it sit still. The definition that follows will be, I hope, a first step toward keeping it from darting away too often. The statement is intended to be neither complete nor even composite. It is simply intended to sum up what Miller, Ulanov, Stearns, and Hodeir have said, to express certain of my own conclusions, and to serve as a point of departure for chapter 3. Here, then, is the working definition: Jazz is the comprehensive name for a variety of specific musical styles generally characterized by attempts at creative improvisation on a given theme (melodic or harmonic), over a foundation of complex, steadily flowing rhythm (melodic or percussive) and European harmonies; although the various styles of jazz may on occasion overlap, a style is distinguished from other styles by a preponderance of those specific qualities peculiar to each style.

chapter 3

UNDERSTANDING
IMPROVISATION

Ludwig Wittgenstein (1889-1951) was a philosopher who devoted much of his life to a scrupulous study of language as we actually use it. He believed that much philosophical confusion could be avoided by not attempting to make pat definitions for even the most seemingly simple things. Morton White, in his book *The Age of Analysis,* tells us that Wittgenstein contended "that to understand a word is to be able to use it in accord with customary social practice," and that Wittgenstein's most famous slogan was, "The meaning is the use." Wittgenstein, himself, put it this way:

> Consider for example the proceedings that we call "games." I mean board-games, card-games, ball-games, Olympic games, and so on. What is common to them all?—Don't say: "There *must* be something common, or they would not be called 'games' "—but *look and see* whether there is anything common

to all.—For if you look at them you will not see something that is common to *all*, but similarities, relationships, and a whole series of them at that.[1]

Difficulties in understanding improvisation arise from the fact that there are different kinds of improvisation; it is, therefore, not enough to offer a pat description of improvisation. What we are seeking is rather an understanding of improvisation as it has been practiced in performance. A dictionary definition—"to compose on the spur of the moment"—tells us only part of the story; "composing and performing simultaneously" tells us still another part of the story. We have also heard frequent references to "free" improvisation and to "collective" improvisation. In addition, every jazzman knows what he means by improvisation, and every writer knows what *he* means, and the result is, of course, an involved combination of meanings leading to unnecessary disagreements and puzzlements.

Basically, there would seem to be two kinds of improvisation: free and controlled. However, to a degree the "free" has controls, and the "controlled" has certain freedoms, and these facts lead us back to Wittgenstein's statement that "we see a complicated network of similarities overlapping and crisscrossing: sometimes overall similarities, sometimes similarities of detail."

Moreover, surrounding the entire question are the value judgments of individuals—and rightly so. When a young child sits at the keyboard and indulges his right to play with the keys, producing haphazard tunes and chords on the spur of the moment, there is no doubt that he is "freely"

47

improvising, unhampered by previously conceived harmonic, melodic, rhythmic, or structural concepts. There are, nevertheless, certain controls. His legs may be too short to reach the sustaining pedal (and this will lessen the possibility of his playing legato, even if he knew what this meant), his fingers may be too short or too weak, or his span may be too narrow for octaves and tenths. Briefly, the child's playing, extemporaneous or otherwise, is controlled by physical limitations that result in technical limitations, not to mention artistic limitations. But, one may ask, what happens when free improvisation is undertaken by a mature performer with relatively no physical or technical limitations? Roy Eldridge, when asked about free improvisation, said: "Clyde Hart and I made a record like that once. We decided in front that there'd be no regular chords, we'd announce no keys, stick to no progressions. Only once I fell into a minor key; the rest was free, just blowing." [2]

When Eldridge "fell into a minor key" he was being controlled by his memory, by the ability of his fingers involuntarily to press down valves in combinations long since automatic, by labial convolutions repeated a hundred thousand times. When he says, "The rest was free," he means free only of certain restrictions—the restriction of a fixed form, perhaps, or of previously established harmonic patterns. The fact is, completely free improvisation is possible only when the creative processes, so to speak, are able to function without the aid of manuscript or memory. Free improvisation bears the same relation to jazz that so-called automatic writing does to prose. Paradoxically, both techniques may be acquired to a high degree by "practicing." Willi Apel has called free improvisation "a 'soapbubble' phenomenon the evanescent nature of which defies documentation and detailed description." We may nevertheless use the term "free" as long as we understand that it indicates a striving on the part of the jazzman to play outside the bounds of his conscious memory.

On the other hand, controlled improvisation, or improvisation on "given" musical materials, is relatively easier to understand. Its *raison d'être* is as old as music itself. In the beginning, music was largely improvisatory, largely supplied on the spur of the moment by primitive folk to accompany the functions of everyday living—work, play, war, love, and worship. Music was not separate from, nor was it simply an adjunct to, these activities; it was rather the force by which were communicated the special, often magical, relationships of man to nature and man to man. The improvised dance music, work songs, war songs, dream songs, love songs, and children's songs of primitive and agrarian societies are more significant to the rise and development of jazz improvisation than the highly civilized, notated complexities of, say, *Le Sacre du Printemps*.

The thread leading from early improvisations to jazz improvisations is a long one and not easily traced; there are entanglements all along the way. A part of primitive (folk) music becomes civilized (art) music and is notated; improvisations are then based on notated music; notated music becomes "frozen" improvisations; and so on through the Middle Ages, the Renaissance, and the baroque period, right up to our own time when, in jazz, the entire process seems to be repeated all over again. Nevertheless, if we are to have a broader understanding of the meaning and function of improvisation in our own time, it is necessary to show the evolution of improvisation, however briefly. And it seems proper here to begin with the words of Béla Bartók, from his definitive study on folk music. In *Hungarian Folk Music* he wrote:

> Performance by peasants, exactly as performance by a great artist, includes a good deal that is almost extemporization; for instance, the same person, performing the same tune, will at times introduce minor, surface alterations, which do not affect the essential quality of this tune. Repetitions of a tune will usually include slight rhythmic alterations; at times the pitch (or perhaps even the note itself) will be changed. It is admissible that a few of these unessential alterations will in the course of time become permanent. Then other performers may introduce other changes of a similar kind; and the last link in this chain may turn out to be altogether different from the first. It is obvious, indeed, that no essential alteration of a musical element can come from one individual peasant. And there can be no doubt that with peasants who people one geographical unit, living close to one another and speaking the same language, this tendency to alter, in consequence of the affinities between the mental disposition of individuals, works in one way, in the same general direction. It is thus that the birth of a homogeneous musical style becomes possible.[3]

What Bartók said of peasant societies holds for higher cultures as well. Two thousand years ago the practice of improvisation among the Greeks was widespread. The bases for their improvisations were called *nomoi*, or what we might call "stock melodies." During the Middle Ages, singers improvised countermelodies against a given melody usually written in a large choir book that all the singers could view simultaneously; some of the singers sang the notated tune while others ornamented the tune according to the prevailing style. There were certain rules to go by— when to use octaves and fifths, special uses of contrary motion, and so on—but no doubt many of the rules were broken in actual performance. Concerning the use of instruments, we know from paintings and manuscripts of the period that during the fourteenth century certain instruments, the drone, for example, were widely used, yet we find written music without parts for these instruments. This would indicate that, whenever improvisation flourishes, the written composition often contains only the skeletal form of the performed composition.[4]

In the early Renaissance, improvisation was such an integral part of the practice of performance that the theorist Tinctoris (*ca.* 1435-1511) felt it necessary to say that " 'counterpoint' is not only a generic term, embracing both improvisation . . . and written music . . . but also a specific term, used as a synonym for 'improvisation.' "[5] The score of the first genuine *ballet de cour,* 1581, contains in places only two outer parts to be used as instrumental accompaniment to vocal music—a clear indication that the performers were expected to fill in, or improvise, the accompaniment. And five centuries before the rise of San Francisco's beat generation, the practice of reciting cellar poetry to an improvised musical accompaniment was a commonplace. There is also an abundance of evidence that dance tunes, the *basse danse* particularly, were played "straight" by some instruments while others improvised around the melody.

Renaissance organists had their own version of the "cutting" contest. In the mid-sixteenth century improvising contests were quite common, especially in Italy, and often were the sole basis for selecting job applicants. The ability to improvise in a fugal style was a standard requirement for all appointments to organ positions, and the ability to improvise ricercaris was particularly important in the free-for-all competitions. Most of the composing of the sixteenth-century organist was therefore accomplished during actual performance, and Gustave Reese tells us:

> The fact that improvisation was an important phase of organ playing may account, in part, for the absence of works by many famous organists of the time. An increased—perhaps excessive —appreciation of performance is shown by a Venetian decree of 1546, providing that no canons or priests should interrupt performing organists, but should remain quiet and patiently await the end of a piece.[6]

A hundred years later improvisation had become one of the cornerstones of baroque performance. Melodies called "grounds" became the basis for much baroque improvisation; "continued" grounds became the basis for extended works. The thorough-bass technique—a method of showing bass notes only, with symbols indicating the proper harmonies—characterized baroque performance. Melodies were improvised upon in various ways: an organist and violist, for example, would offer a performance in which the violist was free to improvise upon the bass line, or melody, ornamenting it without changing its essential contour; or the violist would create new melodies against the bass line, the organist meanwhile improvising on the fixed harmonies, and so on. In his masterful and lucid study, *Music in the Baroque Era,* Manfred Bukofzer illuminates certain aspects of baroque musical practice that, in many ways, are analogous to jazz in the twentieth century. Here, in brief, is the way he summarizes the position of improvisation in the period from about 1600 to 1750:

> The aspects of performance raise a great number of perplexing questions because we have become unfamiliar with the fundamental fact that in baroque music notation score and performance score did not, as a rule, coincide. The notation presented merely a skeletal outline of the composition; its structural contour had to be filled in, realized and possibly ornamented by an extemporizing performer. This practice bears witness to the intimate ties between composer and performer, between composition and improvisation, which makes a clear distinction between the two almost impossible. The division of labor had not yet developed to a point where performing and composing were recognized as fields of specialization, as they are today. Significantly, the great virtuosi of the baroque, like Domenico Scarlatti, Handel, and Bach, were also the great composers of the period.[7]

From Bukofzer's study we may conclude that manuscripts and printed scores of the baroque give us only the vaguest notion of how the music sounded in actual performance. The composer considered his written score as an outline to be interpreted, in full, by the performer—the composer quite often serving both functions. Many scores were little more than what today's jazzmen call "lead sheets." Great improvisation was considered one of the highest forms of musical art, and the ability to improvise, a performer's crowning artistic asset. First-rate musicianship, even virtuosity, was almost a commonplace. Paul Henry Lang tells us that "every member of an orchestra, especially an operatic orchestra, was expected to invent, on the spur of the moment, a free contrapuntal part over the given figured bass." Furthermore, "the operatic scores of the period offer the greatest difficulty for the modern student, for they are little more than general directions for the use of the conductor. In many instances the bass was not even figured, leaving the choice of harmonies to the whim of the continuo player." [8]

This kind of virtuosity and the virtuosity still to come were the result of sixteenth-century musical instruction in ornamentation, seventeenth-century harmonic improvisations on figured bass, and, in the eighteenth century, the improvisations of vocal virtuosi, the whole leading to the fantastic cadenzas of eighteenth- and nineteenth-century solo concertos. After J. S. Bach's time, however, the art of improvisation, as an essential part of the practice of performance, went steadily downhill. (There is little after Bach that can compete with his much-cited two-hour improvisation of a prelude and fugue, an organ trio—a piece in three obbligato parts, a chorale prelude, and a final fugue, all on one hymn tune.) This is not to say that after Bach improvising stopped. It did, however, become a special, rather than a customary, part of a musical performance. History is full of the improvising exploits of Mozart, Beethoven, Paganini, Liszt, and other giants after Bach, but these distinctions are conferred as something apart from their ability to create written compositions; their improvisations became a matter of technical prowess.

As we move into the nineteenth century we find Beethoven, possibly the most gifted and creative of the romantic improvisers, more concerned with getting his ideas on paper than with amazing his audiences with his keyboard fireworks. He worried whether his dynamic signs were where they should be; he fussed over expression marks, tempo indications, and the hundreds of Italian phrases that are intended to illustrate his intentions. But of Beethoven as a performer his pupil Czerny said: "His improvisations were most beautiful and striking. In whatever company he might chance to be he knew how to produce such an effect upon every hearer that frequently not an eye remained dry and many would break out into loud sobs. . . ." [9]

Despite Beethoven's and other composers' concern with the notated composition, improvisation continued to remain a high point of most popular concerts. Such composers as Liszt, Paganini, Mendelssohn, and, later, Franck and Saint Saëns, made the most of their improvising abilities, and the stories of their prowess have been recorded in many sources. For example, from *The Life and Death of Chopin* we learn that during a Vienna concert in 1829 Chopin was given a motif from a current popular opera to improvise upon, and, since the second half of his concert was called *Freie Fantasie,* he proceeded to treat the motif with fantastic variations; as an added gesture, he managed to work in the Polish drinking song, "Hops," no doubt further intoxicating his audience.[10]

At the same time Chopin was playing variations on "Hops" in Vienna, Negroes in the American South were making a music partly their own and partly derived from whatever their musical environment happened to be. To trace fully the rise of jazz improvisation would be to write an exhaustive history of jazz in the United States before 1900, a task already done, in the main, by Marshall Stearns in *The Story of Jazz*. For present purposes, it is only necessary to point out that, especially from the mid-nineteenth century on, the improvisation of untrained musicians was influenced by that of trained musicians who, in turn, adopted some of the devices of untrained musicians. There is little question that during this period both kinds of musicians existed alongside each other and influenced each other. In the South after the Civil War there were field hands who improvised on homemade instruments, and other freedmen in the cities who improvised on "legitimate" instruments. Many big-city bandsmen—right up to the 1920's—knew as little about reading music as their field-hand contemporaries. But a great many of the military bandsmen had training of one kind or another, and eventually these happy few were responsible for the subsequent rise and development of jazz improvisation.

From *Hear Me Talkin' to Ya*, Nat Shapiro and Nat

Hentoff's first-rate collection of reminiscences of jazzmen and their intimates, it is relatively easy to determine the influence of "readers" on "nonreaders." Here are several excerpts from jazzmen born close enough to the beginning to have recollections of it still.

Alphonse Picou, born in 1878, was an important early New Orleans clarinetist who was able to read music; about 1895, after taking lessons for eighteen months, he was asked to play with a band, and he recalls: "That particular style of music was very new to me. I think it was impossible to me! It seemed a sort of style of playing without notes." [11]

Bunk Johnson, born in 1879, a New Orleans cornetist who enjoyed a brief revival in the forties, recalls the Buddy Bolden band of 1895-96: "Now here is the thing that made King Bolden's band the first band to play jazz. It was because they could not read at all." [12]

Richard M. Jones, born in 1889, a jazz pianist and earlier a member of the 1902 Eureka Brass Band, recalls improvisation in New Orleans before World War I:

> Music was different in New Orleans because many were too blamed ignorant to read, not like New York or Chicago musicians. Keppard and others practiced at the 25 Club, in New Orleans. They would all go down there after they got through with their jobs, late at night. I would play over the new pieces because I could read. Then some other pianist would get up and try to play; perhaps he could play it a little better. But they would forget it before they got through and would have to fill in with a break and other stuff. That's where the improvisation came from.[13]

Edmond Hall, born in 1901, self-taught and generally regarded as one of the best of the New Orleans clarinetists, recalls: "In the early days of brass bands, in the 'nineties and even before, the music was mostly written—I mean in the kind of band my father played in. As time went on there was more improvising." [14]

Buster Bailey, born in 1902, one of the important early jazz clarinetists who did not come out of New Orleans, recalls:

> We were playing in Memphis at the same time they were playing in Storyville in New Orleans. The difference was that the New Orleans bands did more improvising. Ours were more the note variety. We played from the sheets.
>
> One of the jobs our band had, for example, was to accompany the draftees to the station in 1917 and '18. We played *Draftin' Blues, Preparedness Blues*, and I jazzed them up. Everybody would follow me. I was the center of attraction. They were playing the straight lead, but I—as the principal of my school said—was embellishing around the melody. I wouldn't have known what they meant by improvisation. But embellishment was a phrase I understood. And that's what they were doing in New Orleans—embellishment.[15]

Early jazzmen—and, for that matter, a good many later ones—had little intellectual awareness of what was coming out of their instruments. They played, as so many of them have put it, what they "felt," but the resulting improvisation was controlled by their technical ability to play their instruments, their musical environment, and their musical knowledge in general. Much of what they knew they learned by imitation and rote, as is true of all early music; much of their jazz was the result of what "lay under their hands" —intervals, scales, and arpeggios natural to the horn, the keyboard, the fingerboard, and, for drummers, combinations of rudimentary rhythmic patterns. The result, however commonplace the materials, was nonetheless exciting. The critic Ernest Borneman, with tongue in cheek as he tries to remember what his teacher, Hornbostel, said to him concerning New Orleans jazz, wrote:

> "Indeed, sir. A *quod libet* of staggering ingenuity. A specimen of collective improvisation that makes your *super librum cantare* sound like amateur stuff. Talk to me of Frescobaldi and Paganini and the rest of your great extemporizers! Why, here you have the transition of primitive heterophony into pure impromptu counterpoint. Here is an urban folk music that makes your *flamenco* guitarists and *cante hondo* singers sound like old-time country musicians! It's the real link between improvisation and composition, folk music and art music, the polyphonic age and the modern tradition. It's *jazz music!*" [16]

Admittedly, Borneman was exaggerating a bit. Nevertheless, much of what he reports Hornbostel to have said reflects the view of many present-day traditionalists.

Just as the performer in the seventeenth and eighteenth centuries created his everyday improvisations on a given bass, so does the jazzman create on given material. In the early days of jazz he improvised on a given melody and, as his musical knowledge increased, on given harmonies. The structural design of his improvised creations was, of necessity, simple—square phrases in an easy-to-remember two- or three-part form able to serve as a framework around a qualified use of the primary triads and a few other chords mostly of dominant function. Two-, four-, and eight-bar phrases were the order of the day, and the bar line was never more tyrannical. This kind of basic structure, however, was necessary if the jazzmen were to play in ensemble or to alternate solos: the structure had to be simple enough to require little concentration; the harmonic progressions had to seem inevitable, that is, be the fundamental harmonic progressions of Rameau. The meter—perhaps under the influence of the military band music most early jazzmen grew up with—was invariably duple.

The twelve-bar structure known as the "blues" is easily the favorite form of jazzmen, followed closely by the thirty-two-bar AABA form of the popular song. A glance at the following example of a blues form makes its structure clear:

The basic blues form

Each of the diagonal lines represents one beat; the letter symbols C, F, and G^7 stand for tonic, subdominant, and dominant seventh in the key of C major, with the C^7 being the dominant seventh of the subdominant. Depending on the jazz style of the improviser, other chords may be substituted for certain of the basic ones. For example, in measure 10, an F^7 may be used in place of the G^7 without implying a change of the harmonic style, in this case New Orleans style; however, substituting a D-flat^{11}, say, for the G^7 in measure 10 does change the style. The harmonic progressions and harmonies implied in improvised melodies are one part of what characterizes a style. It is therefore necessary to point out that the "basic" harmonic progressions shown above are not likely to appear in just that way, except perhaps in early blues improvisations and in the work of later jazzmen intent on imitating the early style. (The various chord substitutions for the "basic" blues will be discussed more fully in their proper places in the chapters on style analysis, since the question of harmonic progression concerns the entire question of style and not just harmonic progression in the blues. For the present, it seems sufficient to say that the twelve-bar blues structure is the jazzman's basic frame of reference.)

The thirty-two-bar AABA form of the popular song, cadential formulas aside, has no basic harmonic patterns; the harmonies and their progressions vary according to the jazz style. Because the so-called standard tunes on which most improvising is done were originally written against simple triads and various chords of the seventh, these simple chords, despite their eventual harmonic expansion, may be considered the "fundamental" chords of a given tune. For example, the basic harmony for the first eight-bar strain of "Sunny Side of the Street," in C major is:

These progressions, characteristic of jazz in the twenties, may with few, but important, changes be made consistent with the harmonic style of jazz in the forties and later. Substitute B-flat[11] for the E^7 in measure 2, and the entire character of the style is changed. If this is done, however, other appropriate changes must be made—for one thing, the more frequent use of chords with an added sixth—otherwise, the result will be harmonically and stylistically inconsistent.

Whatever else it may be called, improvisation is variation; the technique of variation is the essential substance of jazz improvisation, as well as of all music. "The process of improvisation is central to jazz," Sidney Finkelstein has written, "but not so drastically different from the processes that go on in the mind of a composer who writes music." [17] "Processes" in this statement refers, of course, to the composer's intellectual capacity to conceive variations; in addition, the composer has the problem of transferring his conceptions to paper. Leonard Feather in his excellent chapter "The Anatomy of Improvisation" tells us:

> In order to set down jazz on paper and submit it to the microscope, the critic first must be sure that every nuance of the musician's phrasing has been correctly captured, for these are

Understanding Improvisation

the subtleties without which some jazz, on paper, might be indistinguishable from "pop music." . . . Second, he must be equipped with a natural feeling for the texture of jazz improvisation and an understanding of its harmonic substructure.[18]

No doubt something is lost in the transfer of an intellectual concept to paper. When Feather asks assurance that "every nuance" will be "correctly captured," he implies that it is possible to do so. Unfortunately it is not, although the problem of symbolizing concepts is not unique to music, jazz or other kinds. Furthermore, to say that the critic must have "a natural feeling for the texture of jazz improvisation" smacks of the acknowledgment of a mystical, unlearnable quality, the existence of which Feather has correctly denied on other occasions. It would seem that knowledge and perhaps sympathetic understanding are more necessary to the notating of jazz than any "natural feeling." A further and closer look at this problem will be found in the following chapter, in the section on notation; for the present, we shall not be concerned with the notational aspects of improvisation. Rather, we shall concern ourselves with the technique of improvising, with how improvising is accomplished.

Jazz improvisation consists almost entirely of creating new melodic patterns to "fit" a given harmonic foundation that, except in the case of the basic blues formula, usually has a melody of its own; while the harmonic foundation remains fixed, the original melody is varied. ‹Leonard Feather distinguishes three kinds of melodic improvisation:

In the first and simplest, the original written melody is respected completely; the only change lies in the lengthening or shortening of some notes, repetition of others, use of tonal variations and dynamics to bring out its values in conformity with the personality of the interpreter. In the second, the melody remains completely recognizable but its phrases are subject to slight additions and changes; here and there a note is added or subtracted and perhaps a whole phrase is transmuted. . . . In the third type of improvisation the soloist departs entirely from the melody; in fact, rather than using it as a point of departure, he uses instead the chord pattern of the tune. . . .[19]

This third category is further distinguished in three ways, according to the source from which the performer derives the notes he plays:

There are the notes that are decided upon completely impromptu; the notes that are predetermined to the degree that they follow a natural sequence (possibly as part of an arpeggio, chromatic sequence or scalar run), and third, the notes that are played automatically, without real cerebration, because they are part of a previously used sequence at the back of the performer's mind.[20]

Feather's three types of melodic improvisation apparently are based on the degree of recognition afforded, as he puts it, "to the layman listener." The distinction between types one and two—very easily recognizable and easily recognizable—is perhaps a little fine. However, the distinction may be a reasonable one. In the subdivisions of type three, however, I believe there is considerable overlap of those notes that "follow a natural sequence" with those that "happen to lie under the fingers."

Hodeir, writing on the same subject under the heading

"The Melodic Phrase in Jazz," distinguishes between what he calls a "theme phrase" and a "variation phrase." "The *theme phrase*," he writes, "is more stripped, less diffuse, because it has less ornament than the variation phrase." (One wonders, here, whether the distinction between theme and variation is not implicit.) He goes on to say that the variation phrase may be further divided "into two principal types, the *paraphrase* and the *chorus phrase*. The first retains definite melodic affinities with the theme phrase from which it springs; the second, which is a kind of free variation, gets away from it completely. . . ." [21] Thus we find Feather's three types of melodic improvisation in essential agreement with Hodeir's "paraphrase" and "chorus phrase."

Improvisation, then, consists of performing variations on a theme—and the theme may be either a melodic subject or a harmonic progression (or, under certain circumstances, a rhythmic pattern); it may consist of any of these singly, or in any combination. Robert U. Nelson, in his excellent study, *The Technique of Variation*, discusses the "song variation"—a structure common to the baroque period—which bears certain relationships to jazz improvisation. The following description sounds much like what the jazzman sets out to accomplish with an improvised solo. Nelson writes:

The general design of the song variations is simple. In it the theme is followed by a moderate number of units, set off by cadences, which are arranged more or less progressively according to their rhythmic animation and degree of figural elab-

65

oration. The growth in animation is not always steady, being interrupted from time to time by a return to quieter rhythms, yet by and large there is a noticeable increase in activity from the beginning of a set to the end. . . . The component variations keep unchanged the main outlines of the given subject, above all its structure, its tonality, and generally its meter and chief harmonic outlines.[22]

Earlier in his study, Nelson distinguishes three types of variation structures: the *cantus firmus* variation, the melodicoharmonic variation, and the harmonic variation. All three have direct relationship to the Feather and Hodeir classifications: the *cantus firmus* variation corresponds to Hodeir's paraphrase and Feather's type one (for the most part "the original melody is respected completely"); the melodicoharmonic variation corresponds to Feather's type two ("slight additions and changes . . . perhaps a whole phrase is transmuted"); the harmonic variation corresponds to Hodeir's chorus phrase and Feather's type three ("the soloist departs entirely from the melody"). Here is the way Nelson defines the harmonic variation:

We come now to the harmonic treatment of the song variation. In this technique . . . the structural outlines of the theme are preserved, and, as in the melodico-harmonic variation, the basic harmony of the theme remains unchanged. The melody of the theme, however, is either abandoned completely or suggested in a wholly incidental way. Because each variation of a series thus inaugurates a new melodic line, the treatment is unusually flexible in its effect.

It is of more than passing interest that the three structural plans represent three successive stages leading toward the abandonment of the melodic subject. In the cantus firmus variation the correspondence to the melodic subject is literal, save for occasional transient embellishment; in the melodico-harmonic variation the outline of a melodic subject is altered and obscured, generally through figuration; finally, in harmonic variation, the melodic subject is replaced by totally new melodies.[23]

Thus jazz performers build up their own extended, improvised solos: improvisations begin with little or no variation on a melodic subject and, as the performers warm to their job, progress to more elaborate melodic variation until finally the melody is completely abandoned for the harmonic variation. In both the thirty-two-bar form and the basic blues, the performer strives to achieve a balance of rhythmic tension and release as prescribed by the song variation. Above all, the first-rate jazz performer strives to create within the limitations of the style he chooses to work in. Held within the boundaries of a few chords, his imagination soars to melodic heights, driven by the energetic rhythmic force that has given the best jazz its characteristic vitality. The harmonic formulas of jazz improvisation are undoubtedly simple, but then so are the basic formulas for Bach's *Goldberg Variations* and Beethoven's *Diabelli Variations*. A study of baroque theoretical treatises and teaching manuals, for example, is sufficient to show what can be accomplished, artistically, despite rigid formulas. Bukofzer tells us:

> The treatises teach the structural elements of composition by means of cadential patterns, typical bass progressions, and amusing recipes as to how to put them together. . . . In view of the high quality of baroque music the directions seem surprisingly mechanical as though composition consisted of noth-

67

ing more than the word implied, namely the putting together or "com-position" of formulas.[24]

When Feather writes that "no two musicians will react alike to any given set of chords, any prearranged melodic pattern, or even any group of words to be set to music," [25] he is, of course, right. But his statement needs qualifying. Two jazz musicians with about the same musical knowledge, early training, and environment are likely to react to a given set of chords with a similar stylistic interpretation; their individual playing styles and techniques may be quite unlike, but their performances will be similar in style and spirit. The virtuoso jazzmen—men like Louis Armstrong, Benny Goodman, and Charlie Parker—are great because they explored the limitations of the jazz styles they worked in and found ways to turn the limitations to their advantage, always with stylistic consistency. The great jazzman is not born a mature artist; his art evolves. He has transitional periods, of course, during which he is trying to find his means of expression; his greatness comes when he has found what he sought and the means of communicating it through his playing—even when he himself continues the search, unaware of his discovery. The stylistic consistency I am speaking of is manifested most clearly after the discovery is made. It is obviously difficult to evaluate jazz improvisation when it is still in the formative period. We must, therefore, look for the characteristic improvisation of the great jazzman when he is at the peak of his improvisational—that is, creative—powers, and not in periods of evolution or decline.

Understanding Improvisation

As we have pointed out earlier, the possibility of completely uncontrolled improvisation is remote. It is in this sense that what Winthrop Sargeant wrote in 1946 should be taken:

> The much-discussed element of improvisation, too, has been greatly overrated in recent writing about jazz. A false impression has been given that the jazz artist, when he is "in the groove," creates an entirely new musical composition extemporaneously. Actually, this is never the case. Only a small portion of the jazz heard today is improvised, and even in that small portion improvisation affects only a few elements of rhythm and melody. The two most intellectually complex features of music—harmony and form—are never improvised even in so-called improvised jazz. They conform in every case to well-worn standard patterns.[26]

How then, we may ask, do jazz performers create significant compositions on the spur of the moment? The answer is that they do not. That is, they do not compose on the spur of the moment; their significant improvisations are the result of long practice and experience. In the course of years of listening, absorbing, analyzing, and imitating the work of his predecessors and contemporaries (and even his own work), the jazz performer builds up a stock of musical material. He modifies and adapts, to his individual conception of jazz, melodic fragments, rhythmic patterns, and even entire phrases he has heard and admired. All these memories and impressions are assimilated and transformed into music that is fresh, and often, when it is coupled with the spirit of spontaneity, music that is new. The performer's task is to organize his material—however spontaneous his

69

performance may seem—in such a way as to make it appear that the material is, in truth, his own. A phrase he happened upon earlier, consisting of melodic fragments partly under his hand and partly, perhaps, the result of accident, is repeated for a month or a year as well as he can remember it. Then it is further modified in the solitude of individual practice and under the stimulation of rehearsals and public performances until, one evening, it bursts forth apparently new born. Sidney Finkelstein writes:

> When the player arrives at a creation that satisfies him, he remembers it and repeats it. . . .
> To say this is not to detract from the jazz player's originality, but merely to point out the conditions under which every creative mind works. The slow creation of a great jazz solo is a form of musical composition. . . . Hot jazz improvisors are careful workmen and fine craftsmen; they generally know what they are doing every step of the way.[27]

Ironically enough, it is in the few moments of improvisation, when the improvisers actually do not "know what they are doing every step of the way," that something apparently spontaneous is likely to occur. Early moments in improvising sessions usually consist of each performer's blowing himself out, so to speak—ridding himself of those musical ideas close to the surface of his memory, those that come to mind too easily and too readily. As the session progresses, however, and if the performer has any regard for his colleagues' opinion of him, he feels compelled to reach out, or perhaps inward. In such moments great jazz may be born. Gilbert Seldes describes a performance of this kind in the thirties by the jazz violinist, Stuff Smith, and a group at the Onyx Club in New York. Shortly after hearing the performance, Seldes wrote:

> The members of a good swing band instinctively improvise harmoniously. Individuals will no doubt remember a particular hot "lick" and repeat it on later occasions; there will always be tremendous pace, exciting rhythms and counter-rhythms, and in most cases a frenzy of noise. I have heard a swing band rise step by step in speed and tone, repeating some thirty or forty bars of music until it seemed impossible to listen to it any longer. Yet that was only the beginning, and it was after the music had reached apparently its extreme limits that the really expert work began and the effects were multiplied by geometric progression; in this sort of thing the idea of a climax and a quiet ending simply could not exist. When the leader was exhausted, he said "close," and abruptly a shattering silence followed.[28]

Since the early days of jazz, performers have made considerable efforts to explain what they and their colleagues were trying to accomplish in their improvisations. For the most part, their remarks have been colorful but not very enlightening. It nevertheless seems worthwhile to look briefly at some of the statements attributed to jazzmen who spent a good part of their lives working toward a barely perceived, often intangible, goal: the creation of significant improvisation. Johnny St. Cyr, representing the view of many early jazzmen, said:

> A jazz musician have to be a working class of man. . . . The more enthusiastic his audience is, why, the more spirit the

71

working man's got to play. And with your natural feelings that way, you never make the same thing twice. Every time you play a tune, new ideas come to mind and you slip that on in.[29]

Mutt Carey, another pioneer of New Orleans jazz, recalls what he felt after hearing Armstrong perform before the first World War:

> . . . when Louis played that day he played more blues than I ever heard in my life. It never did strike my mind that blues could be interpreted in so many different ways. Every time he played a chorus it was different and you knew it was the blues— yes, it was all blues, what I mean.

> Louis sings just like he plays. I think Louis proves the idea and theory which holds that if you can't sing it, you can't play it. When I'm improvising, I'm singing in my mind. I sing what I feel and then try to reproduce it on the horn.[30]

Armstrong is, of course, a jazz phenomenon. He has been quoted, imitated, and, in certain jazz circles, revered. Armstrong at his best is magnificent, and much of what has been said about him is undoubtedly warranted. Jack Teagarden, a long-time colleague and intimate of Armstrong's, says this about him:

> . . . Louis can't do anything wrong. The sound is there—and the beat. There's never a doubt in his mind as to what he's going to do, and no matter what everybody else is doing, Pops just goes right ahead. . . . Something else, too: I've never yet seen Louis Armstrong fail to please anybody with his playing. It's something innate with him—he just can't miss.[31]

Whether a jazzman is improvising on the primary triads or on a progression of augmented elevenths seems to make little difference in his ability to express what he is trying to say. Charlie Parker recalls a night in December, 1939:

> Now I'd been getting bored with the stereotyped changes that were being used all the time at the time, and I kept thinking there's bound to be something else. I could hear it sometimes but I couldn't play it.
>
> Well, that night, I was working over *Cherokee,* and as I did, I found that by using the higher intervals of a chord as a melody line and backing them with appropriately related changes, I could play the thing I'd been hearing. I came alive.[32]

Parker's talk of "appropriately related changes" and "the higher intervals of a chord" are, in their way, as inarticulate as Teagarden's "he just can't miss." When Parker says, "I came alive," however, he is speaking in the tradition of most jazzmen; and for jazzmen, even those with some academic training, no other explanation is necessary. Miles Davis, who studied. at the Juilliard School of Music, when asked about improvising the blues, said: "You don't learn to play the blues. You just play. I don't even think of harmony. It just comes. You learn where to put notes so they'll sound right. You just don't do it because it's a funny chord." [33]

Despite Miles Davis' assertion that "it just comes," the limitations on improvisation are severe. The performer must accept the discipline of melodic, harmonic, rhythmic, and structural limitations—in short, stylistic limitations—if he is to create significant improvisations. When the performer is not bound by stylistic limitations, his improvisations become sketchy and sporadic, he shows flashes of creativity, he plays an interesting measure or two here and there, but his creation suffers in its total impact. The best improvisation, like the best notated music, comes to the listener as an organized pattern, a unified structure. Music, improvised or written, if it is to be art, must have direction and purpose; one must be able to search for and find the same qualities in jazz improvisation that one would expect to find in the best calculated, notated music. Considering the severe limitations upon the performer, it is remarkable how many fine and sensitive improvisations have been created over the years.

The evaluation of improvisation and other aspects of jazz does not appear to me to be as controversial as certain of the traditionalists would have it. The problems of evaluation are thorny enough without complicating the issues with such questions as "Is oldtime jazz better than current jazz?" There is as little point to such a question as there is to the question of who is the better composer, Tchaikovsky or Ravel. Both questions are based on a false premise. Composers and their music are properly evaluated only in the setting and spirit of their own time; serious evaluators and critics ought not to be permitted to impose the limitations or freedoms of one period on another. Nevertheless, this is exactly what traditionalists and progressives alike have done in the controversy over the relative merits of notated and improvised jazz. Those who see collective improvisation as the foundation of all jazz are understandably nonplussed when asked to evaluate, for example,

Fletcher Henderson's or Benny Goodman's version of "The King Porter Stomp." Those who by some obscure reasoning hold that chords of the eleventh are more musical than chords of the seventh are equally nonplussed when asked to evaluate, for example, Bunk Johnson's solo on the "Saints." The rationale of critics on both sides of the fence is largely fanciful and irrelevant.

As soon as jazzmen learned how to read, the traditionalist view holds, jazz started downhill. Since the basis of jazz is, or ought to be, collective improvisation, individual improvisation leads to inflated egos and undisciplined freedom, which, in turn, deny the value of the musical teamwork essential to the true jazz. The traditionalists consider the short life of swing and the groping for new jazz styles of the following twenty years sufficient proof of the inadequacy of solo improvisation to contribute anything to jazz; on the other hand, the resurgence of the New Orleans, or Dixieland, style in 1946 is offered as evidence that true jazz will prevail.

The progressives, advocates of solo improvisation (with or without the accompaniment of the big band), take little stock in the foregoing views. They see little difference in the kind of individuality required for collective and for solo improvisation; they make a strong point of holding up to ridicule the traditional jazzman's meager musical resources and technical deficiencies; they claim that their kind of jazz requires infinitely more skill, knowledge, and profundity—more art, if you will—to perform. Further, the progressives believe that the large ensemble, with its arrangements and solo performers, serves to unify and display significant characteristics of style; that the big band gives satisfactory form to what the individual or small group initiates; that the big band works toward financial security for the jazzman since it provides more opportunities for playing, through which jazz can be brought more forcibly to the attention of the general public; and that all these factors result in a wider acceptance of jazz. The unprecedented activity during the swing era when, for the first time, jazz and popular music were almost synonymous is considered by the progressives as sufficient evidence of swing's contribution to jazz.

There is much to say for the attitude of both sides. Each side, in its way, sees itself as a defender of jazz; this, in itself, is a good thing. A part of what each side stands for is true. But the traditionalist needs to know that collective improvisation at one time *was* the basis of jazz (and may very well be again), but only during a particular period; and the progressive needs to recognize that during a particular period the basis of jazz may very well be collective improvisation. Both sides need to know that creativity in jazz must be measured according to the musical and technical means available to the creators; that jazzmen are not to be devalued because certain means were not available to them in their time. The art of Giotto is not better than the art of Picasso; the Colosseum is not a better example of architecture than the United Nations Secretariat; the music of Mozart is not better than the music of Debussy. The critic may, for purposes of educating the reader, show relationships between two periods in art, two periods in music, or when necessary between one period in art and another in music. He may compare techniques and materials; he may not, however, concoct an arbitrary scale of values. He may prefer romantic music to baroque music, but he must make clear that this is not a value judgment; it is a matter of taste and preference.

How, we may properly ask, does one evaluate that part of jazz which is written and not improvised? Most critics would agree, I believe, that, when a soloist or even a group of soloists is improvising, one or more instruments are providing a background against which the improvised solo is heard. Are we then to assume that the soloist is playing jazz and the accompanist is not? Or that the whole is not jazz if any of its parts is notated and played as written? If this should prove to be the case, then much that has passed for jazz would have to be discounted.

Without doubt improvisation is not the sole element in jazz, but it is an integral one, and the value of the accompaniment must be assessed according to the manner in which it acts upon improvisation, that is, whether it impels or restrains improvisation. Arranged jazz is only as important as the solos it frames, and unless it does frame one significant solo, at least, it is poor jazz. A background or, for that matter, a foreground, may move with rocking-chair relaxation or swing high and mighty with jetlike force, but without the excitement of solo jazz it will not get off the ground. The qualities of drive, relaxation, and swing in written jazz need to be judged according to their

77

effect on the soloist, and, just as a solo can be ill-conceived, so can a background. According to Ethel Waters, the drive she needs to move her forward comes in great part from what she hears in her accompaniment. In her autobiography she writes:

> I kept having arguments with Fletcher Henderson about the way he was playing my accompaniments. Fletcher, though a fine arranger and a brilliant band leader, leans more to the classical side. On that tour Fletcher wouldn't give me what I call "the damn-it-to-hell bass," that chump-chump that real jazz needs.[34]

Good jazz needs solid support whether it comes from a wire brush accompaniment of indeterminate pitch or from eight brass rocking a C major chord. Benny Goodman, discussing how difficult it is to come by that kind of background, said, "But the art of making an arrangement a band can play with swing—and I am convinced it is an art —one that really helps a solo player to get off, and give him the right background to work against—that's something that very few musicians can do." [35]

It seems that certain jazz soloists do feel a great need for the "proper" accompaniment, while others are relatively unaffected. (It is difficult to imagine, for example, that the accompaniments provided for Armstrong solos in the early thirties on such records as "I Surrender Dear," "Them There Eyes," "Confessin'," and "Basin Street Blues" held him back in any way, or that they provided him with much stimulation. However, it may be that Armstrong's style—one of sticking close to the melody and, in blues, close to the basic blues material—does not require much support and stimulation from outside himself.) There is certainly a relationship between a performer's technical ability and the kind of background he requires for solo work. For example, numerous instances have been mentioned of the importance of the lead cornet in New Orleans style: of the importance to the improviser of having the tune where he could hear it constantly. On the other hand, a bop improviser would no doubt feel somewhat constricted in his playing if he had the tune impressed upon him all the time; more than likely he would be more responsive— that is, more stimulated to get off—to a rich harmonic background and stimulating rhythmic punctuation.

Furthermore, there is a relationship between the kind of background a performer requires and the degree of intellectuality with which he approaches his solo. Armstrong, for example, never one for being concerned with misses and near-misses, requires only a steady two or four; emotional stimulation he apparently finds within himself. A more intellectual approach to a solo is apparent in Benny Goodman's statement: "Teddy Wilson is nuts about accuracy, as I am. He'll never let a bad note get away from him if he can possibly help it, which means that he's always thinking a little bit ahead of what he's actually playing, anticipating the way an idea ought to work out." [36] Armstrong creates, as do Goodman and Wilson, with a full awareness of his technical limitations. Armstrong plays what he feels is right, and it is right just because it pushes at the bounds of his technical and emotional capacity; and, in his genre,

Armstrong is as hard to beat as Goodman is in his. Technical limitations do not limit one's creative ability; they do limit the possibilities of creating in a particular style. Charlie Parker, at the peak of his work, would probably have been as much hampered by a New Orleans style background as Goodman would be by a bop ensemble.

Certain early jazzmen and critics believed that too much technical facility and musicianship were detrimental to a jazzman's ability to create significant improvisation, and they were right for their time and for the jazz styles they represent. In our own time, however, one wonders at Dave Brubeck's curious attack on technique: "It's a very strange thing the way I feel about technique and creativity . . . the idea is that when you have real clean technique and your pride yourself with it and you have certain standards that have to come to what you want technically, you're gonna cut off creativity. . . ." [37] Brubeck's statement would sound more objective if one knew he were not concerned with answering those critics who wish he had greater technical facility. Brubeck's error here is his failure to recognize that, in the past, he has accomplished quite a lot considering his technical limitations, because technical deficiencies did not hamper him in the jazz style in which he chose to work. Many well-wishers believe that if he is to continue to grow he will have to enlarge his technique. His early works deserve credit and admiration, and these he has received in abundance; but, if he wishes to be reckoned among those present-day jazzmen who have an eye on the future (and Brubeck seems genuinely concerned with this), he must expect his technical proficiency to be compared with that of John Lewis, Lennie Tristano, Phineas Newborn, and others. In a jazz style where a high degree of technical proficiency is an established prerequisite to improvising and creating, it is superfluous to ask what one must do first in order to create in that style.

A first-rate performer in one jazz style is not necessarily a first-rate performer in another style; he may, in fact, be quite impotent in a style not his own. This is not to say that a performer may not attempt a style not his own; if he does, however, his listeners should not expect to hear first-rate jazz on order. Chances are that what they hear will range anywhere from mediocre to poor, stylistically speaking. There is no question that there are people who rejoice in hearing certain jazz styles rather than others; these are the listeners most likely to confuse style with quality. For them, any quality of cool jazz, say, is better or has more value or is more significant than, say, any quality of swing; the fact is that examples of artistically superior, mediocre, and poor jazz can be found in all styles, and the acceptance of this simple proposition is indispensable to the making of proper jazz evaluations.

More important than whether a jazz work is in one style or another, once the style has been established, is determining the general level of performance, the soloist's apparent intent, and whether artistic communication has been effected. Only the experienced and analytical listener can determine the degree of artistic success reached by the performer. The analyst has the task of separating the artistic from the

81

inartistic, the experimental from the commercial. He acts as a conscience for those who, once they discover what they believe to be a successful formula, exploit it for all it is worth; he exposes vulgarity, sentimentality, speciosity, and pretentiousness. The analyst attempts to relate technique and depth of feeling. He is constantly aware of Frank Lloyd Wright's "excess never to be mistaken for exuberance," aware that "creative" implies exuberance and spontaneity.

Because of the nature of jazz improvisation, there is much difference of opinion as to what makes significant improvisation. There is one point, however, on which most analysts agree: improvisation, to be significant, must contain the unexpected; it must produce the feeling of excitement and exhilaration that comes from, as Paul Eduard Miller calls it, the illusion of spontaneity. Therefore, when Whitney Balliett writes, "Thad Jones is a brassy, sure-footed trumpeter whose solos are now and then so perfectly structured they appear to have been carefully written out beforehand . . . ," [38] it is not certain in what sense Thad Jones's solos are being criticized. When Bix Beiderbecke took a chorus, Benny Goodman tells us, "We'd just sit back and listen, because you never could tell what he was going to do next." [39] And Milt Hinton says that Dizzy Gillespie's music was exciting for him because "there were things he attempted to do that he couldn't. He didn't wholly make everything he tried but he got to me and I admired him for what he tried." [40] Aaron Copland sums up the case when he says, "When you improvise, it is axiomatic that you take risks and can't foretell results." [41]

What distinguishes superior creative musicians from the mediocre ones of all periods is the manner in which they create resolutions, and to create resolutions it is necessary to set up irresolutions. This perhaps oversimplified statement summarizes the process of creation, which must be understood if its products are to be judged properly. In order to understand what the jazz creator is attempting to resolve, one must determine his intent; knowing the creator's purpose makes it easier to evaluate the end result. Poor and mediocre jazzmen will impose problems on themselves, problems of resolution whose answers are already evident in the irresolutions they set up. Poor and mediocre jazzmen fretfully pursue resolutions that, when accomplished, surprise no one but themselves; their resolutions seem not so much inevitable as commonplace. Jazzmen in these categories often do not understand that the quality of their jazz will depend not on any resolution, however elaborate, but rather on the inherent intricacy of the irresolution. The answer to two plus two is four, and finding a way to solve this by calculus does not make the problem more profound. The first-rate jazzman sets himself difficult examinations. He is not looking for easy solutions, quick formulas, or back-of-the-book answers. Although he is vitally concerned with solving the problem of creativity, he knows that technique and method of operation are the important factors through which he may achieve his end. The approach that engenders comfort and security is not his. He knows that the intangible qualities of imagination, intuition, and inspiration are in part the result of experience and knowledge, and that only through a delicately balanced organization of all these qualities will the spirit of creativity manifest itself.

chapter 4

THE MUSICAL
ELEMENTS
OF JAZZ

A JAZZ PERFORMER USUALLY
improvises on given material, and, while it may be extremely difficult to show an exact written version of the improvisation itself, it is relatively easy to show a written
version of the given material. Jazz consists of musical
sounds, and the basic elements of music—rhythm, melody,
harmony—are shown in jazz in essentially the same way
as in other music. The problems of symbolizing musical
sounds are therefore not unique to jazz, but are present in
all music. The symbol of a musical sound, that is, a note,
is not the sound itself but merely the representation of the
sound. While the note indicates duration (after a meter is
indicated) and pitch (highness or lowness), it seldom provides for either intensity or timbre (the quality, or tone
color, of a sound); if one wishes to indicate degrees of
loudness or softness, additional symbols are necessary.

Even so, there is no assurance that the composer's sign for "very soft" will not be interpreted—at least to the composer's way of thinking—as "loud"; for that matter, there is no assurance that the indicated pitch will be sounded exactly. Microtonic deviations from pitch are a commonplace; furthermore, instruments are tuned higher in the United States than they are in Europe.

The problem of notating the jazz solo does not lie in the technical deficiency of the composer, as some critics believe, nor is it impossible to solve, as others believe; rather, the difficulty lies with the insufficiency of notational symbols. Those who have attempted to notate a composition of large proportions, in whatever musical style, will know that a constant effort to represent what is in the mind's ear with inadequate symbols invariably leads to frustration. There can have been few composers in the history of music who have not at one time or another felt this frustration and known the gross inefficiency of musical symbols. Nevertheless, composers continue to labor over their work and manage to communicate to the performer, with the performer's help, of course, more than the written page indicates. The evolution of this means of communication is a long one, and it may be useful here to summarize how it came about.

Willi Apel, in his *The Notation of Polyphonic Music 900-1600*, lists twenty-one different notational systems that were in use from earliest times. Not all these systems, of course, had equal currency, and not all played a role in the evolution of our present system, but many of them did. Our modern system very likely has its basis in the symbols used in Greek and Jewish speech recitations of the second century B.C. These symbols, known generically as ekphonetic notation, were for the most part short diagonal lines whose direction indicated whether the speaker was to raise his voice or lower it. (Present-day singers of Jewish chant still use ekphonetic signs.) About the sixth century, the ekphonetic notation grew into a system of signs known as neumes, symbols that expressed—though not very clearly —the general outlines of a melody. Neumes, however, represented neither pitch nor duration; a vocalist delivered his chant in the same rhythm he would use for speaking prose. For the performer, neumes were really mnemonic devices; he learned his music by rote, and neumes helped him to remember approximately how the tunes went so that he was able to hand down the oral tradition to the next generation. Later, attempts were made to clarify the vagueness of neumes by adding letters to the symbols (letter notation had been in use since the early Greeks), and, in about the ninth century, additional help came from the use of a horizontal colored line. Eventually two lines were adopted, and only the space between the lines was used. The staff lines increased until the theorist-monk Guido d'Arezzo, in the eleventh century, introduced the four-line staff, alternating black lines with the colored lines of his predecessors, and called the four lines (from the bottom) *f a c e*. When it became necessary to show higher or lower pitches, he merely added new lines.

By the end of the thirteenth century the five-line staff was widely used; the neumes had acquired a square shape and definite rhythmic values based on the repetition of simple ternary metrical patterns; indicating pitch was no longer a problem. Square notation developed into what is known as white mensural notation (larger note values became white shapes instead of black shapes), a system that was established around 1250 by the theorist Franco of Cologne and flourished until the seventeenth century. Franco's system set up a flexible time relationship between note values much like that of our present system. (There were still certain differences from our modern system. While our undotted note is equal to two notes of the next smaller value, in mensural notation certain notes are equal to three of the next value.) Around 1320 Philippe de Vitry, sometimes called the "father of modern notation," developed the principle of binary rhythm, giving it equal importance with ternary rhythm. Later, black mensural notation superseded the white, and the system, in essence, became our modern one. In his definitive volume on notation, Apel writes that "the development of notation from 1100 to 1600 is characterized by a gradual simplification and rationalization, by steps leading from extremely vague notions to the laws and principles prevailing in our days." [1]

It has already been stated that there were other notational systems besides the ones mentioned. For example, the development of systems of tablatures—the notation for solo keyboard and lute music that corresponds in some degree to the guitar and ukelele symbols found in much sheet music of the 1920's—was concomitant with mensural notation. Not until some fifteenth- and sixteenth-century keyboard tablatures are bar lines evident, and then they are inconsistently used and are apparently a matter of convenience in reading rather than a symbol to be placed after each repeated number of definite beats. (This function of the bar line has been adopted by most twentieth-century composers who do not favor the system of changing meters; performers of contemporary music have long since learned to ignore the bar line except as an orientation point and a convenience in counting measures.) The use of the bar line, together with the tie, which appeared first in a sixteenth-century keyboard score, mark the principal distinctions between mensural notation and modern notation. By J. S. Bach's time, a number of dynamic signs and tempo indications were widely used; by Mozart's time, the signs for various kinds of staccato and legato were well established. Small changes and additions continued to be made through the nineteenth century up to our own time, and there is little reason to believe that our present-day notation is the end of notation's evolution.

In the past, systems of notation have had to conform to composers' needs, and, when the needs could not be met, the system was altered to fit. There is a definite need for more serious and concerted effort to adapt our modern system of notation to the needs of jazz if jazz is to be notated properly. However, the imposition of special signs and symbols on jazz will not in itself be enough, so long as jazzmen continue to believe that what they improvise cannot be written down. This will be particularly true as long as reading music is considered a lesser accomplishment than improvising it. Practically speaking, we must admit the likelihood that jazz will always have two types of jazzmen: those who believe a serviceable jazz notation can be evolved, and those who either do not believe it or are indifferent to the problem. It is my belief that a jazz notation will evolve that will serve jazz-oriented performers as well as classical notation serves performers of classical music. Furthermore, this evolution has been proceeding quite rapidly in the past twenty years; many more musicians who ordinarily function outside the jazz scene have become aware of the practice of jazz performance, and it is the combined knowledge of notation and performance practice, not notation by itself, that brings about truthful interpretations of the composer's intent. (This point is of great significance, and we shall have to take a closer look at it further on.)

Let us see briefly which elements of jazz lend themselves readily to our present system of notation and which do not. Of the so-called special effects of jazz the most notable are the glissando, the growl of brass instruments, the fluttertongue of both brass and reeds, absence or exaggeration of vibrato, and slightly flatted notes. (The use of special mutes, while peculiar to jazz, is not a notational problem.) Standard notation provides serviceable symbols for the glissando, fluttertongue, and vibrato. What notation does not provide for is the degree to which these are to be used. The glissando, for example, indicates only a sliding up or sliding down; when the glissando is not immediately followed by another tone, there is no indication where the glissando is to end, or for that matter how rapidly or slowly it is to be effected.

Knowing how these things are done is a matter of knowing the practice of performance. For a musician technically familiar with the practice of a given jazz style, "smearing" a tone, for example, is no problem. If a special kind of glissando symbol is meaningless to a technically proficient nonjazz musician, so may Bartók's notational symbol for playing notes flat be meaningless to the jazz musician. And, even if both musicians understand the significance of the symbols, they must know their use in performance if they are to effect them with the proper style. Further, academically trained musicians do not generally know the meanings of such written indications as "smear," "growl," "bend," and others, not because they are technically incapable of performing them but because they are unfamiliar, first, with the indications and, second, with the proper manner of executing them. Because many nonjazz performers are not willing to devote the necessary time and practice to acquire a sense of jazz style does not mean they are incapable of doing so. (Not all nonjazz musicians are willing to devote the necessary time and practice to acquire a sense of Renaissance style either; it is a matter of preference.) Acquiring a "feel" for playing jazz is possible for any technically proficient musician who is willing to work at it; given the proper musical environment and study, any academically trained musician can learn to perform creditable jazz.

In some ways the problem of notating jazz effects that

concern pitch appears less formidable when approached through the notation of folk music, rather than art music. The reason for this is that, while the flatting of certain tones in jazz is usually related to a preconceived harmonic basis, the off-pitch tones of folk music may be looked at for themselves; folk music is conceived as melody without harmony. In folk song, despite the arbitrary major-minor basis by which most of us understandably relate all music, there is no harmonic conflict. A. H. Fox Strangways tells us:

> No folk-song anywhere recognizes harmony as a positive element. The drone, usually of one note, may add its neighbouring harmonics; voices in duet or chorus may overlap and, especially in pentatonic modes, harmonize for a moment; ancient Greeks magadized (sang in octaves) ; the valleys of the Niger and of the Severn hear some Gimel (singing in thirds). But harmony begins only when voices that have woven two tunes together mentally stop and admire the quality of the sound as such, and distinguish it from some other quality.[2]

Béla Bartók, who probably did as much as anyone in an attempt to notate special musical sounds and effects, recorded thousands of folk tunes on wax cylinders, after which he attempted to set them down on paper. It would seem that the special symbols Bartók had to create to realize even an approximation of the actual recorded performance might well be given further consideration by those who feel the necessity for notating improvised jazz melodies. As an illustration of the problems he was interested in solving, here is an excerpt from Bartók's definitive volume, *Hungarian Folk Music:*

The Musical Elements of Jazz

(2) The sign ⌒ (e.g. ♪, ♩) indicates a slight extension of value, and the sign ⌄ (e.g. ♪, ♩) a slight curtailment. The pause (⌒) gives a note at least twice its original value.

(3) The signs ⌐ and ⌐ indicate a *glissando* or *portamento;* ⌐ indicates a glissando beginning at the pitch of the note, and immediately after the note is given out, extending approximately to the note belonging to the point of the stave at which the *glissando* sign ends (in other words, the *glissando* covers the whole value of the note); ⌐ indicates a similar *glissando* beginning later (approximately with the second half of the value of the note); ⌐ means a *glissando* from the point of the stave from which the sign starts to the note which the sign reaches (the duration of the *glissando* corresponds approximately to half the value of the note). The sign ⌒ over two or more notes (⌐) indicates a *glissando* beginning slightly before the first note and ending slightly beyond the last, the two written notes standing out to a certain extent. ⌐ indicates a faint *tremolando.*

(4) The key-signatures include only such signs as obtain throughout a song. Generally, no time-signature is given for *parlando-rubato* tunes.

(5) The sign ↑ over a note indicates a slight rise in pitch, and the sign ↓ a slight lowering, both smaller than a quarter-tone: b/2 indicates a lowering by a quarter-tone.[3]

Bartók's item (4), dealing with time signatures, is especially important because it brings to the foreground the question of meter and, by extension, rhythm. Although this question is dealt with later in the chapter, it seems proper here to clarify one particular issue. All who have tried to notate jazz know the difficulty of notating its rhythms; this difficulty, as we have pointed out earlier, is not peculiar to jazz; it is encountered in notating all music. Nevertheless, writers continue to report on rhythm and meter in jazz as

93

if they were something unique to jazz. Leonard Feather writes: "The beat is something too subtle for completely accurate notation. Its presence or absence in countless performances has been the subject of dispute among musicians and critics ever since jazz began." [4] The "beat," it would seem, belongs more properly to the practice of performance than to a system of notation. The presence of the beat arises not from notational indications (although these would certainly represent the performer's working blueprints), but rather from the performer's interpretation, from his knowledge of what is expected in a style.

Bartók's "no time-signatures for *parlando-rubato* tunes" (tunes freely sung, almost spoken) shows an attitude that may well serve most jazz composers. A specific time signature ought to be indicated only when it obtains throughout a composition or, at least, when it dominates the music's meter. In other words, the time signature merely reflects the pulsation of the music; we derive the meter not from the time signature, but from the music. (The same principle holds true for key signatures. It may seem unnecessary to point out that the sharps or flats in key signatures do not determine the key, that the key is determined by an analysis of the music; experience with beginning analysts, however, will prove the necessity of emphasizing this seemingly obvious fact. An F-sharp in the signature does not necessarily mean that the music which follows is in G major or E minor; it only means that all F's are to be played as F-sharp unless they are otherwise marked. The key signa-

ture is only a clue to tonality; the time signature is only a
clue to the meter.)

If one insists upon saying, "Jazz is invariably in duple
meter," or, "Jazz can also be made to swing in ternary
rhythm," one runs the risk of confusing the measure of the
music with the 4/4, 3/4, or 2/4 time indicated in the signature; one also runs the risk of confusing bar lines perhaps
intended only as orientation symbols with bar lines intended as measuring posts. Without question, music of certain periods—from Bach to Brahms—used the bar line as
an aid in indicating weak and strong beats. In such music the
preponderance of strong accents is in agreement with the
meter. In 4/4 time, for example, the strong accents in the
music usually fall on the strong first and third beats, and
the weak accents on the weak second and fourth beats, and,
since the bar line is used to measure off every four beats, it
is proper in this style to give more stress to the beat immediately after the bar line and less to the beat immediately before the bar line. However, much twentieth-century
music, as we have already stated, is not controlled by the
bar line; to understand the meter of such music one cannot
simply count bar lines or take time signatures at face value.
One must measure the music, its strong and weak accents,
its entire rhythmic structure.

It is the element of rhythm and the performer's manner
of interpreting rhythmic indications that help distinguish
jazz from other music, and, as Leonard Feather points out,
"the rhythmic characteristics of jazz are those that are

hardest to define and notate and, by the same token, the most difficult to develop in a musician unaccustomed to a jazz *milieu*." [5] If we are to follow the evolution of the rhythmic characteristics of jazz, we may consider Bartók's general conclusion that rhythm, at the outset, was strict and steady, consisted chiefly of equal values, and had its basis in the motions of dancing. When it became necessary to sing, the simple dance rhythms were adapted to the rhythm of words. In the third stage—a return to the dance—the complicated rhythms derived from words were imposed on dance tunes, making the rhythms of the final stage considerably more complex than those of the first stage.[6]

Most observers would agree that the evolution of jazz styles was accompanied by increasingly complex rhythms. One has only to compare characteristic New Orleans rhythms with characteristic bop rhythms to recognize the degree of rhythmic complexity that separates the two. Nevertheless, there are a rhythmic drive and vitality common to the best jazz that force one to seek for some rhythmic device by which all jazz could be characterized. Many who have tried to isolate such a device have done so in vain, for the answer is not to be found in the repetition of particular rhythmic patterns or in the variation of others. Certain writers have searched for answers in Freud; others have tried West Africa; still others have speculated on "psychic tension" and "personal magnetism." If there is an answer to the secret of rhythmic vitality, I believe it lies in a remote region of the listener's mind and is activated only when the listener receives and understands the consummated intention of a jazz performer.

It seems certain that one part of the secret of rhythmic drive concerns the rhythmic element known as syncopation. Much has been written on syncopation, mostly on its effect on the listener; here we are concerned, rather, with the manner in which it may be used. But first it is necessary to remember that there are two types of rhythm: melodic rhythm and harmonic rhythm. Melodic rhythm is the rhythm of the melody, the result of the duration of each successive tone in the melody; harmonic rhythm is the rhythm of harmonic change (change of root). The following example should make clear the distinction between the two:

Walter Piston, in his *Harmony*, writes, "Syncopation, implies a well-established rhythmic pulse, the effect being based on a dislocation of that pulse by giving a strong accent where one is not expected, and suppressing the normal accent of the pulse." He then lists four ways of using syncopation that seem to sum up its possibilities:

1. The principal melodic line may be syncopated against the harmonic rhythm, or pulse. . . .
2. The pulse may not be actually heard but may exist by analogy with the preceding measures. . . .
3. Both melodic and harmonic rhythms may be syncopated against a pulse previously established but not heard at the moment. . . .
4. The harmonic rhythm may be syncopated, while the rhythm of the melody continues to agree with the established pulse. . . .[7]

Jazz has been concerned principally with the simple syncopation (1). The reason is not difficult to understand. In addition to the regularly stated pulse accompanying most jazz, at least up to the forties, the harmonic rhythm was in agreement with the meter, and, if there was to be any syncopation at all, it had to come from disagreement between the melodic rhythm and the established pulse. Although jazz has made great strides in expanding chords from sevenths to ninths to elevenths to thirteenths, including all sorts of alterations, little attention has been paid to the theoretical possibilities of having syncopation result from a manipulation of the harmonic rhythm as defined in (4).

As long as the harmonic progressions of blues—rhythmically the most rigid—dominated jazz performance, there was little room for exploring syncopation based on the dislocation of the harmonic rhythm. The blues progression, and progressions in the standard tunes of the twenties and thirties, with their important root changes agreeing with

98

the meter, required almost total concentration on the rhythm of the melody. By the forties and fifties, however, as jazzmen began working with thematic material in which the important changes did not necessarily coincide with the normal accent of the pulse, syncopations based on dis-location of the harmonic rhythm had a greater opportunity to develop and expand. The principle of simple syncopa-tion, coming as a result of single tones accenting weak beats or weak parts of beats against an established pulse, could now be expanded to a syncopation coming as a result of strong harmonic changes falling on weak beats or weak parts of beats against a melody whose rhythm agrees with the established pulse.

Composers who feel that binary rhythm in jazz may have outlived its usefulness, that binary rhythm restricts jazz, and that new time signatures are necessary if jazz is to continue to grow may do well to put aside temporarily their concern with 3/4, 5/4, 7/4, and other time signa-tures and concentrate their efforts on the potentialities of syncopation through harmonic rhythm. In exploring the pos-sibilities of harmonic rhythm, it is likely they will find that much that previously received little consideration can be done in binary rhythm. For example, Leonard Feather, in-tent on showing that jazz is possible in a ternary rhythm, says:

> Even one of the few apparent constants of jazz, the binary rhythm, has been shown to be less than completely essential. . . . To most of us at present jazz performed in anything but four-four seems unnatural and does not swing. In the future it

is quite possible that jazz and the waltz . . . may prove to be completely compatible.

He then goes on to show an example of a theme in 3/4 time that he derived from a theme in 4/4 time. Here are the rhythms intended to demonstrate how 4/4 may be converted to 3/4.[8]

An examination of the 3/4 structure shows no special evidence that the melodic rhythm is ternary, except for the bar line separating the equivalent of every three quarter notes. The melodic rhythm scans perfectly well as a three-bar phrase in 4/4. It is therefore apparent that Feather determined this particular use of ternary meter not from the melodic rhythm but, first, from a desire to maintain a parallel four-bar structure and, second, from the harmonic rhythm. Both reasons are logical if one takes for granted the traditional agreement of meter and harmonic rhythm. However, it seems that a fresher approach—not only to jazz rhythm but to structural design as well—would be to look at the theme not as a ternary one but rather as a binary one in which a rhythmic "lift" is achieved by a dislocation of the harmonic rhythm, as follows:

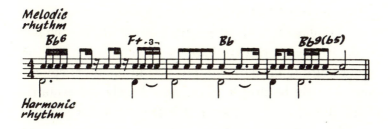

Marshall Stearns is almost entirely justified in saying:

> The criticism that the rhythms of jazz are monotonous is perhaps the most frequent and, at the same time, the most easily disproved. By his own criteria, the classical musician is quite right: he examines a jazz score, notes that the time signature is always 4/4, and concludes that the rhythms are simple. He probably does not realize that jazz cannot be notated accurately or that jazz is almost never played precisely on the beat or that duple rhythm lends itself to infinite complexities. The fact that academic musicians generally find it impossible to play jazz probably has something to do with the nature of jazz rhythms.[9]

This statement needs qualifying. The fact that most academically trained musicians do not play jazz has nothing to do with "the nature of jazz rhythms" except—as we have already pointed out—as the performer is unfamiliar with them. Stearns corroborates this view later when he says, "For in spite of the rapid and continuing fusion of European and West African music, there is no musician in the year, say, of 1955, who can rightly be considered pre-eminent in both fields. That time, however, is sure to come." [10]

101

If the time "is sure to come"—and I agree that it will—it certainly will not be because the nature of jazz rhythms has changed.

In some respects, rhythmic complexities have not had as much fascination for jazzmen, particularly during the past twenty-five years, as have harmonic complexities. But, before we turn to the harmonies of jazz in the twentieth century, it might be proper to consider briefly the evolution of traditional harmony, since it is from this that jazz harmony has been derived. The basis of harmony is the scale. From the scale are derived intervals that, when sounded simultaneously, result in chords. Harmony, sometimes called "vertical" music, is a much later development in music than counterpoint, or "horizontal" music; the system of traditional harmony as we know it is in fact an outgrowth of counterpoint, as is our system of building chords in thirds (tertian harmony). We shall see that the harmonies of jazz have their models in the harmonies of the past, from the tenth century to the twentieth.

The evolution of harmony may be divided into three periods: from 900 to 1450, when harmony was the result of contrapuntal writing; from 1450 to 1900, when harmony consisted of pre-established combinations of sound; from 1900 to the present, when systems of harmony other than tertian were evolved. The three periods may be called pretertian, tertian, and post-tertian. Discussion of the post-tertian period will be found in chapter 10; for the present we shall concern ourselves with the two earlier periods.

In pretertian days a system of scales called modes was

used as a basis for the composition of solo vocal melodies; when one voice was joined by another part, vocal or instrumental, the result was certain "acceptable" harmonic intervals (fourths and fifths in the two-part harmony of the tenth century, followed a century later by a prescribed use of octaves, seconds, thirds, sixths, and sevenths). By the end of the pretertian period there was a wide use of three-part counterpoint that produced open triads (root, fifth, and octave), full triads (root, third, and fifth) in rhythmically weak places, and consecutive triads in first inversion (third, fifth, and octave) that produced an effect not unlike the consecutive minor triads with added seventh that are much favored by many present-day jazzmen.

Around 1450, in the early tertian period, composition in more than three parts was so widespread that the modal scales, originally conceived for the solo voice, no longer served this purpose. When the theorist Glareanus published his book, *Dodecachordon*, in 1547, he added four modes to the eight then current; six scales were called "authentic" and six, the "hypo" scales, "plagal." The scales were all white-key scales and were identified by their final note and range, as follows:

Dorian	D (D to d)	Hypodorian	D (A to a)
Phrygian	E (E to e)	Hypophrygian	E (B to b)
Lydian	F (F to f)	Hypolydian	F (C to c)
Mixolydian	G (G to g)	Hypomixolydian	G (D to d)
Aeolian	a (a to aa)	Hypoaeolian	a (E to e)
Ionian	c (c to cc)	Hypoionian	c (G to g)

By the time Glareanus published the twelve scales, composers and performers had already been using accidentals to alter modal scales to avoid the tritone (F to B became F to B-flat) and to provide a half step between the seventh and eighth degrees of the scale, for example, c to d in the Dorian mode might be played c-sharp to d. At times the accidentals were notated; at other times they were provided by the performer, who raised or lowered tones according to the current practice of performance, with the result that the modal scales usually turned out to be what we now know as forms of major or minor scales. But before the construction of major and minor scales, as such, could become common practice, before scales could be started on tones other than "white keys," the acoustical problems of equal temperament had to be solved. Although these problems were not to be finally solved until the nineteenth century, the process of solution continued through two hundred years. The sixteenth-century modes were eventually replaced by the major and minor modes, and composers became more concerned with vertical combinations of sound.

Although composers had used sections in chordal style alternating with polyphonic style from the thirteenth century on, it was not until the early baroque period that Italian opera composers set the style of melody with chordal accompaniment that was to prevail to our own time. The method for this style of composition, the basis of modern harmonic theory, was formulated by Jean Philippe Rameau in his *Traité de l'harmonie*, published in 1722. In this remarkable treatise, Rameau recognized the necessity for a strong tonal center, presented the theory of chord inversions, and made out the case for tertian harmony. He initiated the relations between I, IV, and V and codified the harmonic relationships we now call "traditional." While he did not create any new chords, he related old ones in a new way, a way that established tonality, or a key. Whereas composers for five centuries previous had heard harmony as the result of combined melodies, Rameau contended that melody was derived from harmony. In his own compositions diminished seventh chords and chords of the added sixth were common, and his modulations were more distant than was customary in his day.

With Rameau's system well established, the chordal style pervaded the work of most composers, and gradually there was a complete transition from modal writing to tonal writing. Between 1750 and 1825 the I, IV, and V became the functional chords around which all others revolved. Modulations to distant keys and chromatic progressions were no longer extraordinary. The nineteenth century saw composers working, first, to expand tonality, and in the end seeking to avoid it; chromatically altered chords and an almost unrestrained use of nonharmonic tones became common practice. The romantic period, characterized by the late work of Beethoven and such harmonic styles as are found in the compositions of Chopin, Wagner, Franck, Strauss, and Debussy, was the culmination of the system developed by Rameau. As we move away from the romantic period into the twentieth century we discover, among certain composers and theorists, a widespread movement to

disestablish—perhaps we should say further disestablish
—Rameau's system of functional harmony. It is therefore
rather ironic that many jazzmen who consider jazz to be
"new" music and classical music to be "old" music choose
to remain harmonically in the last quarter of the nineteenth
century, while classical composers have gone on to such
harmonic developments as quartal harmony, polymodality,
polytonality, and atonality. Jazz composers, in the late fifties at least, have apparently found their wellspring in the
parallelism of Debussy and the chromaticism of Franck,
with an occasional exploratory dip into modal harmonies.

The harmonies of early jazz are much the same as those
found in a large number of eighteenth-century dances and
nineteenth-century evangelical hymns. The early jazzman
accepted the harmonies of his musical environment and
went on to develop what he was mainly concerned with:
melody and rhythm. Since the development of any art
proceeds slowly, it is no surprise to find that most jazzmen
still rate harmony after melody and rhythm. They are concerned with harmony, but not in the same creative sense
they are concerned with melody and rhythm. Aside from
harmony's function as a base for their improvisation, jazzmen believe that harmony serves best when it is strengthening and maintaining the fundamental tonality; that is why
their harmonic frame of reference is the progression dominant to tonic, or, more specifically, dominant-function
chords to tonic-function chords. If a jazz composition is
constructed on this harmonic basis the result, of course, is

not as simple harmonically as certain eighteenth-century compositions built on the same harmonies, but this is only because the concept of dominant function has been expanded to include any combination of tones that, in the traditional sense, require resolution. Relying on dominant-function chords to provide newness can be successful provided the chords do not fall on ears already jaded by these harmonies. Diminished chords, augmented chords, secondary dominants, and a good many chromatically altered chords may occasionally be satisfactory substitutes for a dominant chord, but they add little to harmonic depth —at least in our time.

Except for relatively few jazzmen, the approach to jazz harmony has been naïve in the extreme. After only thirty years of hard use by jazz composers, the primary triads, diminished seventh chords, and secondary dominant sevenths were expanded into a "modern" jazz harmony that is still being purveyed in little pamphlets at anywhere from fifty cents to two dollars each. For one dollar, for example, Johnny Warrington's twenty-four-page *Modern Harmony* (published in 1948 by Bregman, Vocco, and Conn) informs the anxious student about the whole-tone scale and its augmented chords; chords with added notes ("Adding notes to major and dominant 7th chords provides one of the most modern devices in scoring for large dance bands"); parallelism; the modes ("The six principal Greek modal scales form the basis of our present-day harmony. The purpose of this study is to show how they can be applied in a modern manner"). The last statement is

107

followed by a two-page study. The remaining sixteen pages cover, in the language of the author's subject headings: "Superstructure Chords," "Contrapuntal Writing," "The Minor Dominant Seventh Chord," "Impressionistic Motion of Chords," "Chromatic Alteration of Scale Chords," "False Progression of Dominant Chords," "Tonic Harmonization of Scales," "Free Chords," "Dissonant Seventh Chords," "Chord Substitutions," "Complete Modern Reharmonization."

Until one thinks about it, there seems little harm in this sort of thing, but its pretentiousness is certain to repel some students and discourage others. It is true that the author is not a jazz composer, and his pamphlet does not emphasize any appeal it may have for jazz students. But what innocent jazz student would not be attracted by its title? There are too many pamphlets of this kind. Perhaps some of them serve a good purpose, but one wishes that their authors had more regard for the printed word. It is one thing for a jazzman to be inarticulate—he has tradition on his side—but an inarticulate author writing a jazz teaching manual is quite another thing. Usually the musical examples are clear enough, and if the student can avoid reading the text he is less likely to be confused A good example of ambiguous language and confused terminology, in an otherwise quite clear musical context, can be seen in Van Alexander's *The Be-bop Style*, published in 1949 by Criterion Music Corporation with endorsements attributed to Pete Rugolo, Miles Davis, Babs Gonzales, and Tadd Dameron. On page 2 Alexander writes:

Bebop may be analyzed by these steps:

1. The melodic framework (tune) which helps determine the character, mood, and tempo.
2. The harmonic sequences, which give the key to the improvisation.
3. The rhythmic pattern of the original theme sets the new structure. While bebop is basically four, it is usually an implied beat and is usually sparked with counter rhythms by the piano and bass. It is also colored by sporadic beats and chords.
4. The instrumentation of the performers, which determine the color.

Probably the worst confusion of terms arises out of step number two. Obviously what is meant is not "the harmonic sequences," but the harmonic *progressions;* and to use "key," a term of technical significance, in a loose, popular sense, can only heighten the confusion. (If the ultraconservatism of jazz harmony could be attributed to any single compositional device, the sequence would surely rate as high as any. The sequence, not a bad thing in itself, is too often the method taught by the pamphlets in question. Given a one- or two-bar cliché, the unimaginative composer or performer is led to believe it will gain in strength if repeated two, three, and even more times at different pitch levels. The compilers of these works are apparently unaware that a mere change of pitch or key does not enrich what may be, at best, a banal motive.)

The study of harmonic practice is the study of consonance and dissonance. It is necessary to remember that these qualities are relative—what is dissonant in one musical style may be consonant in another. Furthermore, the

109

question of consonance and dissonance seems to depend as much on the harmonic conditioning and experience of the listener as on scientific analysis. For most listeners, an interval of a third or a sixth is more consonant—more "pleasant," as they would put it—than an interval of a fourth or a fifth; yet, in the earliest periods of music history, fourths and fifths were considered consonant, and not until the fourteenth century were thirds so considered.

Consonance and dissonance are determined by context: the interval of a perfect fourth, for example, takes on a relative feeling of repose when preceded by a series of consecutive minor sevenths. Similarly, the minor seventh takes on a relative feeling of repose when preceded by a series of major sevenths.

In short, even among the traditionally acknowledged dissonances, there are *degrees* of dissonance. And, if there are degrees of dissonance, there may be degrees of consonance. A listener may hear the fourth and minor seventh in the above example as a lessening, although not necessarily a resolving, of the dissonance created by the intervals preceding them. According to one's experience, then, the resolutions may be heard as a lesser degree of consonance or a lesser degree of dissonance. Add more voices to two-part writing and the difficulties become more complex. Prearranged combinations of sound (chords) are not intended to stand by themselves but rather are conceived as a foundation on which to build melodies, and, when melodies are not made up entirely of chord tones, their disagreement with the harmony must be justified according to the harmonic style. Walter Piston puts it this way:

> The question of deciding whether a tone is a chord factor or a nonharmonic tone comes often to the fore in the study of harmony. More important than the decision of this question is the appreciation of both sides of the issue. Let us repeat that all chords are the product of the momentary coincidence of melodic parts. A vertical cross-section of the music at a given instant is undeniably a chord, but we notice that some of these chords are constantly recurring under different conditions whereas others seem to depend on some other simpler chord for their existence.[11]

Before proceeding to the problem of melodic dissonance it may be helpful to list the most common chords and their symbols, as found in jazz notation.

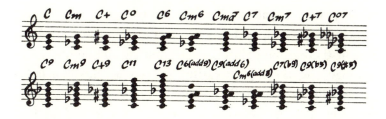

Jazz notation is not much concerned with correct chord spellings, and enharmonic spellings, particularly in diminished seventh chords and altered chords, are a commonplace. In chords of the eleventh the symbol occasionally implies the augmented eleventh instead of the perfect eleventh (the eleventh in C^{11}, for example, may be an F-sharp). Symbols for chords of the thirteenth are often ambiguous; they may be used, for example, to show chords that contain a thirteenth, but no eleventh and no ninth (the seventh, however, is almost invariably present). Since the position of the thirteenth in the chord is apparently of no consequence, one often finds C^{13} and $C^9(\text{add}^6)$ used interchangeably. (Also, because chord symbols make no provision for chord inversions, the tones DFAC may be symbolized either as Dm^7 or F^6, depending on the context; one supposes that C^7 would be followed by F^6, and A^7 by Dm^7, but this is not always the case.) The added-note and altered-note symbols provide for any combination of sounds; if the composer is unable to analyze a particular combination of tones because, for example, the root is only implied, he need only find a combination he recognizes, show its symbol, and then show the remaining tones in parentheses.

The system of chord symbols serves satisfactorily nonetheless and, in practice, is understandable to all. Whatever deficiency there may be is not in the system of symbols, but in their often arbitrary selection by the composer or arranger. Jazz composers often neglect to distinguish between what is essentially harmonic and what is essentially melodic. Jazz melodies, like those of the period of harmonic common practice, either are derived from established chords with the addition of nonharmonic melodic tones or—in the work of certain jazzmen of the late fifties —imply established harmonies. Whether a melodic tone is nonharmonic depends, of course, on its context. Harmony, we recall, evolved as a result of combining melodies. Eventually contrapuntal tones that created dissonances as they passed over established harmonies became an integral part of those harmonies. Sevenths and ninths, for example, may in certain past styles be analyzed as dissonant nonharmonic tones; in other styles their harmonic functions may depend on their rhythmic value. Many jazz composers are inclined to overlook these aspects of chord building. If the tones CEGB, for example, have been established as a chord, their reasoning goes, then it is a simple matter to show this chord as a Cma^7 wherever it appears. And they do so. However, it is necessary to remember that the tones CEGB may be shown as a Cma^7 only if the B has the necessary duration to be considered part of the harmony.

This distinction will not make much impression on composers who care little whether they write C or Cma^7, or on accompanists who would just as soon play the one chord as the other and who would defend to the death their right to play *all* the notes in a given symbol. It *should* make an impression on jazz soloists searching for fresh melodic tones —a confounding task when the accompanying background consists of skyscraper chords already commandeering most of the available sounds. If a soloist is set on improvising against a traditional tonal background, his chances of turning a fresh phrase depend mainly on his use of nonharmonic tones. The fewer the number of nonharmonic tones he is permitted, the fewer the opportunities for freshness. The vitality of so much eighteenth-century music is due in part to its being constructed on simple harmonic foundations around which the composer or performer could embellish freely. Similarly, much of the vigor and freshness of early jazz is mainly due to an observance of this principle. The principle is illustrated in its best use by the manner in which composers of the past characteristically resolved the appoggiatura. (In certain later harmonic styles, of course, resolving the appoggiatura is not *required*.)

The appoggiatura, king of the nonharmonic tones, is capable of producing the strongest possible dissonance in combination with simple chords. In addition, the effect of its resolution—if done properly—intensifies the dissonance in retrospect, so to speak. It is therefore essential that the note of resolution, when sounded, be fresh, unless the note of resolution is also the root of the chord to which it is resolving, in which case it is considered esthetically correct to double the root. The characteristic resolution is as follows:

It is not necessary to show these chords as C^9 or C^{11}, as is so often done. The listener is interested only in the sounds, not the symbols; and the jazz soloist is interested in accompaniment that will stimulate him. Most of the stimulation he has received in the past has been rhythmic; perhaps in the future he will receive in greater measure the harmonic stimulation that comes from sounding a note that is exactly right and belongs, so to speak, to him. This could only happen, of course, with the help of accompanists who themselves are imaginative enough to sense harmonic and melodic possibilities.

As a reference for accompanists, and perhaps future jazz analysts, the following brief definitions of the most-used nonharmonic tones may prove helpful.[12]

A passing tone is a nonharmonic tone derived by step and resolved by step in the same direction. It is usually rhythmically weak, but if it falls in a strong place it may be called an accented passing tone. If a passing tone is derived by leap instead of by step, it is called a free passing tone.

The auxiliary tone, sometimes called neighboring tone or embellishing tone, is a nonharmonic tone derived by step and resolved by step in the opposite direction. It is rhythmically weak. Consecutive upper and lower auxiliaries are known as changing notes.

The suspension is a nonharmonic tone derived from the tone that precedes it and resolved down a step. It is rhythmically weak and is characterized by a tie, which is often implicit. Infrequently the suspension is resolved up a step instead of down; it is then known as a retardation.

The anticipation is a nonharmonic tone derived from the tone that follows it. It is rhythmically weak. In jazz the anticipation is frequently tied to its resolution as a device for rhythmic anticipation; harmonically the effect is rather like that of the suspension.

The *échappée* is a nonharmonic tone derived by step and resolved by skip (usually a third) in the opposite direction. It is rhythmically weak.

The *cambiata* is a nonharmonic tone derived by skip (usually a third) and resolved by step in the opposite direction. It is rhythmically weak.

The appoggiatura is a nonharmonic tone derived in any manner and usually resolved down a step; it may, on occasion, resolve up a step. It is rhythmically strong and often has the effect of a suspension in which the suspended tone is struck again instead of being tied over.

Nonharmonic tones may, of course, be used either singly or in any combination; they may appear consecutively and without immediate resolution; they are then being directed toward an ornamental resolution. The following phrase shows this analysis of nonharmonic tones.

The use of nonharmonic tones is intimately connected with tonality and modality, two aspects of harmony whose technical qualities have often proved troublesome to jazz

117

analysts. Chords, as we know, are derived from scales, and scales are arbitrary successions of horizontal intervals. It has been the practice during the history of tonal music to select one scale tone, called the tonic, and to use it as a base to which all the other tones must find relationship. When this is accomplished according to prescribed rules, tonality is established, that is, the music has a tonal center and a key. While scales may be constructed on any number of tones in any intervallic relationship, only three of the scales that have come down to us have had wide and important use: the pentatonic (a five-tone scale), the diatonic (a seven-tone scale), and the chromatic (a twelve-tone scale). A form of the diatonic is the basis for jazz.

In one of the earliest books on jazz theory, Winthrop Sargeant, concerned with the "scalar structure of jazz," tells us how he went about reconstructing a scale for jazz. He "selected particularly hot passages from fourteen recordings highly regarded by swing enthusiasts, and notated them with incidental indications of pitch variation." After listing the titles of the recordings and reasons for their selection, Sargeant goes on to say:

> In the process of these observations and computations a definable scale began to take shape, and certain traits of melodic movement began to establish themselves as universally characteristic. The tones comprising the scale may be indicated as follows:

For convenience, and because it is associated with the performance of the blues as well as with hot jazz proper, we will call it
the blues scale.[13]

The "blues scale" is a reasonable enough term for this
scale, but in addition the minor third degree and minor
seventh degree are often referred to as "blue notes," a less
happy term. Marshall Stearns, in an attempt to merge the
blue note and the blues scale, refers to them in combination as "blue tonality." He asks, "Where does blue tonality
come from?" And his answer is, "It can't be found in Europe. Something very much like it occurs in West Africa. . . ." [14] I suggest, first, that the term "blue tonality"
is incorrectly used and, second, that what is "very much
like it in West African music"—variations in pitch, "worried" tones, and other peculiarities of intonation—are part
of the practice of performance and cannot be part of the
notation of the blues scale. The principal point of conten-
tion, however, is Stearns's use of "blue tonality," and before we continue it will be necessary to prove its misuse.

Tonality refers to a tonal center, and the tonal center of
the blues scale is the tonic—C, in Sargeant's example. The
size and quality of the various intervals between middle C
and its octave in this scale in no way affect the tonality. In
brief, the tonality of a C major scale is C, and the tonality
of a C minor scale is C. When one is concerned with the
size and quality of the intervals, one is concerned with
modality. The tonality of a C major scale, for example, is
C, and its modality is major; the tonality of a C minor
scale is C, and its modality is minor. It seems, therefore,

119

that what Stearns is concerned with is not tonality but modality.

The blues scale, as we have mentioned, may be a reasonable term, but it is not a correct one. It is not truly a special ten-tone scale, as some writers have suggested, or even a nine-tone scale. If we accept the harmonic practice of composers in the past, it becomes evident that in the blues scale we are dealing with a simple diatonic scale subject to the same harmonic and melodic manipulations as any diatonic scale. The problem posed by the blues scale is based, I believe, on the seemingly ambiguous intervals between the C, or root, and the third and seventh scale degrees. Thirds and sevenths, the reasoning goes, ought clearly to be part of a major scale or part of a minor scale; since the scale is not clearly major or minor, it is proper to call it something else, namely, the blues scale. If we examine a blues scale we recognize that the minor third and seventh degrees were drawn from the minor mode, while the remaining tones were drawn from the major mode. There is sufficient evidence in the works of nineteenth- and twentieth-century classical composers to show that this situation is not peculiar to the blues scale. Walter Piston tells us:

> Major and minor modes are not as distinct in usage as their two scales would seem to indicate, and it is sometimes uncertain which impression is intended by the composer.
> Fluctuation between major and minor has always been common.[15]

It is easy to lose sight of the fact that the practice of jazz preceded the construction of the blues scale. Early jazzmen probably saw little distinction between major and minor modes and used the major and minor thirds interchangeably. The minor seventh degree of the blues scale may be analyzed as the seventh degree of the descending melodic minor scale (the minor seventh may also have come about through a need for V^7 of IV, which almost invariably precedes the IV in blues). In any event, if the blues scale needs further to be characterized, it would not be improper to refer to it as being in the major-minor mode, or, more simply, bimodal.

chapter 5

UNDERSTANDING
STYLE

IN SOMETHING LIKE SIXTY years, jazz has divided itself into four significant periods encompassing a number of styles. A full understanding of the evolution of jazz from 1900 to the present time is possible only through a careful analysis of the characteristic style in each period. Manfred Bukofzer wrote, "A musical era receives its inner unity from the musical style and can be historically understood only in terms of stylistic development." [1] We might add that one cannot understand the development of a style unless one is willing to study the various theoretical aspects of jazz; theory attempts to provide the technical reasons for music's sounding as it does, and helps illuminate the fundamental qualities that characterize a musical style. The study of theory is therefore essential to those who wish to understand the musical history of jazz or any other music.

A musical period may extend over many years, or even centuries, and during one period there may be numerous changes in the music, the manner in which it is played, and so forth. How, then, is it decided when one period ends and another begins? In the broadest view the periods were distinguished when the music being composed and performed was so "new" that current writers and critics apparently felt compelled to say so. This wholesale critical phenomenon, as Willi Apel has pointed out, occurred once every three hundred years, starting with Guido d'Arezzo's introduction of the four-line staff in the year 1000. Approximately three hundred years later, composers thought of their music as new and music before 1300 as old (*ars nova* as against *ars antiqua*). Around 1600, Italian composers, prompted in part by the title of a published volume of music called *Nuove musiche*, broke from the traditional "old" music and went on to compose thousands of *nuove musiche* operas, oratorios, and cantatas that are now considered old by those who around 1900 decided that old music had had its day, particularly old romantic music. About 1925, or about the time Louis Armstrong was contemplating something "new," someone in Germany designated the period from 1900 to that time as the period of *Neue Musik*. And so it goes. Hodeir has written:

> Certainly, a very curious similarity between the evolution of jazz and that of European music has often been noted. Beginning at the same point (popular and religious vocal music) and passing through the same stages (instrumental polyphony, accompanied melody, symphonic music, and so on), jazz does in-

123

deed seem to have retraced in five decades the road that European music took ten centuries to cover.[2]

To regard the sixty-year history of jazz as a miniature history of music in general is, of course, an oversimplification. It is true that jazz, like classical music, has gone through a number of "periods" in its relatively short span, but only time can tell whether the various kinds of jazz represent true periods or are only a number of jazz styles that may in the future all turn out to belong to one or two periods.

Each of the so-called new-music periods may be considered a musical and historical point of departure. Each new-music period fostered lesser periods—identified mainly by terms borrowed from poetry, painting, and architecture—which, in turn, resulted in an array of musical styles, many of which are still practiced, at least in part. For our purposes the periods of music may be enumerated as follows: the Middle Ages (600-1450), the Renaissance (1450-1600), the Baroque era (1600-1750), the Classic era (1750-1825), the Romantic era (1825-1900), the Modern era (1900-   ). As we know, each period embraced many styles, and jazz has come under certain influences from a number of them, particularly the harmonic and contrapuntal style of the baroque period as characterized by the music of J. S. Bach, and the impressionistic style of the romantic period as characterized by the music of Debussy. The special influences of various periods and styles on jazz will be discussed more specifically in the chapters devoted to each jazz period. For the present, we need only discuss briefly what we shall call the four main jazz periods.

Until time has made sharper distinctions among jazz styles and periods, we prefer to think of jazz as having four main periods: the New Orleans period (the name is a useful one; it is *not*, however, a geographical distinction), which starts about 1900 and ends about 1926; the Preswing period, which continues to about 1934; the Swing period, which continues until about 1945; and the Modern period, which has not yet ended. The dates are, of course, approximate, and there is always an expected overlap when one is distinguishing periods. The New Orleans period contained the earliest jazz, a music that was to attain its characteristic form and content, its characteristic style and breadth, in the early twenties with the work of King Oliver and his Creole Jazz Band. Before the first World War jazz was embryonic and, while deserving of careful study in its own right, must not be confused with the music it became. (Some writers have labeled this early jazz "archaic," "primitive," or "preclassic.") The earliest years are important historically, but artistically the peak of the New Orleans period must be sought in the early twenties. I believe that the jazz of this time characterizes the New Orleans period, and this style is known as New Orleans style. (The so-called Dixieland style and Chicago style are, in the main, other names for New Orleans style; specifically, Dixieland is New Orleans style imitated by white musicians, and Chicago style

125

is New Orleans style as performed by white musicians in Chicago immediately before and after the first World War.)

The Jazz Age—F. Scott Fitzgerald's term—saw, in its second half, a flowering of jazz characterized by the solos of Louis Armstrong and such exponents of *le jazz hot* as Duke Ellington and Fletcher Henderson; the most distinctive jazz of 1927 to 1934 is called the preswing style—the style of a transitional period more fully discussed in chapter 7. The characteristic music of the decade 1935-45, as performed by such jazzmen as Benny Goodman and Count Basie, is called swing style. In the so-called modern period it is much more difficult to distinguish a characteristic style because it is probable that not all the plays, so to speak, have been made yet. At the present time, however, the characteristic style of the middle forties and fifties must encompass both bop and cool jazz, even though it seems likely that bop, together with the most significant elements in the so-called progressive jazz, will eventually be absorbed into the cool style. The men of bop and cool are not as yet firmly established historically. There seems little question, however, that such names as Charlie Parker, Dizzy Gillespie, Miles Davis, Bud Powell, and Thelonious Monk will hold high positions in future evaluations of both styles.

In any discussion of jazz styles, one is bound to omit the names of some jazzmen and include others; there may be only subjective reasons for these omissions and inclusions. Even Leonard Feather, in the exhaustive biographical section in his *Encyclopedia of Jazz,* and Panassié and Gautier, in their *Guide to Jazz,* were compelled to omit the names of certain jazzmen, besides devoting more space to some than to others. The task of comparing the number of words devoted to various jazzmen would seem to be a futile one, nevertheless one does notice obvious relationships. For example, the *Guide* (English edition published 1956) devotes ten columns to Armstrong (about 200 words to the column), two columns to Goodman, and half a column to Parker; the *Encyclopedia* (published 1955) devotes three columns to Armstrong (about 1,350 words to the column), two and a half columns to Goodman, and one and a half to Parker. It is plain that the encyclopedists agree that Armstrong, Goodman, and Parker are significant jazzmen historically and musically, perhaps even in that order. On the other hand, when the *Guide* devotes half a column to Frank "Big Boy" Goodie, who receives no mention in the *Encyclopedia,* it seems reasonable to assume that Big Boy Goodie is a historical figure whose artistic contributions to jazz are either questionable or unknown to Leonard Feather, this last being a surmise not readily acceptable. (Goodie was a member of the original Tuxedo Orchestra who afterward spent most of his life playing in Europe.)

When one sets out to enumerate jazzmen, of whatever caliber, there are likely to be not only omissions but unfortunate comparisons. In any consideration of the jazzmen who were responsible for bringing a style to its peak, there are bound to be those transitional figures who, with their

127

feet in two styles so to speak, never become as famous as those who make an abrupt entry onto the jazz scene. Both types are hard to rate: the transitional figure often spends himself without ever achieving the fame that may rightly be his, while the true value of the jazz star may be lost in the dazzling brightness of his publicity. The most difficult men to rate are those who are considered dyed-in-the-wool jazzmen by some and out-and-out businessmen by others— the men who have sought to reconcile the commercial and artistic sides of jazz. And many of these figures are still caught up this way, men with an eye to popular acceptance who came onto the jazz scene in the thirties and forties when, for the first time in the history of jazz, little distinction could be made between what was popular and what was jazz. Here, for example, is the way Whitney Balliett rates Stan Kenton:

> Kenton's music, in spite of all the organlike talk that has surrounded its "progressivism" in the past ten years, fits roughly into the tradition of the silvered semi-jazz bands of Larry Clinton, Glen Gray, Glenn Miller, the Dorseys, and Ray Anthony. This tradition, although kneaded from time to time by the energy of Bunny Berigans and Bobby Hacketts, is parallel to, and quite different from, that of the genuine big jazz bands cradled by Fletcher Henderson and Duke Ellington, and maintained since by Goodman, Lunceford, Calloway, Basie, and Woody Herman. Kenton does not fit easily into the white-collar jazz of the former tradition, however, for he tried, with the help of extracurricular seasonings, in his fashion to combine the two movements into something new. This he did, in part by allowing many soloists ample space within glistening limousines of sound that, in the end, tended to stifle and stiffen whatever potentiali-

ties for jazz there were on hand. He also created, as a result of purposely and confusedly trying to be a kind of musical refractor of his times, a self-conscious music that was caught—strident and humorless—somewhere between the pseudo-classical, jazz, and popular music.[3]

Balliett may have overextended himself in this view of the Kenton band. Another equally valid view is that the Kenton band at its peak produced a sound, a big-band sound, unique for its time, that was the logical outcome of the big-band jazz of the Goodman era. The ultimate weakness in Kenton's position was brought about not because he helped create a sound identifiable as "Kenton" but rather because he did not continue to develop. Early in his career he discovered a formula for big-band jazz that turned out to be commercially successful and, despite numerous financial and artistic setbacks in recent years, Kenton has continued to promote and sponsor a type of big-band jazz that has now become only curious and unprovocative.

Kenton is considered by some to be the outstanding exponent of the so-called progressive jazz; André Hodeir lists Kenton and Brubeck as the leaders of progressive jazz. Unquestionably, Kenton and Brubeck have had considerable influence, but on whom? I believe the answer will have to be recorded in the social history of jazz rather than in the musical history. If jazzmen had been as eager to acknowledge the influence of Kenton and Brubeck as the public was to acknowledge their impact, Kenton's and Brubeck's positions in jazz history would be as secure as Goodman's or Tatum's. In selecting the names of a few jazzmen as representatives of the styles in the chapters to follow, my intent is to hold up to the light those who have made artistically significant contributions to jazz, particularly those who, while perhaps not always the creators of a style, nevertheless brought a style to its peak by molding its characteristics into a unified whole, thereby communicating the meaning of the style in its highest sense.

Style, according to the *American College Dictionary*, is "a particular, distinctive or characteristic mode or form of construction in any art or work." Part of the theorist's job is to isolate the distinctive qualities of each style and to group those qualities which will then characterize or denote this style. This backward-forward-backward practice usually ends when the theorist arrives at what he considers a logical classification and terminology—in our case, for example, "New Orleans," "preswing," and so forth. The theorist is not always completely satisfied with his classification, and, even after he has apparently accepted it, he continues searching for more logical ways to classify his material, perhaps with the hope that he will eventually create, if not simpler classifications, at least self-explanatory ones. Athanasius Kircher, a seventeenth-century archeologist with an interest in musical styles, believed that styles were best classified in three main orders: individual style, national style, and functional style. A contemporary illustration of Kircher's classification might be: individual style—jazz as played by Gillespie or Armstrong; national (regional) style—jazz as played in Kansas City or Los Angeles; and functional style—jazz as played by big dance bands or small pit bands. In his last order Kircher enumerated nine styles, such as dance, theater, and others. Later, the Italians also classified music according to three styles: church, chamber, and theater. Their criteria, however, were not functional in Kircher's sense, but rather were technical, dealing with such musical aspects as harmony and rhythm. Johann Matheson, an eighteenth-century opera singer, composer, and theorist, combined the Italian point of view with Kircher's, and the result, as Bukofzer writes, "has served as the basis of our modern concept of musical style." [4]

Matheson's synthesis notwithstanding, we go on classifying and analyzing. Some jazz writers continue to classify all jazz as either solo improvisations or collective improvisations, while others, seeking broader relationships, find reason in "hot" jazz and "sweet" jazz—the hot jazz presumably encompassing the solo and collective improvisations and allowing room for whatever it is the classifier considers "sweet." In the thirties certain enthusiastic if somewhat inept classifiers found a solution in "white" jazz and "Negro" jazz. Fortunately, this distinction is no longer valid. A system of classification by Aaron Copland, however, deserves wider attention. Concerned with clarifying the confusion in the minds of a great many listeners of contemporary music, he writes:

> It might be helpful, therefore, to start by trying to bring some order into the apparent chaos of contemporary composition by dividing its leading exponents according to the relative

degree of difficulty in the understanding of their respective idioms:

Very Easy: Shostakovitch and Khatchaturian, Francis Poulenc, Erik Satie, early Schoenberg and Stravinsky, Vaughan Williams, Virgil Thomson.

Quite Approachable: Prokofiev, Roy Harris, Villa-Lobos, Ernest Bloch, William Walton.

Fairly Difficult: late Stravinsky, Béla Bartók, Chavéz, Milhaud, William Schuman, Honegger, Britten, Hindemith, Walter Piston.

Very Tough: middle and late Schoenberg, Alban Berg, Anton Webern, Varèse, Krenek, Charles Ives, Roger Sessions.[5]

What, one may ask, makes Milhaud, or William Schuman, "fairly difficult"? It is necessary at once to make it clear that Milhaud and Schuman have written compositions that range from "very easy" to "very tough"—Milhaud a considerable amount in all categories; however, the music we think of most often as being Milhaud's or Schuman's, the music that is *characteristic* Milhaud and Schuman, is fairly difficult for the layman to understand. Granted, Copland's distinctions may be considered arbitrary by some; nevertheless, the principle on which they are based has much merit. Returning to the principal question, we may again ask, What makes certain music easy and other music difficult? The answer must be sought in the technical musical aspects of dissonance, texture, structure, and the many others that in their totality make up the form and content of style.

Barry Ulanov, attempting to analyze three general standards of evaluation—freshness, profundity, and skill—writes:

It seems to me that we can do no more than compute mathematically in this branch of musical activity—but that is not so little. It is altogether possible to name the figures a man plays; to compare his phrases with all those that have gone before, and to make a firm quantitative judgment and the beginning of a qualitative one as a result. In poetry or painting so much has gone before that just naming the stock phrases and figures, tropes and images and textures and color combinations is an impossibility; but in jazz the process is not so difficult. The thirty, forty, fifty or sixty years of jazz, depending upon how you date its history, can be totted up, listened to for the most part on records, and at least outlined on paper. It is possible to follow the blues tradition, the common variations on the even commoner themes, the rows of familiar riffs, and the mountains of only slightly different solos, and from this it is further possible to come up with common sounds, with basic ideas, to note one long curve on a graph, reaching to bop and then changing shape and direction abruptly, whether for good or bad. The very least, then, that we can do with freshness of idea or inspiration is to name the changes wrought by musicians to discover exactly what they are doing with notes and chords and rhythms, and to make public that discovery. In the next category of standards we may find some way of deciding the value of those changes.[6]

In short, Ulanov is making a plea for an analysis of the qualities that make up a style. Once the spotlight is turned on "notes and chords and rhythms" and the entire method of developing musical materials, we can then proceed logically to weld the technical style criteria to the functional. When this is accomplished, a musician will have to show more than a New Orleans birth certificate to warrant his being called an exponent of New Orleans style, and more than membership in the Los Angeles musicians' union will

133

be necessary for those seeking sanctuary in West Coast jazz. The style of a jazzman will be based first on what he plays, not on what he would like to play or where he plays or with whom he travels. Properly speaking, it is only after an analysis of the jazzman's characteristic handling of musical materials that other, functional style points may be studied; characterizing the musician as a player of ballads or jump tunes, or as hailing from Copenhagen, has no immediate bearing on the question of his style, while his use of the appoggiatura or his avoidance of diminished seventh chords does.

In 1911 Guido Adler, the founder of the modern system of style criticism and analysis, presented the basic principles of style criticism in his book *Style in Music*. He later summarized the part dealing specifically with musical criteria:

> The fundamental question is: What determines style? At the focal point are the specifically musical criteria—those of melody, tonality, harmony, polyphony, thematic material, and timbre. These are the antecedents of style-definition. From this focal point proceed the rhythmic and formal criteria. Analysis of form . . . taking all these elements into consideration, is the point of departure in the style-critical process. With it is associated analysis of content . . . which inquires into the psycho-intellectual side of music. By considering the reciprocation and correlation of the analyses of form and content we arrive at authentic style-criticism of a higher order. . . .[7]

Much jazz criticism of the past seems to have been more concerned with individual style traits than with general characteristics. This has been particularly true among writers who, week after week, have been compelled to analyze subjectively, for the edification of the jazz fan, the playing of individuals. Even so, occasional notices have implied, correctly, that an individual's particular style traits were the property of others as well. No creative jazzman likes to think he is borrowing or imitating another jazzman's style; nevertheless, at any given time there is a common cache of chords, chord progressions, ornaments, and a host of other musical properties available to all, and it is the frequency with which these materials are used by all that identifies them as general characteristics; but it is the manner in which they are used by the individual that identifies his individual style.

The real error arises when a writer's view of the general characteristics of a group is obstructed by the height of one great jazzman. The writer's intention is commendable; he wishes everyone had the genius of the genius. The fact is, however, that a genius is unique: there is only one Armstrong, one Tatum, one Parker. The genius is ahead of his time, and it is unfair—incorrect, in fact—to compare his style traits with those of jazzmen playing characteristically for their time. However, the history of jazz shows that imaginative jazzmen eventually do catch up to the genius, that is, they begin to understand what he had in mind, what he was trying to do, and they set about achieving the same end, and from this moment starts the development of the characteristic jazz of the period. Sometimes the genius goes on to greater accomplishments, and the growth of a characteristic jazz is halted; sometimes he is cut off by sickness or death, and the jazz he originated seems to shoot up as if a great pressure had been removed, and for a time jazzmen seem to be clambering over each other to complete the structure that is to be a characteristic jazz until another jazzman, a genius, perhaps, breaks loose and the whole process is again set in motion.

The complete story of jazz style is to be found not only by analyzing the individual styles of such jazzmen as Count Basie, Sidney Bechet, Cootie Williams, and Dizzy Gillespie, but by analyzing and isolating those characteristics of their individual styles that eventually passed into the jazz mainstream. Aside from the pleasure the individual may give to listeners, his eventual position is usually determined by his influence on his less gifted colleagues. The combined influences of the men at the top help determine the general characteristics of a style. Certain ones, like Armstrong, may be the fountainhead in their time; others, like Basie or Gillespie, may contribute a rhythmic idea or a melodic idea that swirls around the mainstream until it is absorbed by the general flow. So-called mainstream jazz is neither better nor worse than old-time jazz or jazz of the future. It is simply the characteristic jazz of its time, moving along with the current now smoothly, now roughly, occasionally listlessly but always with direction however imperceptible it may be at the moment. It is the mainstream jazz that must inevitably be the point of departure for new styles, and to understand the evolution of style one must stand in midstream, so to speak, and look both ways.

Definition with respect to Time [Adler wrote] is the essence of independent style-criticism. We arrange the several style-varieties in periods and study their mutual relationship and opposition, their individuality, their rise and fall. We survey the complexity of the occurrences within a period and seek to isolate the basic style with all its attendant phenomena.[8]

Style criticism or analysis, as we know, must begin with the individual. Analysis with respect to the individual can be criticism in its highest form provided the investigator's study does not degenerate into a recounting of the subject's love life, what he thinks of Lollobrigida, of the Yankees, of pizza. This is not to say that biographical studies are something less than style studies; on the contrary, they can be wonderfully illuminating in the hands of writers who seek to present their subjects as man and artist. But we are a little ahead of ourselves here.

The immediate problem is one of selecting individuals for style study, and here we have a choice of two types: the innovator or the representative. In instances where the innovator is also an outstanding representative of the style, the choice may be a simple one; on the other hand, a strong representative of a given style can be a satisfactory subject for style analysis even if style innovation is not his forte. It is not necessary for a jazzman to help originate a style in order to be highly creative within it—Tony Scott and Chu Berry illustrate this. Restricting oneself to studying the work of Armstrong, Ellington, Parker, and a few other innovators can lead to valuable individual style criticisms. However, such studies must then be used as a basis for wider studies of the characteristic jazz styles.

Furthermore, it is likely that an innovator's reputation may be based not on any sustained creativity, but on only one invention. This is not to disparage such an invention, but merely to point out that perhaps more emphasis should be placed on the invention and less on the inventor. Certainly this has been the case in classical music where, in the early days of twelve-tone composing, Schoenberg dominated the entire genre. His influence was so great and his utterances seemed so profound that studies, writings, and analyses of and about Schoenberg became required reading for all conscientious composers. As time went on, however, it became apparent that many were to surpass Schoenberg in the handling of his own technique, and today Schoenberg's name is identified not so much with the personality that was his as with the style he initiated.

In one sense, what is true of Schoenberg is fast becoming true of Armstrong. There are many who believe that Armstrong's rise and influence ended in the early thirties, and that he has been in a decline since, except for rare flashes of the qualities that made him the best-known name in jazz. At his peak he was an outstanding representative of New Orleans style and a major preswing innovator; in addition to his musical talents, he was endowed with an unusually robust personality. Armstrong's personality is as radiant now as it ever was, and it is this quality that keeps him in the front line of jazz today.

In the days before mass communication facilities and internationally sponsored geophysical years, there was a school of thought that believed that there was a proper time for discovery and invention, and that when this time was at hand different inventors would be found at work on the same invention in different places, each unaware of the others. This theory probably had a measure of truth. The fact is, there are few innovations that are the sole property of one man. This is particularly true in jazz: no one man was responsible for New Orleans jazz—despite Jelly Roll Morton's exaggerated, good-natured claims—or for swing, or bop, or cool jazz. There are, of course, those to whom writers have attributed the discovery of these styles, and there is a measure of truth in this also. As we know, a style evolves; it may receive impetus from the contributions of an individual or, as is more likely, from a number of individuals, each aware of the other's work, reacting to the other's intention, and, in turn, being reacted upon. Those jazzmen who received their early musical training in the marching bands of the 1890's and early 1900's—Buddy Bolden, Freddie Keppard, and Joe Oliver, for example—learned something from the straightforward rhythmic and harmonic style of the march as utilized by the men to whom the march and marching band were the culmination of musical training and thought. Bolden (1878-1907), to use one example, "was heir to all the musical influences that survived in and around New Orleans," as Marshall Stearns points out.[9] And Bolden apparently influenced many of the next generation of jazzmen who heard him. The evidence of his influence offered by those who heard him play around the turn of the century is conflicting and unreliable, to say the least; however, the reports seem to agree that he played an exceptionally "loud" horn for his time.

Later in the century, evidence of the influence individual jazzmen may have had on their colleagues is easier to find. The earliest jazz recordings, while incapable of faithfully reproducing the quality of a jazzman's tone either in a solo or in ensemble, nevertheless were able to establish, reliably and as never before, who were the innovators and who were the imitators. And from this point on the contributions of Armstrong and the subsequent emergence of the solo improvisation as the first real break with the past are available for all to follow. The part played by Fletcher Henderson in the evolution of swing, for example, and by Duke Ellington in the evolution of jazz orchestration may also be followed. Goodman, whose discipline and dedication brought a style to its peak; Basie, who managed to remain distinctive while those about him were being nudged into commonplaces; Tatum, Coleman Hawkins, Gillespie, Parker, Miles Davis, and many more jazzmen whose influence is solidly established—the work of all of these is available for everyone to follow and study.

Valuable deductions and contributions in the study of jazz may come as a result of comparing individual styles: the harmonic style of Tatum compared to the harmonic style of Theolonious Monk; the use of the saxophone section in Ellington's band compared to its use in Lunceford's; the degree of contrapuntal independence in Gerry Mulligan's duet performances compared to that in the Modern Jazz Quartet. These and similar comparisons can provide wide areas for study and exploration, and by exposing the strengths and weaknesses in individual styles such investigations can become the foundation for broader, more comprehensive studies of entire periods and their characteristic styles.

(With the initiation of the *Jazz Review* in November, 1958, edited by Nat Hentoff and Martin Williams, it is plain that studies much like those suggested above will eventually be published in that journal. For example, the first few issues offered carefully prepared articles—on Count Basie, by André Hodeir; on Erroll Garner, by Mimi Clar; and on Cecil Taylor, by Gunther Schuller. Future issues will no doubt include pieces on the styles of Ellington, Henderson, Tatum, Parker, and others. The first issue —December, 1958—of the new *Jazz: A Quarterly of American Music,* edited by Ralph Gleason, indicates that it too will no doubt continue to publish serious and provocative jazz studies.)

There are, of course, other kinds of studies, nonmusical or, rather, nontechnical studies, what we may call jazz studies, studies that grow out of a writer's desire to explain what Adler calls "the flowering of artistic accomplishment." Style criticism with respect to place comes under this category. The state of jazz in a nation, a state, a city, a district may be studied in the light of the people and the language peculiar to the region. The relationship of the jazzman to the general citizen may be investigated where the similarities and differences in physical and intellectual environment bear on the creation of jazz. Political events may also be studied for their influence on jazz. What, we might ask, were the consequences of the opening of the Storyville district, of its closing? What influence did the Pendergast regime have on jazz in Kansas City? What was the state of jazz before and after World War I, World War II, the Korean war? How was jazz affected by Prohibition, the Depression? The necessities of local demand may prove upon study and synthesis to be not unique, but part of a larger scheme. What historical events may have had a peculiar influence on one jazz style and perhaps not on another? What general educational facilities are available to the jazzman in some regions and not in others? To what extent is jazz self-taught? What have been the influences of private jazz schools, jazz courses, and even jazz degrees in higher education?

In what way has the course of jazz been affected by music publishers, instrument manufacturers, and public school administrators? To what extent has jazz been influenced by one-night stands, the death of vaudeville, the Carnegie Hall concerts, the summer festivals, and Jazz at the Philharmonic? To what extent does the jazzman's economic condition affect the quality of his playing? What has been the influence of the musicians' union on jazz? Certainly any explanation of "the flowering of artistic accomplishment" will include studies of the position and influence of radio, the movies, television, the popular press, and the jazz fan magazines. (A question has already been raised concerning the propriety of critics who write liner notes for record jackets and afterward review the records. What is the influence of these critics on the jazz fan, whose support often determines a jazzman's position?) The influence of the recording industry on jazz has been approached gingerly by a few, but much more needs to be done. (There is no doubt that the form of much jazz has been influenced by the time restrictions and limitations of the various sizes and speeds of records.) John S. Wilson, a critic whose "social" jazz writing may well serve as a model of its type, shows how records help influence the development of jazz styles, in this case Chicago style. He writes:

> In its beginnings as an instrumental music, jazz had been played by self-taught Negro musicians, men who had to create their own ways of playing their instruments, ways inevitably at variance with "correct" techniques. This very incorrectness contributed to the flavor of jazz and established a pattern of aiming at something and getting a result just a bit different, which has constantly enriched the music. Similarly, when the early white New Orleans jazz musicians tried to play what they heard their Negro contemporaries playing, the result didn't come out *quite* the same, but it had enough validity of its own to form the basis for what is now generally identified as Dixieland. And when the Austin High School gang in Chicago was intent on imitating the records of an early Dixieland group, the New Orleans Rhythm Kings, their own personalities came through so strongly that they missed the mark as imitators but created Chicago style jazz in the process.[10]

But in the end, unless we are to be sociologists, we must realize that the kind of studies we have been speaking of cannot be considered as terminal studies; we must use these studies as a frame of reference for the theorist's main business: studying the evolution of musical style. If the

143

critic points out that there are differences in periods, in styles, the theorist analyzes and catalogues the differences and sets up the criteria for style. The astute critic will refer to the theorist's work and use it as a basis for making critical evaluations. The imaginative theorist, it is hoped, will realize the use to which his work will be put and understand that his studies, like those of the nontechnical writers, are not intended to be terminal. He will recognize that it is proper and desirable for his work to be the point of departure for esthetic analysis, and he will hope that his work can eventually dispel the ambiguity in much critical writing. The theorist will understand that subjective writing and evaluation are necessities if jazz is to continue to flourish, and that his work can be an aid to those writers and critics who guide and mold public opinion. He can stress constantly the difference between objective and subjective evaluation, the difference between what may be artistically significant and what may be historically significant. In the past jazzmen and certain critics have tended to confuse a jazzman's style with his excellence according to their personal taste and preference. This is a natural and understandable error that, unfortunately, leads only to misunderstanding and puzzlement. The theorist will emphasize that a statement such as Ellington's "Jelly Roll played piano like one of those high school teachers in Washington; as a matter of fact, high school teachers played better jazz" [11] is a personal and subjective evaluation that may have little to do with whether Jelly Roll actually played that way or not.

The jazz of any period needs critical comment and evaluation, but criticism must be based on something more than personal preference or personal opinion. The jazz fan who prefers swing to bop need not justify his taste; it is a choice for which he need not apologize. The professional jazz writer who prefers swing to bop is, however, in a different position. While he has as much right to his opinion as the jazz fan, he has the responsibility of justifying his taste if he is going to impose it on impressionable, susceptible readers whose taste is perhaps in the formative stage. It is obvious that Ellington's opinion of Jelly Roll Morton's playing would have considerable weight with many who are faithful fans of Ellington's music, and it is likely they would accept his view without question. However, it must be remembered that it is not Ellington's point of view that is in question, nor his influence on others; what is in question is the method by which he arrived at his conclusion and the method by which his followers may arrive at the same conclusion. The function of a critic—and when a man of Ellington's position makes a public statement on jazz he is a critic—ought to be to teach, to persuade, and to encourage the jazz public, lay and professional alike, to study jazz, to explore it, to become acquainted with its rich history, its various styles, and the contributions of individual jazzmen old and new. In order to make pertinent critical judgments one must listen not only to the words of those who have the public's ear, but above all to the music under discussion, for it is only by listening that one may arrive at sound reasons for one's preferences. This is what Schoenberg meant when he said: "Yes, the role of memory in music evaluation is more important than most people realize. It is perhaps true that one starts to understand a piece only when one can remember it at least partially." [12]

It is the responsibility of the theorist—and, by extension, of the critic—to impress upon the world of jazz that the quality of jazz does not depend on its chronological position in jazz history. "Art is not a question of precedence," George Antheil wrote, "but of excellence." Swing is not in itself "better" jazz than New Orleans jazz or modern jazz. (It was not too long ago that swing, itself, was "modern" jazz.) The fact is that the quality of jazz may vary within a given period and even within a given style. The history of jazz consists of countless examples of good jazz and bad jazz, and discussion and debate over the relative merits of different kinds of jazz can be healthy and rewarding provided they are based not merely on opinion but on significant analysis and interpretation.

The theorist will seek ways to define and illustrate those aspects of jazz which in the past have seemed not to be demonstrable; he will attempt to clarify problems even when they seem insoluble; he will attempt to express clearly in prose what the jazzman finds it difficult to say but nonetheless "digs." He will try gradually to bring scholarship and the general level of jazz information and communication closer together, and at the same time avoid the dangers of both intellectual and anti-intellectual snobbery, but he will be prepared to receive the rebuffs of both sides. Finally, he will be as convinced of his position and the importance of his work as the jazz connoisseurs are of theirs, and he will proceed with his work according to his disposition—nimbly or cautiously, hopefully or apprehensively, humbly or arrogantly, conservatively or radically—but always with style.

chapter **6**

NEW ORLEANS
STYLE

THERE IS SUFFICIENT EVI-
dence to indicate that the style we know as New Orleans is
more directly connected with military band music of the
late nineteenth century than with any other single source.
From shortly after the Civil War to the end of the century
the United States stood in the front rank of military music,
and there was scarcely a village or a town whose musicians
did not come under its influence. In the 1890's the band of
John Philip Sousa, for example, played Fayetteville, North
Carolina; the St. Louis Exposition; and the Cotton States
Exposition. "In 1899," Sousa wrote in his autobiography,
"our tour stretched from coast to coast and from the St.
Lawrence to the Gulf." [1] Richard Franko Goldman wrote
about Sousa's band that "it is probable that no musical organization in history was known to as many people,
or held in greater popular affection. . . ." [2]

Sousa's band was the most popular, but Patrick Gilmore's band set an early precedent. Gilmore, born in Dublin in 1829, went to Canada with an English band, and organized his own band in Massachusetts in 1859. During the Civil War he and his band served in a Massachusetts regiment. In 1864 he was bandmaster in the Federal army in New Orleans. Goldman tells us, "His first immense festival took place in New Orleans in 1864, where he celebrated the inauguration of Governor Hahn with a chorus of 5,000 adults and children, a band of 500, a huge trumpet and drum corps, and lots of artillery." [3] In the 1870's Gilmore and his men traveled throughout the United States, often playing "When Johnny Comes Marching Home Again," his best-known march.

An incident that took place in 1861, shortly after the Civil War began, illuminates certain aspects of military band practice and its probable influence on the pioneers of jazz. The story, recounted by Louis C. Elson, concerns the origin of the Civil War march we know as "Glory Hallelujah":

> ["Glory Hallelujah"] was begun as a hymn-tune in Charleston, South Carolina. . . . The song was used at many a Southern camp-meeting before the war, and was also employed in many of the colored congregations. It even made its way into the Methodist hymnals at the North.
> . . . We therefore find "Glory Hallelujah" closely entwined with the history of the Twelfth Massachusetts Regiment, as the following (gathered by the author from Captain Henry J. Hallgreen and other officers of the regiment) will clearly show.
> One day, while the regiment was still at Fort Warren, Cap-

149

tain Hallgreen heard two new recruits from Maine, in the throes
of homesickness, most mournfully singing the hymn, "Say,
Brothers, will you meet us?" He was struck by the melody, and
taught it to some of the "Tigers." It spread like wild-fire, and
at once became a camp tune. As there was no rhyme or complex construction to the words, the men soon found they could
add their own improvisations to the tune, a fact which made
it all the more popular. Meanwhile Gilmore, who frequently
came to the fort with his band, caused his men to "vamp" the
tune (that is, to improvise harmonies to it), and often accompanied the singing of it.

[Shortly after, in New York] the regiment was halted on
Broadway, and there again they sang their song amid the
wildest frenzy of the public. It mattered little that the people
could not fully comprehend the words, the tune was one of the
"swingiest" of marches, the whole affair was redolent of the
camp, and "Glory Hallelujah" was sung by the Twelfth Massachusetts Regiment from city to city, from camp to camp, until
it became national.[4]

This example of the practice of improvising harmonies
with band instruments precedes by twenty years, at least,
the work of such famous New Orleans pioneer groups as
the Olympia Band, the Eagle Band, the Imperial Band,
and the Superior Band, not only in spirit but in instrumentation as well. There is little doubt that the standard New
Orleans instrumentation and its function have their foundation in the last strain of band marches where characteristically the melody is carried by the cornets or trumpets
against a countermelody in the low brasses and a florid
embellishment in the high woodwinds. The most famous of
the New Orleans marches is Porter Steele's "High Society,"
in Alphonse Picou's treatment, while Sousa's "The Stars

and Stripes Forever" is the most famous of the standard marches; it is not difficult to hear the relationship between the treatment of the last strain in these two examples, and many other similar ones. Picou's clarinet solo in "High Society," however, must not be considered typical of the technical ability of early jazzmen. Picou was a trained musician. He tells us, ". . . my father did not know *I* had taken lessons from a flute player at the French Opera House. I did not explain him nothing, but one time I just sat down and played *Cavalleria Rusticana.*" [5] As a descendant of early French settlers, a so-called "Creole," Picou had certain advantages not available to the freedmen who flocked to the cities and river towns after the war, for Creoles had many of the privileges of the whites. Alan Lomax tells us that "cheap instruments left behind by the Confederate Army bands, filled the pawnshops. Creole freedmen could afford to buy instruments and pay for music lessons as few other Southern Negroes could. Almost any Creole oldtimer can recall his childhood musical instruction—given in the strictest style of the French Academy." [6]

It is interesting to compare Picou's conception of "High Society" with the "Gettysburg March" as performed by Kid Rena's Jazz Band in a recording made in New Orleans in 1940, in which Picou plays clarinet. According to Frederick Ramsey, Jr., the "Gettysburg March" is "of the sort reported to have been played by Civil War bandsmen." [7] The impression one has on listening to the "Gettysburg March" is of its authenticity—the small town band spirit that can only be manifested by exuberant amateurs. One can see the parade of half a dozen players, inspired by the jaunty beat of the snare, stepping along the cobbled street. Picou's fluffed notes, Ed Robinson's stylish trombone, the straight trumpet of Kid Rena, the rousing forte of the last strain, and the delightful innocence of the last two bars all seem to give off the light of truth.

But their playing is not the source of New Orleans style; it is more likely once removed from the source. It is the second step; the first is the performances of marching bands and performers that inspired imitation. Kid Rena's performance is an imitation that has become, for some people, the real thing. It is possible that these people are correct; in the process of jazz evolution who is to say, once imitation has set in, what is being imitated? We know that many Creole musicians received sound musical training; we know, too—if Picou may be used as an example—that imitation by trained musicians is often difficult to distinguish from its source; we also know that, at a certain time after the war, Creole musicians played with relatively untrained Negro musicians who must certainly have been influenced by the Creole technique and knowledge of instruments. It would seem, therefore, that the pioneers derived much of their manner of playing and the major part of their instrumentation from military bands.

The Negro's immediate response to freedom was to leave the rural areas and head for the cities and river towns. In 1865 he was intent on being footloose. As he moved around the countryside he neither sought nor was interested in employment; he extended his new-found freedom to include freedom from work, and life away from the farm held a strong attraction. Once he had reached a city he found occupation in domestic service or just loafing, seeking only those jobs that required a minimum of responsibility. The work, of course, was in keeping with the almost total lack of education among Negroes just emerging from slavery; nonetheless, a number of the more persevering did manage to support themselves in small business enterprises. To call the Negro's desire for freedom "irresponsibility" is perhaps too strong. He was not so much irresponsible as he was irregular; since he was now free, he saw little reason for working six days a week when he could support himself on what he could earn in two or three days. Actually, he needed very little. He ate cheaply, with little variety, and usually lived in a ramshackle, one-room cabin on the edge of town, or in a squalid slum flat, often with six, eight, or a dozen of his friends and relatives—all apparently happy and contented. Marriage and the home meant little. Under slavery such arrangements were informal: men and women lived as husband and wife by permission of the master, and divorce was by mutual consent or occurred when one of the parties was sold to another master. After emancipation, therefore, it was only to be expected that the traditional marriage customs would be continued. Desertion and divorce became commonplaces, and the Negro, having just emerged from slavery, had no family life. Moreover, there was little in his religion to control his conduct. Christianity, as he practiced it, was a code of beliefs, not of morals.

Being a Christian meant praying and singing in church and, when life in this world was over, traveling to another world; life was grief and sorrow, and death was a welcome, perhaps happy, relief. Meanwhile, he could console himself with recreation, a part of life for which, until emancipation, he had had little time, and to which, after emancipation, he devoted himself wholeheartedly. Henderson H. Donald tells us:

> It is highly probable that the great majority of the forms of recreation were originated by the Negroes themselves. They seemed generally to harmonize with the Negroes' temperament, inclinations, and peculiar life conditions. It should be noticed also that the recreation of the Negro freedmen for the most part was of the active rather than of the passive type. They preferred amusing themselves to being amused by others. In time, however, they adopted many of the forms of recreation prevailing in the general society.[8]

Music has always been an acceptable form of recreation, and the postwar South apparently had almost as many bands as there were towns—the number of bands in New Orleans alone invites special study. The freedmen of the South—as has been pointed out by many writers—were particularly fond of organizing and joining societies and were never quite so happy as when they were marching in a parade, and they could find some joy in any sort of parade. Secret societies and marching societies (they were often, no doubt, the same) were formed in Maryland, Virginia, District of Columbia, Florida, South Carolina, Louisiana—in short, throughout the South. As Donald wrote: "Likewise, the Negroes of middle Georgia were particu-

154

larly fond of parades, and were constantly organizing societies. And it seemed that they did the latter mainly to get an opportunity to march about after a fife and drum." [9] They followed much more than "a fife and drum" when it was available, and in New Orleans, at least, instruments and subsequently players and bands were plentiful.

Even a hasty study of New Orleans bands shows an extraordinary amount of musical activity. Thumbing through jazz histories, newspapers, and volumes of reminiscences brings to light the St. Joseph Brass Band, the Imperial Band, and the Excelsior Band, all of the 1880's. (It is sometimes difficult to establish the names of the leaders in these and subsequent bands, since the bands often met without schedule for funerals and for special celebrations. Usually the leader was the contractor, as is still the case in union "pick-up" bands.) There is reason to believe, however, that Claiborne Williams led the St. Joseph Band and Immanuel Perez the Imperial Band; the Excelsior Band, which continued to flourish through the 1900's, may or may not have been led by the renowned John Robechaux—there is little question that he played in the band, at one time or another, with such pioneers as Louis and Lorenzo Tio, Picou, and Perez. Jelly Roll Morton, who didn't pass out compliments lightly, said, "John Robechaux probably had the best band in New Orleans at the time, a strictly all-reading, legitimate bunch." [10]

The 1890's saw the flourishing of such New Orleans bands as the Peerless, Indian, Columbus, and Diamond Stone; the Onward Brass Band with Perez and Joe Oliver;

Adam Olivier's Band with Bunk Johnson; and, continuing through the decade, the already mentioned Excelsior Band. In the 1900's the Olympia Band was led by Freddie Keppard and had Picou and Louis "Big Eye" Nelson; the Eagle Band had Sidney Bechet, "Papa" Carey, Bunk Johnson, and, from 1907 to 1915, Keppard, who also played for a while with Bill Johnson's Original Creole Band. From 1905 to 1912 the Superior Band had Bunk Johnson, and this period also saw the ascendancy of the Magnolia Band with Joe Oliver. An important white band of the period was "Papa" Laine's Reliance Brass Band, which included Nick LaRocca, later the leader of the Original Dixieland Jazz Band.

Before the Storyville district was established in 1897, there was a much clearer distinction between bands than there was afterward. In the eighties and nineties most of the bands were just marching bands that paraded for social functions including funerals and special celebrations, and, when the celebrations called for dancing, the bands were able to provide dance music of a sort. But dance bands, of the kind that had an influence on New Orleans style, were relatively few in this period. Papa Laine is reported to have had a ragtime band in 1888, but the most important was Buddy Bolden's Ragtime Band of 1893. Bolden, who had a brass band before he had his ragtime band, was an untrained musician who played a "powerful" trumpet. He was able to draw on legitimate players for his band because New Orleans Creoles of the 1890's who earlier had practiced music as a matter of culture now needed money as badly as the Negroes did. The Creoles came to Bolden, and they played his way. Wallace Collins, a New Orleans musician who claimed to have played in Bolden's Ragtime Band, told Rudi Blesh that Bolden's was the first band to play rags. Collins also described Bolden's teaching methods:

> To "rag" a tune, Collins says, "he'd take one note and put two or three to it. He began to teach them—not by the music— just by the head. After he'd get it down right, he'd teach the others their part.
> "They had lots of band fellows who could play like that after Bolden gave 'em the idea." [11]

Paul Dominguez, a New Orleans violinist, corroborated Collins's testimony when he told Alan Lomax that "Bolden cause all that. . . . He cause these younger Creoles, men like Bechet and Keppard to have a different style from old heads like Tio and Perez." [12]

While the influence of the marching band was directly responsible for the manner of performing New Orleans style, the players came to the marching band with a wealth of musical background both secular and religious. Starting with a background of West African culture, for about two centuries they had heard and made music at Saturday night dances, weddings, baptisms, candy stews, corn shuckings, evening gatherings, picnics, parties, and funerals; they knew work songs, love songs, devil songs, jigs, quadrilles, and stomps. They had heard the folk tunes of Scotland, Ireland, and England, the art songs of Italy and

157

Spain, the melodies of French operatic arias, and the bright tunes of minstrel shows. The heat of plantation religion brought them the spirituals based on the simple harmonies and ardent spirit of the evangelical hymn. And, above all, they knew the blues. Add to these ragtime—the notated piano music that originated in the Midwest and flourished throughout the South about the same time Storyville did (1896-1917)—and all the ingredients are gathered in. What the Storyville bands and their immediate successors played must be sought in the conglomeration of religious, secular, notated, and improvised music.

Joseph "King" Oliver and his Creole Jazz Band brought the New Orleans style to its peak. Why Oliver's band should have been responsible for this is not difficult to understand in retrospect. By 1923, the year of the culmination of the New Orleans style, Oliver and the band members had among them all the qualities and influences of the period from the end of the Civil War to the end of the first World War. The personnel of the band—which included Louis Armstrong on cornet, Honore Dutrey on trombone, Johnny Dodds on clarinet, Baby Dodds on drums, Bill Johnson on banjo, Lil Hardin Armstrong on piano, and of course Oliver on cornet—had participated in just about every kind of musical organization that had anything to do with the evolution of New Orleans style. The Creole musician, Dutrey, had played with Oliver's band in New Orleans. Johnny Dodds, a self-taught musician who had played with many New Orleans bands, had been in Chicago twice before, once on his own and once with Oliver;

both times he went back to New Orleans, and in 1920 he returned once more to Chicago to join Oliver's band. His brother, Warren "Baby" Dodds, a longtime friend and colleague of Armstrong's, had played in marching bands and in ragtime bands and had worked the Mississippi riverboats. Bill Johnson, born in 1872, was an old hand with the "spasm" instruments: harmonica, guitar, and banjo; around 1900 he took up the bass fiddle and created the organization whose name Oliver was to assume in 1920. Lil Hardin Armstrong (she married Armstrong in 1924) had studied piano at Fisk University and later was a member of Freddie Keppard's band in Chicago. The history of Louis Armstrong's rise is too well known to be recounted again here; it is sufficient to say that his experience before he joined Oliver's band included playing with marching bands, dance bands, and riverboat bands. The total experience of the Original Creole Jazz Band, in short, encompasses the history of New Orleans style specifically and early jazz in general; and it took a man of Oliver's wide experience and theretofore untapped organizational ability to weld the 1923 organization into the most important exponent of New Orleans style.

King Oliver was born in New Orleans in 1885. Little is known about his youth except that by the time he was in his early teens he was already involved in a brass band. While he may have received spasmodic instruction from any one of a dozen oldtimers, chances are that his musical education was picked up on the run or, perhaps more correctly, on the march. Soon he was sharing solo cornet hon-

159

ors with Perez in the Onward Brass Band. Like most of his contemporaries Oliver played music for extra money; he was regularly employed as a butler. But his outstanding work with the Eagle Band and later with the Magnolia, Olympia, and Kid Ory bands made his playing a full-time job. Barry Ulanov tells us:

> Sometime after 1910 Joe made his way into Storyville and played with a variety of bands. One night he stood on Iberville Street, pointed across the street to Pete Lala's Cafe, where Freddie Keppard was playing, and farther down the street to the spot where Perez was entrenched, and blew the blues. Loud and true he blew and loud and clear he shouted "There! That'll show them!" This exhibit of lung power and daring established Joe Oliver's majesty, and from then on he was "the King." King Oliver moved into Lala's with a band that featured Lorenzo Tio on clarinet, Zue Robertson on·trombone, Buddy Christian on piano, and Zino on drums.[13]

By the time Storyville was closed down in 1917, King Oliver was reputed to be the best cornet player in New Orleans. Although he was playing with Kid Ory's band along with Johnny Dodds, and enjoying a reputation envied even by Louis Armstrong, the idea of leaving New Orleans and going to Chicago was in his mind. Before the outbreak of the first World War there seemed little reason for King Oliver, or any other Negro, to leave the South and head for Chicago. But by 1918 there were two good reasons: Storyville had been closed down; and Chicago's war industries, which had absorbed tens of thousands of Negroes from all over the South, seemed to have room for many more. (Between 1910 and 1920, fifty thousand Negroes came to Chicago.) Long before the Storyville days, Chicago had had a reputation for bigness, wickedness, and violence. When the war in Europe began, the citizens of Chicago, tired of depression and repeated vice crusades, elected "Big Bill" Thompson, an uncommonly exuberant Republican, as their mayor. Thompson promised them a big city, and by 1922 he had given it to them. Chicago has always enjoyed the reputation of being a wide-open town with a sporting tradition, and to those who work the shadowy side of the street Chicago has always been a sanctuary. "The sporting spirit," Lincoln Steffens said, "is the spirit of Chicago." King Oliver was obviously a man who had the sporting spirit; besides, 1918 seemed like a very good time to go to Chicago.

Once he was in Chicago, Oliver's ability enabled him to work in shifts between Lawrence Duhé's New Orleans Jazz Band and Bill Johnson's Original Creole Band, and in 1920 he took over Bill Johnson's band. About a year later he apparently found Chicago less taken with his new band than he had hoped, and off he went to California, where during the next year he played in various dance halls and night spots in San Francisco and Los Angeles. In 1922 he returned to Chicago and persuaded Armstrong to leave New Orleans to join his band, and it was at the Lincoln Gardens Cafe that the band finally hit its stride. After Oliver and Armstrong had played together for a year, there was not a jazzman in Chicago, colored or white, who was not aware of the transformation that had taken place in what was now "the best band in the land," Alexander's

Ragtime Band notwithstanding. The Lincoln Gardens could accommodate between six and seven hundred dancers, and the band played regularly to a capacity house. Frederick Ramsey, Jr., describes a typical evening at the Lincoln Gardens:

> There were no waltzes played at the Lincoln Gardens, the customers liked the Bunny-hug, the Charleston, the Black Bottom. A stomp ended; a minute's silence broke in on the din, then Joe tooted a few notes down low to the orchestra, stomped his feet to give the beat, turned around, and they were off on a new piece, first impatient for a release from the stiffness of the opening bars, then relieved to be tearing through fast and loud in their own way. Lil Hardin bit hard on her four beats to a measure, while the deep beat of Bill Johnson's string bass and the clearly defined foundation of Baby Dodds' drum and high-toned, biting cymbal filled out the "bounce" and kept the others sweeping forward. This motion led to a climax, a point beyond which the breathless pace of the music seemed doomed to fall, unless something would intervene. Then Joe and Louis stepped out, and one of their "breaks" came rolling out of the two short horns, fiercely and flawlessly.[14]

There has been much conjecture on the reason for the band's success in 1923. Some writers have attributed it to the social atmosphere in Chicago and have suggested that the band's music reflected the spirit of the times; others have suggested that the arrival of Armstrong provided the band with the spark it needed. There is, of course, some truth in both these conjectures. Certainly the social atmosphere of the period was friendly and encouraging, and there is little doubt that Armstrong lent a certain solidity to the ensemble. Sidney Finkelstein, however, points out still another aspect of the question:

> The Negro community for whom Oliver played in Chicago was different from the Negro community in New Orleans. The music that Oliver played was still New Orleans in its march tempo, its rag, blues and stomp content, its collective music making and self-absorption in the music on the part of the players; but it also reflected the new Chicago audience. The opportunity to make records, as well, induced a greater attention to technical detail and formal organization, making the music a founded out unity with beginning, middle and end.[15]

The main clue to the truth may be in the words "formal organization." Probably of the highest significance is the fact that the band had stayed together long enough for its individual members to know each other's minds, musically speaking, and in a band where the emphasis was on playing collectively, this knowledge was all important. Baby Dodds said, "Those of us who worked with the King Oliver Band had known each other so long we felt that we were almost related. That outfit had more harmony and feeling of brotherly love than any I ever worked with. And playing music is just like having a home." [16]

In the postwar period Chicago was well on its way to becoming the national headquarters for jazz and aspiring jazzmen. Oliver was king, but his position was not unchallenged. Nor had he, in 1918, come into virgin territory. Perez had come to Chicago two years earlier and had operated out of the Deluxe Cafe with a band that included Sidney Bechet. And even before that, in 1915, Tom Brown, a white New Orleans trombone player who had played with Papa Laine's band, came up to Chicago with a band to take a job at the Lambs' Cafe where they had the distinction of being advertised as "Brown's Dixieland Jass Band." The following year, 1916, Alcide "Yellow" Nunez, a white New Orleans clarinet player, came up to Chicago with a band that later, after some shifting of personnel, became the Original Dixieland Jazz Band with Nick La-Rocca on cornet, Larry Shields on clarinet, Eddie Edwards on trombone, Henry Ragas on piano, and Tony Sbarbaro on drums. In 1921, while Oliver was trying to impress Californians with his band, a group led by Paul Mares came up from New Orleans and opened as the Friars Society Orchestra; they later called themselves the New Orleans Rhythm Kings. While groups like these were very popular with the general public, Oliver probably worried little about them. In fact, the members of these groups, after playing on their own jobs, would gather at the Lincoln Gardens to listen to the Oliver band. It is likely that the only band that caused Oliver concern—if any band in 1923 did—was "Doc" Cook's Dreamland Orchestra, mainly because Cook was using Freddie Keppard on cornet. In New Orleans Keppard had carved himself an important reputation, and some thought him far superior to both Oliver and Armstrong. Jelly Roll Morton said, "I never heard a man that could beat Keppard—his reach was so exceptional, both high and low, with all degrees of power, great imagination, and more tone than anybody." [17]

At any rate, King Oliver ruled a musical domain that

included the most significant jazzmen of the period. Chicago had taken up where Storyville ended, and in 1923 the Creole Jazz Band was the royal representative of New Orleans style. Before we move on to the technical aspects and characteristics of New Orleans style, it seems proper to point out that the early Dixielanders—Tom Brown, Nick LaRocca, Larry Shields, and others—receive little attention here because, properly speaking, they helped neither to formulate nor to fix New Orleans style. Dixieland, as we have already stated, is an imitation of New Orleans style by men who, because of their race, lack the social, musical, and religious background to do anything more than copy the superficial aspects of the style. These men did, however, have some small weight in the development of style during the preswing era, and they will be treated in more detail in the next chapter.

New Orleans style is characteristically an instrumental style performed on three or four wind instruments: one or two cornets or trumpets, a clarinet, and a trombone; and a combination of various other instruments carrying out a rhythmic function: piano, bass, drums, guitar, banjo, and tuba. Ernest Borneman outlines the New Orleans instrumentation and the function of the individual instruments:

> Since the elementary laws of harmony require a minimum of three notes to form a chord, the essential jazz orchestra should have three wind instruments—no less and no more; and since jazz is essentially rhythmic music, a rhythm section made up of drums, bass, and guitar or banjo should be added. The piano

165

is optional, and the sole function of the rhythm section should
be to mark the beat and the basic chords. The modern tendency
of the piano, the bass, the guitar, and the tuned drums to act as
solo instruments and play whole melodies on their own is ab-
horred by the Fundamentalists as an essentially unorganic use
of jazz instrumentation. The organic use of the basic instruments calls for the cornet or trumpet to play the melodic lead,
the clarinet to play a syncopated obbligato, and the trombone
to fill in the harmony with propulsive glissandi.[18]

The cornet stays close to the melodic line even on those infrequent occasions when it has a solo. Although the ensemble characteristically plays collectively, and each of
the three wind instruments is thought by many to have
equal independence, the fact is that the clarinet and trombone play "around" the cornet. For this reason, the cornet
may not stray very far; in practice New Orleans clarinetists
adjust their "syncopated obbligato" according to the degree of floridness the cornetist bestows on the melody, and
the trombonist also varies his bass line accordingly. The
success of collective improvisation, therefore, is the responsibility of the cornetist because, in his way, he initiates
the musical texture. The function of the rhythm section is
to maintain a steady, unaccented 4/4 meter and occasionally to emphasize the harmonic rhythm while varying the
rhythm between bar lines.

To understand the various musical textures characteristic of New Orleans style it is essential to understand the
difference between polyphony and heterophony. Heterophony is a singularly rudimentary form of polyphony and
not, as some writers have implied, a somehow advanced

form of polyphony; it is the result of combining two instrumental parts, one of which is not a truly independent part but rather a slightly altered version of the other part. Polyphony, on the other hand, is the result of combining two or more independent parts. Rudi Blesh, in a chart intended to show "African Survivals in Negro Jazz," writes of "the development of polyphony into heterophony"; later on, while discussing the qualities of New Orleans style, he writes, "The three voices together create a polyphony, fervent, eloquent, and logical, in which the harmony, while felt, is never in the focus of consciousness; this polyphony veers continuously into heterophony." [19] The implication one is forced to draw from these statements is that Blesh believes heterophony is properly a higher form of polyphony—which it is not. Here is an example of a tune treated first heterophonically and then polyphonically:

Heterophony—one of the principal characteristics of New Orleans style—is no better or worse than polyphony, just as New Orleans jazz is no better or worse than bop, or a major chord is no better or worse than an augmented eleventh chord. Heterophony is a primitive form of polyphony; it is a technique that has been used successfully by such sophisticated composers as Brahms and Stravinsky, and it should need no apologists. When used properly, heterophony can provide interesting textural contrasts to both homophony and polyphony. In a proper context heterophony can be an extremely useful compositional device; often it can provide a much-needed tensional transition from the accompanied solo to the polyphonic collective improvisation. The secret of its successful use lies in the dependence of one part on another. Grossman and Farrell, in their *Heart of Jazz*, seem to think that having voices with dependent parts, or in imitation of each other, would in some way diminish the New Orleans style. They write: "In New Orleans jazz, voices (instruments) rarely imitate each other, and the melodic lines are noted for their mutual contrast and independence. Thus there is greater emphasis on diversity than in most polyphony." [20] What, we may ask, is the criterion of diversity? The answer, of course, would have to be *unlikeness*—in short, the greatest possible independence between parts, the greatest possible disagreement between parts. Walter Piston, in his *Counterpoint*, summarizes the qualities that distinguish heterophony from polyphony:

. . . dependence, or agreement, would be supplied harmonically by the use of consonances and by coincidence of harmonic rhythm with melodic rhythm. In rhythm, there would be coincidence of stresses or strong beats, and of rhythmic activity. In the melodic lines, there would be what is called similar motion, and the climax, or peak, would be reached simultaneously by different voices. These features detract from the contrapuntal nature of the texture.

On the other hand, independence, or disagreement, is obtained by the use of dissonances and non-harmonic tones; by avoiding coincidence of rhythmic stress and rhythmic patterns; by opposition of the melodic curves, making use of oblique and contrary motion. These are some of the means contributing to the contrapuntal style.[21]

Certain writers have said that it requires as much musical training and intellect to listen with understanding to a New Orleans ensemble improvising collectively as it does to listen to a Bach fugue. One has only to listen to a great deal of both kinds of counterpoint to know that these writers have understated their case. It is easier to follow and understand a Bach fugue (or, for that matter, any premeditated, composed fugue) than a collective improvisation because the trained composer is concerned with keeping the various strands independent of each other; he knows that comprehension comes from the listener's being able to distinguish each part from the others. Since rhythm impresses itself on most listeners before pitch, the simplest music to understand is homophonic or chordal, where, despite the use of three or more individual voices, there is really only one part, one rhythm to follow. Even in polyphonic music, where the parts are truly independent, the listener is able to separate the parts in his mind because the composer has worked to distinguish them from each other, to give each part independent melodic and rhythmic activity, direction, climax, and so forth. With concentration and experience, the strands of a composed fugue can therefore be followed with relative ease, especially if the fugue is performed by a group of instruments, each with its own tone color.

Despite the advantages of having three distinctive tone colors to distinguish its lines, New Orleans heterophony is more difficult to follow and comprehend than a Bach fugue. The reasons are not difficult to understand when we consider three individuals trying to achieve on the spur of the moment, often publicly, what the composer is able to calculate privately and at his own pace. It is no wonder, then, that much of what is created by the New Orleans ensemble, when they are improvising collectively, is, so to speak, heavy, dense, not easily penetrated, and often without apparent direction. If one is to understand the structure and design of New Orleans jazz—and there is a design—one must hear it as a chiaroscuro: as a pattern of light and dark sections, what Italians call "clear dark."

The characteristic New Orleans forms are blues, stomps, rags, and marches; these forms, however, are not structurally fixed. The blues chorus, for example, while it is twelve bars long, may be preceded or followed by interludes or transitions in four-, eight-, or sixteen-bar sections; and, when the melodic and harmonic materials in these latter sections are similar to the chorus material, it is often difficult to determine exactly where one section begins and another ends unless one is able to see a notated outline of the work. Perhaps it is proper here to point out that, while New Orleans jazzmen may on occasion have improvised on the traditional harmonies of the blues, they more often worked with specific blues pieces such as "Jelly Roll Blues," "West End Blues," "Buddy Bolden's Blues," "Dippermouth Blues" (also known as "Sugarfoot Stomp"), or such pieces with twelve-bar choruses as "Snag It" and "No Easy Rider." Many of these blues included—in the printed version or traditionally—eight-, twelve-, or sixteen-bar verses that, in performance, were not only often repeated but sometimes returned to after a number of repetitions of the chorus, giving the impression of a modified ternary structure or a long bridge propped up on either end by two short pillars.

Stomp pieces, except for a characteristic stomp section, are cast in a great variety of forms. Not counting introductions and endings, and such transitional material as interludes and episodes, it may be said that stomp pieces are constructed in sections of eight and sixteen bars, with individual sections occasionally repeated with variations, following the general plan AABBCC, the C section consisting of the stomp itself. Occasionally there is a return to the beginning—a *da capo*—that arbitrarily goes on to the end of any of the sections. Rags, like stomp pieces, are sectional forms with each section having its own tune. New Orleans style marches may be just a sixteen-bar strain repeated over and over, as in Kid Rena's version of "Gettysburg March," or they may be given the full treatment of introduction, repeated first strain, repeated second strain, transition, and trio, with everyone having a go at it, as in Kid Ory's version of "Panama" in a Good-Time Jazz recording, "Tailgate!" Furthermore, it is more than likely that the length of a piece and even its structure were subject to the time and place of its performance. Everyone has heard of the legendary one- and two-hour sessions of blues improvisation in honky-tonks and dance halls. But the fact is that a great many recorded New Orleans style, medium-tempo blues have the same format: a four-bar introduction, nine choruses of blues, and a two-bar tag, and the reason for this is the three-minute recording. In spite of the limitations of recording, however, the New Orleans jazzmen were little concerned with questions of formal structure. They were too busy learning how to finger and blow their instruments; they were still much taken with the curious musical sounds and noises their horns could, on occasion, produce—and they were learning to control them. They were too busy exploring the melodic possibilities of the basic chords to think about formal structure. They did, however, have a feeling for design, for the light and shadow, the chiaroscuro we have already mentioned.

The New Orleans ensemble was able to provide a number of musical textures of varying weight and density, the heaviest texture coming as a result of the polyphonic *tutti*, and the lightest as a result of the unaccompanied solo "break"; in between we may list the heterophonic *tutti*;

the concerted, chordal, or homophonic *tutti;* the solo against the polyphonic, heterophonic, or homophonic *tutti;* and the solo against only the rhythm section. Without attempting to set up a system of measures and color intensities, it appears reasonable to divide the New Orleans sound patterns into dark, medium, and light. Working mostly by feel and head arrangements, the ensemble leaders often managed to achieve logical and sometimes even interesting designs. While they may have known little of structure, they knew the value of contrast. When one considers how often these contrasts were initiated on the spot, so to speak, the balance is quite good, and—in the work of Oliver's Creole Jazz Band, as we shall see—remarkably deft. With the possible exception of the four-bar homophonic introduction and the two-bar tag, New Orleans jazzmen followed no established formula; it was usual to begin with the polyphonic ensemble, but a piece could just as easily start with a clarinet solo. The number and placement of solos depended to a degree on the color and weight of the ensemble preceding it, the color and weight to be intensified and multiplied by consecutive choruses of the same type. When the chorus itself was divided into multiples of two or four, the rapidly alternating, contrasting short phrases seem to come in an arrangement of black and white squares.

In constructing melodies, the New Orleans jazzman is characteristically short-winded; he seldom thinks more than four measures ahead, more often only two. This method of constructing melodies usually results in aimlessness in the melody as a whole, that is, there is apparently

no direction, no flow, no melodic curve. In its place, however, one finds an abundance of perfectly structured two-
and four-bar phrases; the best work of the period may occasionally encompass eight bars, but seldom more. The
principal melodic curves may be shown as

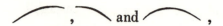

the latter usually covering four bars while the ascending
and descending curves cover two bars each; on the other
hand, a great many two-bar phrases have little consistent
upward or downward motion and either merely undulate
or consist of a vibrant rhythmic variation on a single tone
or perhaps two. Characteristic melodic curves may be
shown as follows:

The shape of the melodic line will depend, of course, on
the shape of the tune being improvised upon and how

closely the performer decides to stick to it. "Jelly Roll Blues," for example, has little motion within each two-bar phrase and does not encourage much exploration by the performer, at least not the first time through. On the other hand, "Wolverine Blues," with its successive two-bar descending curves, invites a similar improvised treatment.

Throughout New Orleans style melodies, the tonality is firmly maintained; it is not uncommon to hear the tonic note ten or twelve times in as many measures of a blues chorus. On occasion there will be a single modulatory passage to a next related key, but in general pieces begin, continue, and end in the same key. Of the nonharmonic tones, the anticipation, the passing tone, and the auxiliary tone have the greatest frequency; of the passing tones, the unaccented ones appear with considerably more frequency than the accented ones. Appoggiaturas appear occasionally, and when they do they are more likely to form a consonance with the root than a dissonance—an *a* sounding against a C chord, for example, instead of a *d* or an *f* sounding against a C chord. (Accented passing tones coming in strong places are often considered appoggiaturas by some theorists; however, the rhythmic value of such tones must be seen, or heard, in relation to the rhythmic value of the preparatory note and to the note of resolution.) *Cambiatas*, *échappées*, and escape tones are infrequent, and the suspension is rare; but ornamental resolutions are quite common, particularly in the penultimate bar of the final cadence of individual solos.

The principal mode of New Orleans jazz is major, but

175

with frequent interchange of the major and minor third scale degrees; the major and minor seventh scale degrees are also used frequently, but not interchangeably, the minor seventh occurring most frequently—as has already been pointed out—in V^7 of IV. A good example of the interchange of the major and minor third is found in the beginning of a characteristic blues solo by Armstrong, as follows:

The harmonies of the New Orleans style are the harmonies of the marching band. The primary triads (I, IV, V) are the foundation for each composition, and the secondary triads (II, III, VI) are used considerably less frequently, as is the augmented triad; diminished seventh chords are fairly common (the four-bar introduction to "Dippermouth Blues" provides a well-known example), and secondary dominants enjoy wide usage. Of the latter, the most common is the V^7 of IV; a favorite harmonic progression is the series of consecutive secondary dominants: V^7 of II, V^7 of V, and V^7, followed of course by the tonic chord (A^7, D^7, G^7, C). This series of sevenths appears frequently not only in tunes that are constructed in eight-bar sections, but in the twelve-bar blues as well; examples may be seen in the chorus of "Chimes Blues" in bars 8 to 11, and in the verse to "Dippermouth Blues," bars 8 to 11.

The standard blues progression, however, remains predominant, that is, three bars of C, one of C^7, two of F^7, two of C, two of G^7, and two of C, with a G^7 added to the last measure when the chorus continues into another.

The harmonies and harmonic progressions used by solo pianists of the period are another matter. Jelly Roll Morton, for example, was quite capable of constructing major seventh chords and chords with added ninths not simply as ornaments, but with sufficient duration to give them a life of their own, as can be plainly heard in "Kansas City Stomp." Ragtime, however, while it had an influence on New Orleans style—rhythmic mostly—is essentially a notated music that grew up separately from but alongside the New Orleans style; it is basically keyboard music, and its harmonies are thus naturally more sophisticated than those implied in New Orleans solo instrumental music.

Perhaps the most frequent rhythms of the New Orleans style are the dotted eighth note followed by the sixteenth (♪♫),, and the syncopated quarter note (♪ ♩ ♩ ♩ 𝄾); one-beat triplets are fairly common, and two-beat triplets are rare. The rhythms of the collective improvisation, between bar lines, usually add up to a straightforward combination of eighth and sixteenth notes, and except for unaccented upbeats the rhythms are fairly square, that is, they agree for the most part with the meter. There is very little significant rhythmic activity across the bar line because, as has already been pointed out, melodies are generally conceived in two-bar phrases. For this reason, the rhythmic effect of melodic improvisation is stop-and-go rather than a rhythmi-

177

cally flowing motion; this is particularly true in solo work. The flow, however, is provided by the steady, unaccented beat of the rhythm section. The following example shows a number of characteristic rhythms drawn from solos in the New Orleans style.

In the New Orleans ensemble, as we know, the cornet provides the melodic lead, the clarinet embroiders the cornet lead, and the trombone underlines the harmonic basis. The variations supplied by the trio depend, of course, on how "straight" the cornet plays his lead. In the main, variations consist of arpeggiolike figures, scale figures both diatonic and chromatic, the rhythmic variation of a tone or two, as well as variations of tone quality, and the use of such special instrumental effects as the growl, produced by simultaneously blowing and humming into the instrument; the shake, produced either by an exaggerated hand vibrato or by jaw vibrato; lipping, controlling the pitch by stiffening or slackening the lip muscles; and fluttering, produced by vibrating the tongue against the roof of the mouth. The glissando, produced by sliding from one tone to the next—more properly called portamento—is the favorite effect of the trombonist and, to a lesser degree, the clarinetist. (Leonard Feather, in his chapter on the trombone in *The Book of Jazz*, implies that the reason for the trombone's glissando lies in the early jazzman's incapacity to manipulate the slide with the proper degree of control. "In order to lead to a melodic creation of any substance," he writes, "the manipulation of the slide and the control of the embouchure must be expert and highly professional." [22] This statement would be true if everyone agreed on the meaning of "substance." Feather's implication seems to be that a glissando scale is something less than a legato scale because the legato is more difficult to achieve.)

Between March and November of 1923 the Oliver band made thirty-nine known recordings, according to Charles Delaunay's *New Hot Discography*.[23] Except for occasional changes in personnel (Charlie Johnson, bass saxophone, replaces Bill Johnson, banjo; Jimmie Noone replaces Dodds on clarinet; and so forth) the band's personnel, as listed earlier in the chapter, remained the same. The thirty-nine recordings include what many consider to be the outstanding examples of New Orleans style: "Mabel's Dream," "Riverside Blues," "Froggie Moore," "Canal Street Blues," "Workin' Man's Blues" (with its two-bar tag that foreshadows the Ellington of the thirties), "Dippermouth Blues" (with Oliver's swinging muted cornet solo), and perhaps the finest of all, "Chimes Blues" (with Armstrong's first recorded solo). Practically every one of Oliver's recordings of 1923 is noteworthy, and all deserve to be better known (Riverside's lp "Louis Armstrong: 1923," which contains eleven reissues of the Oliver recordings, should help give them a wider audience). "Chimes Blues" has been singled out for special attention here, not because it is the best jazz of the period—although this position may well be defended—but rather because it manages to encompass during its three minutes of playing time a great many of the characteristic New Orleans features as they were handled by the outstanding exponents of the style at the culminating point in its history.

"Chimes Blues," like "Dippermouth Blues," "Canal Street Blues," and other Oliver medium-tempo blues, opens with a four-bar introduction followed by nine choruses of blues and a two-bar tag. Since the composition is Oliver's, the arrangement follows the plan of his original four strains: each strain is repeated once, and it closes with an additional repetition of the second strain, a triolike tune, giving us the curious structure AABBCCDDC. The form is not as diverse as it seems, because the harmony is fixed in the ABC strains and has important changes only in the D strain. The harmonic progression for ABC is basically three measures of C, one of C^7, two of F, one of C, one each of A^7, D^7, G^7, and the last two of C; the D strain—Armstrong's solo—uses A-flat^7 instead of C in measure 2, and Cdim^7 instead of F in measure 6, and these changes provide an interesting and relatively colorful harmonic contrast to the six choruses preceding it.

180

While there are important melodic and rhythmic devices that help create an impression of unity and purpose in Oliver's "Chimes Blues," the total direction of the arrangement is mainly dependent on contrasts of sound. The introduction consists of two bars played by Oliver and Armstrong, followed by two bars of full ensemble in a figure that has long since become a cliché but that nonetheless kicks off the ensemble in an authoritative fashion. Chorus 1 presents the ensemble in rich but lucid polyphony lightened somewhat by the clickety-click of Baby Dodds's wood block; in the second chorus the ensemble continues, but the clarinet is now brought to the fore while the rest melt into a heterophony which, while making their parts more difficult to isolate, creates a warm background for Johnny Dodds's pushing arpeggios. Choruses 3 and 4 are obviously intended to be in the traditionally homophonic ensemble style of the march trio, and for the most part they are; Dodds's clarinet, however, is perhaps not quite finished with its job and sporadically leaves the ensemble and spills over into inviting spaces, filling them with warmth and exuberance. And underneath it all, firmly but without dominating, are Lil Hardin's "chimes" in an adumbration of the next two choruses—5 and 6—that are to be hers alone. The chimes of choruses 5 and 6 are played in even quarter notes in descending arpeggios ending with a characteristic stomp rhythm, while the ensemble drives the solo piano forward with concerted staccato chords on each downbeat, an extra upbeat-downbeat push between measures 8 and 9, and Oliver's muted triplet filigree imposed on the stomp rhythm. Armstrong's open horn for the next two choruses is a strong contrast to the quarter-note flow of the chimes; angular, frenetic, pointedly coarse, his twenty-four-bar solo seems the inevitable result of the six choruses preceding it. The repetition of chorus 3 by the homophonic ensemble—this time with Johnny Dodds's clarinet above the lead—is a proper coda, and Dutrey's two-bar solo tag is a good-natured imitation of the two bars preceding it.

In the foregoing I have tried to summarize those qualities of Oliver's Creole Jazz Band that, in 1923, enabled it to bring the New Orleans style to its highest peak. Performances like those of "Chimes Blues," "Dippermouth Blues," and others, were the culmination of a quarter century of sorting out what were to be the essential ingredients of jazz. The brief analysis of "Chimes Blues" is intended as a guide to the melodic, rhythmic, and harmonic riches inherent in the best New Orleans jazz. This analysis barely touches the problem of rhythmic development, for example, and it is hoped that students of New Orleans jazz will continue to study Oliver's complete works of 1923 until the essentials of the style are available for all who wish truly to understand the technique of New Orleans style. A version of "Jelly Roll Blues" performed by Sidney Bechet and his New Orleans Feetwarmers on a Jazztone Society recording is especially curious in the degree to which it follows the publisher's sheet music version; it is as if each player had been provided with a copy of the music, notified what parts were his, what cuts were to be made, and who was to take which chorus. It is only fair to say that the performance was nonetheless first-rate, and as stylistically consistent as it is possible to be thirty years after the culmination of a style. In addition to Bechet, the performers are Wild Bill Davison on cornet, Wilbur deParis on trombone, Ralph Sutton on piano, George Wettling on drums, and Jack Lesberg on bass.

After 1923 the Creole Jazz Band disbanded, and Oliver, having breathed the heady air on the summit, started the long, dreary descent. By the end of 1924 the Dodds brothers and Dutrey were playing with a new group, Armstrong and Lil Hardin were married and Armstrong was playing lead cornet with a new group, and Oliver was playing lead cornet with a new group—Dave Peyton's Symphonic Syncopators. The descent was slow but steady: Oliver went from one group to another, tried the publishing business, one-night stands, New York, New Jersey, Pennsylvania, and West Virginia; in April, 1938, after fifteen years of disappointment, confusion, and poor health, he died in Savannah, Georgia. It is not likely that he was aware of his contribution to jazz. A simple man, he thought of himself as an individual, as "the world's greatest jazz cornetist"—a title by which he was often billed. When the band broke up he was certain its members could not go anywhere without his guidance and discipline, and none of them, except Armstrong, did. The Dodds brothers, Dutrey, and the rhythm section were substantial musicians, and Oliver and Armstrong had stood on their shoulders. After the breakup Oliver moved downward, the rest of the band remained on a sort of dead level, and Armstrong, radiantly optimistic, set out to see what it was like on other, perhaps higher, peaks. His new adventures belong more properly to the preswing era.

chapter 7

PRESWING

THE MEN WHO SHAPED AND
influenced the course of jazz in the preswing era were Louis
Armstrong, Fletcher Henderson, Duke Ellington, and a
number of other, less substantial figures. The period between 1924 and 1934 is difficult to evaluate. New Orleans
style was losing ground and by the mid-twenties had little
consequence. Jazzmen, both Negro and white, moved back
and forth between Chicago and New York capriciously,
while jazzmen from West Virginia, Tennessee, Georgia,
and other southern states congregated in New York and
played a notated music as unfamiliar to the musically un-
lettered New Orleans jazzman as New Orleans style was
to the New York jazzman. But, before the decade was over,
the direction jazz was to take became clear. It is impossible
in a work of this size to treat at length the accomplishments
of the period's major figures—those whose work, in the

confusion of a transitional period, had direction. However, if we are constrained to treat them briefly, we must nonetheless be aware of their significance. Let us start with Armstrong.

When Armstrong left Chicago and the Creole Jazz Band in 1924, it may have been because Lil Hardin could not tolerate his playing second cornet to anyone—even King Oliver. Armstrong, however, could not have been induced to leave if he did not himself believe in his individuality. The breaking up of the Creole Jazz Band and Armstrong's leaving to play with Fletcher Henderson's band are in many ways symbolic of the crumbling of the New Orleans style, with its emphasis on collective improvisation, and of the rising emphasis on solo improvisation which was to be brought to its highest point more than a decade later. The solo improvisation was, of course, nothing new; but in New Orleans style it had been used primarily as a contrast—an interlude, perhaps—to the polyphonic sections. In a great many performances, however, even in the so-called polyphonic sections, one instrument often dominated the musical texture, and a musician of Armstrong's individuality could not long be kept subordinated to the group. It was therefore more than coincidence—more likely good timing—that, when in 1924 Henderson asked Armstrong to join his band (he had asked Armstrong the same question in New Orleans several years before, and Armstrong had almost accepted the offer), Armstrong felt ready, even anxious, to leave the comparative protection and security of Oliver, who had brought him to Chicago, for the somewhat insecure but more exciting position in New York with Henderson, a man who would allow him to blow his own horn, so to speak.

Before Armstrong joined the Henderson band, it had already enjoyed a modest success as the Club Alabam Orchestra, and when Armstrong was ready to join them they were moving into their second season at Roseland, New York's immense dance hall. The group Armstrong went east to join consisted mainly of musicians trained in the East, and many of them were to dominate the New York jazz scene for years to come. By the time Armstrong made his first recording with the Henderson band, in the same year he joined them, the band included Elmer Chambers and Howard Scott on trumpet, Charlie Green on trombone, Buster Bailey on clarinet, Don Redman on alto saxophone, Coleman Hawkins on tenor saxophone, Henderson on piano, Charlie Dixon on banjo, Bobbie Escudero on tuba, and Kaiser Marshall on drums. The men in the Henderson band were all in their early twenties (Hawkins, the youngest, had just turned twenty), and Armstrong, who had been the youngest man in the Oliver band, now found himself exceeded in age only by Henderson. But there were further distinctions.

Of the eight members of Oliver's Creole Jazz Band, seven were born in New Orleans and received their musical education there; Lil Hardin was born in Memphis. Of the ten men Armstrong joined in New York, two, or perhaps three, were born in New Orleans, while the others were born in various southern states. The trombonist, Big Charlie Green,

187

and the tuba player, Bobbie Escudero, knew the New Orleans style for certain. Green was born in New Orleans, and Escudero came to New York with A. J. Piron, the New Orleans clarinetist who led the first Negro band to play at Roseland. Buster Bailey had played clarinet with a band led by W. C. Handy in 1917, and joined Oliver for a brief spell after Armstrong left; he could play a refined New Orleans style when the occasion demanded it. But primarily Bailey was a "reader"; five years before he joined the Henderson band he had taken clarinet lessons in Chicago with Franz Schoeppe, first clarinetist with the Chicago Symphony. (Some years later Schoeppe also gave lessons to Benny Goodman.) The rest of the Henderson band certainly knew that a New Orleans style existed, but there is little evidence, in the recordings they made at the time, to show that it had influenced them, at least so far as the style of improvisation is concerned.

The Henderson band of 1924 probably had more academically trained musicians on its roster than most of the other Negro bands combined. Hawkins had studied cello in his youth and later attended Washburn College in Topeka, Kansas; Redman had been a child prodigy who played piano and trumpet at eight and continued with a substantial early training in theoretical subjects that ended, academically speaking, with additional studies at Storer College and schools in Boston and Detroit; Dixon, the banjoist, apparently had sufficient theoretical knowledge to do some orchestration for the band and later some arrangements for Chick Webb; and, finally, there was Henderson himself.

Fletcher Henderson was born in Cuthbert, Georgia, in 1898. From his mother, who was a piano teacher, he learned to read music and play classically; from his father, a school principal, he apparently acquired a faint academic air he carried with him everywhere. His early formal training took him through Atlanta University, where he studied chemistry and mathematics. He graduated in 1920 and came to New York ostensibly to further his scientific studies, but a part-time piano-playing job with W. C. Handy's publishing company soon led to a full-time job as staff pianist with Black Swan records, another Handy enterprise. In short order he toured with a group of jazzmen as accompanist for Ethel Waters and later played accompaniments for Bessie Smith and most of the important female blues singers of the time. In 1923 Henderson auditioned for and received the job at the Club Alabam. It is apparent that from the start Henderson was a note man; it is no surprise to find him at first attracted to Handy, another note man. However, the tours with Ethel Waters and his subsequent record dates where he came to know many important jazzmen certainly added to his growth; he learned much from his relationship with Redman, who did all the early Henderson band arrangements. Not an especially engaging pianist, Henderson spent most of his time gathering potentially good jazzmen and giving them the opportunity to express their individuality; he brought them together where they could influence each other and where—most important for Henderson—they could influence him. He listened carefully, and when he was ready he wrote and arranged music that eventually influenced not one jazz-man or one jazz band but a whole jazz generation. As John S. Wilson put it:

> Henderson holds a remarkable place in jazz as a catalyst, as the attracting force that brought together the fantastic pool of talent which made up the Henderson band in the middle and late twenties, and as the creator of that bridge between popular dance music and jazz which made possible the Swing Era in the middle and late thirties. . . .[1]

Henderson's education, however, might not have been complete without the opportunity of hearing Armstrong during that one important year. And Armstrong's influence was just as important to Redman and the rest of the band as it was to Henderson. Not only did he bring with him the vitality and exuberance of his solo playing and his personality, but he brought ideas that he had himself learned from Joe Oliver. In his excellent survey on Fletcher Henderson, Wilson tells us that

> . . . Armstrong brought with him a number by Joe Oliver which the Oliver band had played as *Dippermouth Blues*. Rechristened *Sugarfoot Stomp*, set in a framework by Redman and featuring some inspired playing by Armstrong, it became the prototype of the Henderson big-band style with its mixture of driving beat, swinging ensembles, and brilliant solo work.[2]

Similarities between Henderson's 1931 recording of "Sugarfoot Stomp" (with Rex Stewart on trumpet) and the Creole Jazz Band's recording of "Dippermouth Blues" make comparisons inevitable. It is no wonder that at least one critic, Charles Edward Smith, found reason to say that "the King Oliver style, in fact, formed the basis of swing jazz." [3] However that may be, it is unquestionable that Armstrong influenced the Henderson band. It is also certain that the year he spent with Henderson's group added to his own development. Henderson gave him a chance to sing with the band, and, since Henderson's was a reading band, Armstrong was compelled to improve his reading. The state of his reading ability when he first joined Henderson—and the kind of music the band had to play on occasion—is made clear by Henderson's anecdote concerning Armstrong's first rehearsal with the band:

> The band at first was inclined to be a bit reserved toward the new arrival and there seemed to be a little tension in the air. At rehearsal he was perplexed by the trumpet part I gave him to a new arrangement of a medley of beautiful Irish waltzes. Now, those parts were well marked with all the dynamics of the music, and at one point the orchestration was indicated as fff with a diminuendo down to pp.
>
> The band followed these notations and was playing very softly, while Louis still played his part at full volume. I stopped the band and said, "Louis, you are not following the arrangement."
>
> Louis objected, saying, "I'm reading everything on this sheet." I said, "But, Louis, how about that pp?" and Louis broke us all up by replying, "Oh, I thought that meant 'pound plenty.'" There was no tension after that.[4]

In the fall of 1925 Armstrong returned to Chicago where he underwent a strengthening or weakening, depending upon whether one sees Armstrong during the middle twenties through the eyes of the traditionalists or of the progressives. Apparently still uncertain where his future lay, for the next several years he alternated between New Orleans groups such as his Hot Five and Hot Seven and Johnny Dodds's Black Bottom Stompers, and groups where he was permitted the freedom of the soloist, such as the bands of Erskine Tate and Carroll Dickerson (who had Earl Hines on piano). The Dickerson band was the one Armstrong kept intact in 1927 when he opened at the Sunset Cafe. By 1929 Armstrong was back in New York where he played at the Savoy Ballroom and then at Connie's Inn; after a trip to California he returned to New York and then went on triumphantly to Europe, leaving his mark wherever he played. By the end of the decade he had made his choice for Armstrong the individualist, and so it has been since.

The year Armstrong returned to Chicago, 1925, saw the dissolution of Nick LaRocca's Original Dixieland Jazz Band and the end of Paul Mares's New Orleans Rhythm Kings. Dixieland, or Chicago style as some call it, had by the end of the decade little force. An imitation of New Orleans style to begin with, it was destined to remain on a dead level until it reached its apogee in the much-publicized revival after the second World War. The group of young musicians known as the Austin High School Gang—Bud Freeman, Jim Lannigan, Jimmy and Dick McPartland, and Frank Teschemacher—who set out in 1922 to imitate the New Orleans Rhythm Kings and later the Wolverines (white bands that themselves were imitating Negro bands), went their separate ways and by the end of the decade had lost whatever New Orleans characteristics they may have picked up even at two removes. Their main distinction in this period seems to lie in the enthusiasm for jazz they generated among many of those they associated with, such jazzmen as Goodman, Dave Tough, Joe Sullivan, George Wettling, Pee Wee Russell, and Eddie Condon. Like the Austin High boys, the Wolverines and the almost legendary Bix Beiderbecke spent much of their time trying to sound like the New Orleans Rhythm Kings; however, one has only to listen to the profusion of ninths, elevenths, and thirteenth chords of Beiderbecke's "In a Mist" to know in what direction his interests lay. Beiderbecke left the Wolverines about the time Armstrong returned to Chicago; George Hoefer tells us that "some of the Wolverines themselves admitted that Bix left the band . . . because he felt they were too far behind him musically." [5]

The middle and late twenties were a curious time for jazz—a period of transition when jazzmen were divesting themselves of the jazz they thought they knew and were struggling to replace it with a music more restrictive. As if the search for a new jazz style were not enough of a problem in itself, there arose in the middle and late twenties the added difficulty of choosing between jazz, with its minimum financial security, and the lush, full-blown, popular sounds being promoted and dispensed by such solvent groups as those led by Vincent Lopez and Paul Whiteman. The choice for many was a simple one. The names of those who played with the Whiteman band of the twenties, for example, reads like a list of the most important white jazz-

men of the swing era. (Whiteman bought twenty arrangements from Don Redman for two thousand dollars, but it
seemed more like a gesture to justify his self-bestowed title
"King of Jazz" than evidence of a true desire to play
mainstream jazz.) Despite the money problem, which
plagued most jazzmen, there was nonetheless a continuous
movement toward the new jazz style. The recording industry was at its peak, and if the prices paid for recording
were not precisely munificent there was still something for
anyone who wished to preserve his sound on wax. Apparently all the jazzmen who could read—and many who could
not—found their way to recording studios in New York,
Chicago, St. Louis, and Richmond, Indiana. As Ulanov
points out: "In 1926 phonograph records had hit an
all-time high. Americans gobbled up 100,000,000 of
them. . . ." [6] And Red Nichols, a not particularly distinguished trumpet player, did his share toward supplying
those recordings.

Nichols started recording in 1925, but in 1926 he went
at it in earnest, recording as Red Nichols and His Five
Pennies. Between 1925 and 1932 he recorded about 250
sides—half by the Five Pennies and half by assorted
groups known as the Louisiana Rhythm Kings, the Wabash
Dance Orchestra, the Six Hottentots, the Midnight Airdales,
and others. The original Five Pennies were Jimmy Dorsey
on clarinet and alto saxophone, Arthur Schutt on piano,
Eddie Lang on guitar, and Vic Burton on drums. As time
went on the Five Pennies varied in number from six to ten,

for Nichols added and subtracted personnel so often that playing with Red Nichols often meant little more than a day's work. Those who managed to play with Nichols frequently enough at the start to be considered associates included, besides those mentioned, Miff Mole, Joe Venuti, Adrian Rollini, Fud Livingston, and several others. In 1929 a typical Red Nichols ensemble might include Nichols and Manny Klein on trumpet, Jack Teagarden and Glenn Miller or Tommy Dorsey on trombone, Benny Goodman on clarinet, Fud Livingston on tenor saxophone, and Gene Krupa or Dave Tough on drums. It is obvious that Red Nichols brought a lot of jazzmen together and for this must be considered at least a minor influence on the development of a jazz style. He gave potentially important jazzmen an opportunity not only to hear one another's individual style, but to perform together and, no doubt, influence one another. The value of the kind of training and performing center Red Nichols conducted is in the long run inestimable.

In Detroit in 1921 William McKinney, a drummer, organized the Cotton Pickers, a band that was taken over by Redman in 1927 and later drew sidemen of the caliber of Rex Stewart, Fats Waller, Joe Smith, and Bennie Carter. The same year, 1927, was the year for wide-open Kansas City, where the Pendergast machine created an atmosphere not unlike that of Storyville, and in 1929 Bennie Moten had his Kansas City Orchestra there—a band whose main influence was to come when its piano player, Count Basie, took over in 1935. Marshall Stearns summarizes the dance-band activity in and around Kansas City during Boss Pendergast's regime:

> A fairly regular circuit for Negro dance bands existed from Houston and Dallas to Kansas City and Oklahoma City, and a series of stomping bands swung along this circuit; the Terrence Holder band from Dallas; the Jap Allen band (with Ben Webster) from Tulsa; the Troy Floyd band from San Antonio; the Alphonse Trent band from Cleveland; the George Morrison band (with Jimmy Lunceford) from Denver; Bat Brown, Gene Coy, Pardee's Footwarmers, and many more. And a new, more powerful style was evolving, as old recordings demonstrate.
>
> Soon after 1927, Walter Page and his Blue Devils were touring Arkansas, Oklahoma, Texas, and Missouri with Lester Young playing tenor sax and—later—Count Basie playing piano. Basie was from Red Bank, New Jersey, and Young was from Woodville, Mississippi, but, like many others, they were attracted to the Southwestern renaissance. By 1929, Andy Kirk and his Clouds of Joy came up to Kansas City from Dallas with a girl named Mary Lou Williams playing piano. . . .[7]

Back East, Henderson was about to enter the most productive phase of his band-leading career. After Armstrong had left the Henderson band and Redman had shaped the big-band arrangement that would show off soloists—both vocal and instrumental—to their best advantage, Henderson proceeded to staff his band with the best available jazzmen, and they in turn sought to play with Henderson. By the time Redman was ready to move on to the Cotton Pickers, Coleman Hawkins's drive was helping to carry the Henderson band to its highest point. (Henderson's 1926-28 band is considered by many to have been his best, but others believe his band of 1932-33 was superior.) In December of 1928 Henderson's band included Russell Smith, Bobby Stark, and Rex Stewart on trumpet; Jimmy Harrison and Benny Morton on trombone; Buster Bailey on clarinet; Hawkins on tenor and Bennie Carter on alto saxophone; June Coles on bass; and Kaiser Marshall on drums. Carter, who had replaced Redman's successor, Don Pasquall, was also a first-rate arranger who had attended Wilberforce University in Ohio and later became one of the outstanding alto jazzmen in the swing era. By the time the Henderson band had run its course, it could boast alumni that included J. C. Higgenbotham, Dickie Wells, Edgar Sampson, Ben Webster, John Kirby, Chu Berry, Russell Procope, and Roy Eldridge. The best were drawn to Henderson because they knew him as a gentle, easygoing leader who was happiest when his musicians were expressing their individuality. Henderson's wife, Leora, tells us: "The men liked to work for him. He'd exploit their names and bring them out so people would know them. And he had an easy disposition and a nice way about him. In fact, I never, in all the time I knew him, knew him to get real mad about anything." [8]

It was not until 1933 that Henderson started arranging in earnest, but it was soon obvious to all that Henderson had mastered the technique of big-band jazz. Barry Ulanov has summarized the main qualities of Henderson's big-band writing:

> Drive was the overwhelming point of Fletcher Henderson's music, and there was plenty of competition to establish the point,

197

each soloist vying with the others in half-serious and sometimes dead earnest instrumental battles. Fletcher scored his arrangements to give the same quality to section choruses, so that brass and reed phrases sounded like spontaneous solo bursts. With this band, the exciting reiteration of two- and four-bar phrases, usually built on a blues pattern, became a basic big-band jazz formula. All of this drive and reiteration had become ordinary jazz currency by the time swing appeared, but none wrote it better than Fletcher, which is why Benny Goodman sent for him when the Goodman band was on its way to success.[9]

For many the most important figure in this period—perhaps in all jazz history—is Edward Kennedy "Duke" Ellington. Born in 1899 in Washington, D. C., Ellington started piano lessons at seven and played piano for money at seventeen. In high school he became interested in commercial art, and his parents, who were reasonably well off, gave the young man the freedom of choosing his profession. At eighteen he played in dance groups that included Sonny Greer, Elmer Snowden, Arthur Whetsel, and Toby Hardwick. By the time Ellington was twenty-four he had gone off to New York with these musicians, had been rebuffed by the big city, and returned home. But once more, at the behest of Fats Waller, he returned to New York to try his luck. In September, 1923, after lucklessly working Harlem nightclubs, Ellington opened on Broadway at the Hollywood Cafe, later called the Kentucky Club, where his band played for almost five years. The big break came in December, 1927, when, with the help of Irving Mills, he opened at the Cotton Club with a band that was to remain there, on and off, until 1932. During this period the band acquired many of the men whose names were always to be associated with Ellington. In 1930, for example, one of Ellington's best works of the time, "Rockin' in Rhythm," was recorded by Cootie Williams, Arthur Whetsel, and Freddie Jenkins on trumpet (Williams had replaced the growl trumpet of Bubber Miley only a year earlier); Tricky Sam Nanton and Juan Tizol on trombone; Barney Bigard on clarinet; Johnny Hodges on alto saxophone and Harry Carney on baritone saxophone; Freddy Guy on banjo; Wellman Braud on bass; Sonny Greer on drums; and Ellington on piano.

Whetsel and Greer had, of course, grown up musically with Ellington. Braud and Bigard, however, were both New Orleans men—Bigard was born there—and most certainly must have had a small influence on the band. Bigard had studied with Lorenzo Tio and before joining Ellington had played with many New Orleans-style groups including King Oliver's and, later, Luis Russell's; Braud, at this time, was almost forty years old, and his experience had been mainly with New Orleans-style groups. At the opposite extreme were Hodges, who, except for a short spell with Chick Webb, had had little experience; Jenkins, whose experience was with Fletcher Henderson's brother Horace at Wilberforce University; and Carney, who had joined Ellington's band at sixteen and had had no significant experience. Tizol had come up from Puerto Rico, and his experience had been with a concert orchestra in San Juan and with legitimate reading groups in the States; Williams, too, had had legitimate playing experience in school and a later stint

199

with Fletcher Henderson; Nanton and Guy had taken their training in Harlem's night spots. It was this seemingly awkward and curious combination of talents that Ellington molded into an instrument for jazz that in its time was incomparable.

Ellington's working method has been commented upon in many places. After Billy Strayhorn joined him in 1939, Ellington himself described it in brief:

> The music's mostly written down, because it saves time. It's written down if it's only a basis for a change. There's no set system. Most times I write it and arrange it. Sometimes I write it and the band and I collaborate on the arrangement. Sometimes Billy Strayhorn, my staff arranger, does the arrangement. When we're all working together, a guy may have an idea and he plays it on his horn. Another guy may add to it and make something out of it. Someone may play a riff and ask, "How do you like this?" The trumpets may try something together and say, "Listen to this." There may be a difference of opinion on what kind of mute to use. Someone may advocate extending a note or cutting it off. The sax section may want to put an additional smear on it. . . .[10]

This kind of composing-arranging worked for Ellington and his men. Certain writers believe that Ellington's work is unique in that he created music apart from the usual jazz of the period. This may be true in part; however his influence on others is unquestionable. Sidney Finkelstein tells us:

> His influence was considerable upon the general run of popular band music, and for good. Fletcher Henderson used his style in such performances as "Hot and Anxious" and "Coming and Going," Charlie Barnet in many rearrangements of Ellington

works and original conceptions, Benny Goodman in performances of Ellington works, Louis Armstrong, Bob Crosby, Woody
Herman, Benny Carter, Will Hudson, Artie Shaw, Jimmie
Lunceford, Eddie Sauter, Raymond Scott. A great many "tone
poems," riff compositions, atmosphere and "mood" pieces were
inspired by Ellington.[11]

Ellington, who has been heard to say, "I'm not worried
about creating music for posterity, I just want it to sound
good right now!"[12] has received—despite his apparent but
not very credible unconcern with the future—more effusive
and unqualified critical praise than any other jazzman in
the history of jazz, with the possible exception of Louis
Armstrong. When Dave Dexter put his *History of Jazz* on
four lp's for Capitol, few thought there was anything unusual in the fact that Ellington or his men appeared on
three of them. Before we turn to the general characteristics of the preswing era and a close look at a specific Ellington work, it seems proper to close this section on Ellington
with a statement by Whitney Balliett that reflects the opinion of most serious jazz critics: ". . . the truth is," he
wrote, "that Ellington inescapably remains after almost
thirty-five years as a professional the richest figure in jazz
as well as one of the most inventive, original minds in
American music."[13]

In New Orleans style, with its emphasis on individual
melodies and counterpoint, it was natural for the musicians
to seek to create their jazz on such diverse instruments as
the cornet, clarinet, and trombone—instruments capable
of remaining tonally independent of each other. With the

201

decline of New Orleans style and the move toward the swing era, with its emphasis on a collective harmonic style, musicians like Redman and Ellington set about composing jazz for groups of like instruments rather than for individual instruments. (Even when, as in Ellington's case, he continued to score for trumpet, clarinet, and trombone, he arranged them homophonically, that is, in three parts rhythmically identical in effect.) The result was a division of the band into three units: the brass section, consisting of trumpets and trombones; the reed section, consisting of saxophones and including the clarinet; and the rhythm section, including piano, bass or tuba, banjo or guitar, and drums.

Keepnews and Grauer, in *A Pictorial History of Jazz*, offer a logical explanation for the advent of the big band and its subsequent division into sections:

> So, while there may be many other ways of explaining the differences between early traditional jazz and this Negro big-band music of the middle and late 1920s and thereafter, the latter is, above all, the kind of music that develops when you play at big dance halls and at night clubs with fairly fancy floor shows, when you provide the size and the sound that such circumstances demand.
>
> Instrumentation can provide a valuable clue to the nature of the differences. To continue with Henderson as the prime example: he opened at the Club Alabam in 1922 [1923] with a ten-man group, which isn't much more than the eight with whom King Oliver was playing in a strictly traditional vein in Chicago at the same time. But those two added men were both saxophone players; the total of three, instead of a single clarinettist, made a "section." That of course is one of the key words, one of the fundamentals of big-band music. Soon enough there

were also at least three trumpets and two trombones. Added to the four rhythm instruments, this means a dozen or more men working in unison.[14]

Of the individual instruments to come into their own during the twenties, the most significant are the saxophone and the piano. By the end of the twenties the use of the saxophone was so widespread that it became for many a symbol of the Jazz Age along with F. Scott Fitzgerald's novels, John Held, Jr.'s, bobbed-haired flappers, the shimmy, the Charleston, and the black bottom. The instrument in use here was, of course, the Rudy Vallee type of saxophone and in fact had nothing to do with jazz as music. The saxophone, an instrument of jazz practically unknown in New Orleans style, became in the late twenties an instrument capable of producing important and expressive jazz in the hands of such players as Don Redman, Coleman Hawkins, and Harry Carney. The piano, whose function in New Orleans style ensembles had been mainly to thump out four-to-the-bar rhythm, became in the hands of Earl Hines a solo instrument capable of producing jazz melody in an instrumental as well as a keyboard style. Using his right hand to play melodies in single notes and, when he felt it necessary, in octaves, Hines produced a so-called "trumpet" style of playing solos that subsequently influenced many pianists of the swing era.

For the composer-arranger of the period, the combinations of brasses, reeds, rhythm, and solo instruments eventually provided a wide variety of sound and texture from which he could fashion his music. In the first half of the decade he moved slowly, feeling his way, seeking to combine brasses and reeds first for themselves and second for the impetus they offered soloists. The earliest arrangements in which these effects were attempted and occasionally brought off were by Don Redman. Leonard Feather points out:

> The earliest Redman works, of which the recording of the Armstrong-Oliver *Sugar Foot Stomp* is a prototype, showed that he had captured what was then the first essential of jazz arrangement: to express in sectional and ensemble terms the same nuances of phrasing and melodic construction that gave jazz improvisation its character. There were passages scored in simple harmony for three clarinets, or three saxophones, or for the brass section; there were rhythm breaks and background riffs behind the ad libbing soloists. Three-part harmony prevailed.[15]

Before the end of the decade, Redman and others had learned to manipulate the big-band components in a manner that was to remain unchanged until the end of the swing era. A brief look at the development of numbers in big-band sections may help to indicate the direction composer-arrangers took in moving away from the New Orleans style and moving toward swing.

As we have already noted, the King Oliver band in 1923, in addition to its rhythm instruments, included two cornets, clarinet, and trombone; and Henderson's Club Alabam orchestra included two trumpets, clarinet, trombone, and two saxophones (alto and tenor). The same year Cook's Dreamland Orchestra, with Freddie Keppard, included two cornets, trombone, clarinet, and three saxophones, or, to put it another way, three brass and four reeds. When, a year later, Henderson brought in Armstrong, his band included three trumpets, trombone, clarinet, and two saxophones, or four brass and three reeds; by 1930 another trombone had been added, and by 1936 another tenor saxophone, and, since the clarinet was expected to double on alto, the reed section was basically two altos and two tenors opposing a brass section of three trumpets and two trombones. When Redman left Henderson for the Cotton Pickers, he recorded in 1928 with a band that included two trumpets, trombone, and four reeds; three years later his band included three trumpets, three trombones, and four reeds.

The increase in instruments is also clearly pronounced in the bands of Duke Ellington. His Washingtonians in 1926 included two trumpets, two trombones, and four reeds; during the same year he dropped a trombone and a tenor to give his Kentucky Club orchestra three brass and three reeds. He was not to replace the reed until 1935; apparently satisfied with an alto, a tenor doubling on clarinet, and a baritone, he spent the preswing period seeking what would be for him the proper brass section. Here is the development at a glance:

Year	Trumpets	Trombones	Reeds
1926	2	1	3
1929	3	1	3
1932	3	2	3
1933	4	3	3
1935	3	3	4

Ellington's replacement of the extra reed may seem rather late when we consider that Redman used four reeds in 1928, Charlie Barnet used five reeds in 1933, and Goodman used five reeds in 1934. The Barnet band, however, had no trombones (they played mostly commercial dance tunes), and the Goodman band used only five brass; furthermore, Redman, Barnet, and Goodman were all reed men and functioned as reinforcements rather than additions to the reed section.

Most critics agree that Don Redman was responsible for working out the big-band jazz arrangement. Barry Ulanov tells us that, in 1930, "just about always he opened with a chorus by the saxes, prepared the way for the vocal with a trumpet or trombone solo, scored some easy riffs back of the singer, and either carried the singer to the end of the arrangement or climaxed the vocal with a clean rideout ensemble chorus." [16] And Marshall Stearns writes:

> Given these two powerful voices, the brass and the reeds, the trick of making a big band swing had been amazingly simple. With the help of arranger Don Redman, Fletcher Henderson had figured it out in the early 'twenties. First a hot solo line was harmonized and written out for the whole section, swinging together. Then arrangers returned to the West African pattern of call-and-response, keeping the two sections answering each other in an endless variety of ways. There were still hot solos on top, with one or both sections playing a suitably arranged background, but that was not new. The repeated phrases which the brass and reed sections threw back and forth became known as "riffs," and "riffing" developed into a fine art which built up each number, chorus after chorus, in the manner of a *bolero*.[17]

Characteristic orchestration of preswing jazz includes numerous combinations of sound of which the following seem to be a fair sample. The solos are improvised, of course, and each combination endures two, four, eight, twelve, or sixteen measures:

muted trumpet solo against sustained chords in saxophones and trombones,

trombone solo against sustained chords with solo trumpet fill-ins,

tenor solo against muted trumpet fill-ins and full ensemble rhythmic punctuation,

saxophones in ensemble against brass ensemble punctuation and fill-ins,

muted trombone solo against sustained chords in saxophones,

trumpet ensemble riffs against trombones and saxophones,

saxophones soli in homophonic ensemble,

saxophones soli against brass rhythmic punctuation and riffs,

saxophones soli against muted brass riffs and fill-ins,

trombone solo against rhythm section,

trumpet solo against riffs in saxophones soli,

piano solo against rhythm section.

While occasional use is made of combinations of unlike instruments (particularly the clarinet, trumpet, and trombone), the rule is to keep the sections intact. Trumpets can be used, of course, without trombones, and trombones are often used to reinforce the saxophone section. All instruments can solo; however, solos on rhythm instruments, except the piano, are infrequent and usually restricted to two- or four-bar breaks. Backgrounds are essentially rhythmic chords or sustained chords and—when the top voice of sustained chords has direction—melodic chords or harmonized countermelody. Although backgrounds are usually in chordal style, infrequently one may hear sections or parts of sections in unison or octaves, but seldom for more than a few measures. The riff background is effected by having one section of the ensemble play slightly modified repetitions of an initial figure or phrase against a "lead" in a solo instrument or in another section; riffs may also be used to oppose each other, as in the call-and-response, where each section may have riffs based on different initial figures. While the riff is sufficiently prominent

in this period to warrant making it a part of the period's characteristics, it was not to reach the peak of its use until the swing era. For the purpose of clarification, here are examples of the most common types of background in this period and the next, and their terminology. It is to be understood, of course, that these are heard in conjunction with a soloist or another section.

Preswing forms are not substantially different from those of New Orleans style, with the exception of the increase in the use of the thirty-two-bar AABA popular song form, which during this period started a rise that together with the blues was to dominate jazz to the present. The forms of the preswing period include those of the earlier New Orleans style: blues, stomps, marches, and rags. The blues continued to be a favorite with jazzmen; stomps began to lose ground; and marches and rags, except perennials like "High Society" and "Tiger Rag," were played mostly by those Dixieland musicians intent on keeping their hands in old-time jazz while they promoted what has happily been called the "vo-de-o-do" style. In general, the Dixieland bands played more commercial song hits than the Negro bands because their appeal was primarily to white listeners and dancers who regarded these tunes, along with the saxophone and Paul Whiteman, as representatives of jazz.

The popular tunes themselves were to remain in the repertoire, and many of them became standards as more and more their simple structure and harmonies were found to serve well as a basis for jazz improvisation. As early as the first World War the Original Dixieland Jazz Band was playing "Indiana" and "Darktown Strutters Ball"; in 1920 they worked on "Margie" and "Palesteena," and in 1922 they made a good thing of Sophie Tucker's favorite, "Some of These Days." Many Negro bands, apparently hoping to attract solvent dancers, tried hopping on the commercial bandwagon, and so we discover Cook's Dreamland Orchestra in 1923—when Freddie Keppard played lead cornet with them and King Oliver considered them his greatest competition—playing tunes like "So This Is Venice" and "The One I Love." At the same time in New York the Henderson band recorded "Somebody Stole My Gal" and, after Armstrong joined them, "How Come You Do Me Like You Do," "I'll See You in My Dreams," "Sleepytime Gal," and "Who?" In the next few years such significant jazzmen and bands as Armstrong and the Hot Five, Jimmie Noone and his Apex Club Orchestra, Redman and McKinney's Cotton Pickers, and Ellington recorded tunes like "You Made Me Love You," "Once in a While," "I Can't Give You Anything but Love," "Sweet Sue," "Sweet Lorraine," "She's Funny That Way," "Supposin'," "Ain't Misbehavin'," "Cryin' for the Carolines," "There's a Rainbow Round My Shoulder," and "Stardust." The height was probably reached in 1930 when the Ellington orchestra accompanied Bing Crosby and the Rhythm Boys in "Three Little Words."

The desire for commercial success notwithstanding, the main body of Negro big-band jazz in the preswing period was not based on the thirty-two-bar commercial dance tune. Its jazz was constructed sectionally on two, three, or more strains consisting of four- and eight-bar phrases that occasionally appeared on either side of standard twelve-bar blues phrases. It was characteristic throughout the period, however, for big-band jazz to seek the balance of ternary form, and unifying devices such as the repetition of introductions and the repetition of orchestrational techniques were quite common. Ellington's work of this period is by far the most advanced structurally and shows a concern for form that has been a part of his work to the present time. In the twenties not only was he concerned with the over-all semblance of ternary form, as were others, but the separate sections of his compositions are also internally well balanced. His recording of "Mood Indigo," for example, shows a classic handling of the small form. An over-all ABBA structure, each of its sections is a miniature aaba and each unit a four-bar phrase. In "The Mooch," as another example, he places a series of eight-bar phrases on either side of four twelve-bar blues choruses for an exceptionally well-balanced form, which may be shown as: Introduction; A (aab); B (blues); Introduction; A (aa).

Tonality remained as firmly established in the preswing era as it had been in New Orleans style, and again, as in the previous period, the prevailing mode remained major, although reference to the minor mode becomes more frequent as we approach the end of the period. And here again Ellington seems to lead the way with such pieces as the just-mentioned "The Mooch," where minor material appears on either side of the major blues, and once more in his "Black and Tan Fantasy," where the minor mode, while used sparingly, has an integrating influence nonetheless. Opening with a B-flat minor blues (A), Ellington then moves sleekly into B-flat major, where, after a sixteen-bar section (B), he returns to the blues while maintaining the major mode; after four choruses of blues he sets up a closing section of fourteen bars, the last four of which slip ingeniously back to B-flat minor, creating an impression of unity that might otherwise seem lacking. Others, of course, made occasional use of the minor mode—Redman, Henderson, and Armstrong, to name the best known—but Ellington seemed to consider the minor mode a primary source of composition, perhaps not equal to the major mode, but important nonetheless. It may be that his early concern with "jungle" effects brought forth a rather nebulous association between "jungle" and "minor." At any rate, he has used the minor mode frequently and successfully, while others have used it only infrequently.

The melodies of this period are either arranged or improvised, and melodic ideas tend to be longer than those of the previous period. The tunes are nevertheless constructed in short phrases, particularly the arranged ideas; the improvised solos, however, often extend over the normal phrase line, giving the impression that the soloist intends to play perhaps sixteen bars instead of the two or four of the earlier period. Preswing jazz lines show quite good direction and, in the hands of first-rate jazzmen, melodic curves that are impressively worked out. Almost all of Armstrong's solos from 1927 on show an over-all direction that somehow does not seem proper in presumably improvised solos, and yet they manage to create an air of free swinging. Particularly noteworthy for this quality is his "Struttin' with Some Barbecue" with the Hot Five, where he starts the piece with a little run up to the E-flat in the top space of the staff; twelve bars later he has worked his way up to G, and twenty-four bars later up to A-flat, where he is interrupted by sixteen bars each of clarinet and trombone solos, but only momentarily. Starting where he had stopped, he moves down and up the scale again, embroidering and spinning until at last he shoots forth two climactic high C's; thirty-two bars later he has gracefully descended to the tone with which he opened the piece. The creation of such melodic direction and tension is not, of course, an everyday occurrence; a great many jazzmen who heard Armstrong during the period, however, were influenced by his style, and, after he was once established as a soloist, length of line and over-all conception of a solo must certainly be considered part of his individual style.

The harmonic foundation of preswing is considerably more sophisticated than harmonies of the earlier period, although a large part of preswing harmonies remains the same for both periods. This is particularly true in the work of jazzmen whose early influences came from New Orleans and Chicago; jazzmen without substantial influences from these sources began, in this period, to draw heavily on the traditional European system of harmony, and their harmonic materials were enlarged to include all the harmonies up to nineteenth-century impressionism. (In fact, Ellington in this period already dips lightly into the impressionistic well.) In the middle twenties, Redman used a major seventh in the penultimate chord of "Sugarfoot Stomp"; Armstrong, in his wife's composition "Struttin' with Some Barbecue," played a number of consecutive G's against an A-flat major chord several times in the piece; and Beiderbecke used a major seventh to end "Thou Swell," but then a year earlier (1927) he had recorded "In a Mist," with its appoggiatura ninths, elevenths, thirteenths, and profusion of augmented, altered, and major seventh chords—in short, the bulk of characteristic impressionist harmonies. The difficulty here is that "In a Mist," as jazz, is questionable. More to the point are the consecutive chromatically descending sevenths in Ellington's "Sophisticated Lady," "Cincinnati Daddy," and "Jubilee Stomp"; the consecutive chromatically descending ninths in his "Birmingham Breakdown," "East St. Louis Toodle-Oo," and "Blue Bubbles"; the consecutive chromatically descending thirteenths in his "Sloppy Joe"; the augmented eleventh in "The Mooch"; and the many unresolved ninths scattered throughout his work.

The harmonic stockpile of most jazzmen was not as varied as Ellington's; nevertheless there is, if not a greater variety of chords than the New Orleans style employed, at least a wider use of those which had been less frequent. Diminished sevenths, which were common enough previously, become practically ubiquitous; augmented chords become more frequent; and secondary dominants become the easiest way to go anywhere. (In his "Black and Tan Fantasy" Ellington uses the following progression of consecutive sevenths: G^7, C^7, F^7, B-flat^7, E-flat^7, A-flat^7, D-flat^7, G-flat^7.) Secondary triads and sevenths are also used with greater frequency, mainly because of the period's greater preoccupation with things minor. The nonharmonic tones appear with great frequency, much as they did in New Orleans style, but *cambiatas, échappées,* escape tones, and suspensions remain infrequent. The appoggiatura, however, has greater incidence than before; furthermore, whereas in New Orleans style appoggiaturas were likely to form a consonance with the root, in this period they are more likely to form a dissonance with the root.

The most significant harmonic change in the blues of the period is the increase in the use of the minor blues. The standard blues progression remains the most characteristic, of course, although small variations and alterations, particularly in the addition of ninths to dominant chords, become increasingly more frequent as the period progresses. For one thing, instead of sounding the tonic for the first four bars, there is a greater tendency to use a new chord in measure two—the subdominant, for example; there is also rather frequent use of substitute chords on the second and fourth beats of some measures, especially measures 7 and 8. Many preswing jazzmen took their harmonic cues from Ellington, and for two interesting variations on the standard blues progression we may again turn to him.

Jazz rhythm in the preswing era was directed in part by the necessity of controlling the instrumental section; therefore, while one generally finds more rhythmic freedom and complexity in the improvised solos, the arranged rhythms for the ensemble are relatively square. Because of rhythmic restrictions in writing for jazzmen with little or no tradition of a collective harmonic style, and certainly with little experience until late in the period, arrangers during the twenties drew up a body of rhythmic and melodic formulas that served the average jazzman rather well (many of these clichés, with slight variation, are still current). An engaging improvised phrase from Armstrong's trumpet or Hawkins' tenor was sure to find its way eventually to the score paper where the figure, break, or rhythmic pattern soon after became part of the public domain, so to speak. The borrowing of such material by lesser jazzmen is not, of course, to be disparaged—borrowing musical material has an honorable tradition.

In addition to the rhythms shown in the chapter on New Orleans style, the following rhythms and their variations had wide currency in the preswing era.

At the opposite extreme, two eight-bar phrases from Armstrong's "Tight Like This," in Lee Castle's transcription (*Louis Armstrong's Dixieland Trumpet Solos*, Vol. I [New York: Leeds Music Corporation, 1947]), give a reasonably accurate example of the type of rhythmic freedom and complexity to be found in the best improvised solos of the period. The entire composition is worth study as an example of a masterful variation on only the tonic and dominant chords.

Similar rhythmic treatment of material may be found in Armstrong's "I'm Not Rough," "Gully Low Blues" ("S.O.L. Blues"), and "West End Blues." As a means of observing the wide use of characteristic melodic and rhythmic figures, compare the following phrases extracted from Armstrong's "Cornet Chop Suey," first recorded in 1926, Ellington's "Down in Your Alley Blues" of 1927, and John

Kirby's "Opus 5" of 1939. In its original key the phrase is an essential part of each of these pieces.

One of the high points in the jazz of the preswing era is Ellington's arrangement of "Rockin' in Rhythm," a tune composed by his baritone saxophonist Harry Carney and originally used as an accompaniment for Snakehips Tucker, a vaudeville dancer. For this 1931 recording the band included Cootie Williams, Arthur Whetsel, and Freddie Jenkins on trumpet, Tricky Sam Nanton and Juan Tizol on trombone, Barney Bigard on clarinet, Johnny Hodges on alto saxophone, Harry Carney on baritone saxophone, Fred Guy on banjo, Wellman Braud on bass, Sonny Greer on drums, and Ellington on piano. The form is characteristically ternary, but with some interesting deviations. It is an AABA structure, with the opening A and final A preceded by a four-bar introduction for piano and trombones; the over-all structure may be shown as: Introduction; A (*abcd*); A (*abc*); B (*e*); Introduction; A (*dabc*).

The introductions are four bars long; *a, b,* and *c* are

eight-bar phrases, with the *c*, however, extended to ten bars; and *d* and *e* consist of two eight-bar phrases each. The A sections are in C major (an uncommon key for jazzmen in this period), and the B section is in the relative minor. After the introduction, *abc* is played by the saxophones soli, with solo trumpet fill-ins on the sustained half-cadences of *b*. The solo trumpet in *d* is heard above the saxophones, whose whirring bears a close rhythmic resemblance to the solo, the total impression being one of a four-part voicing with trumpet lead; however, the impression is quickly erased because the saxophones also serve to punctuate the rhythm on the offbeat every two bars. Cootie Williams' brief solo moves along jauntily and, as Dave Dexter, Jr., has pointed out, sounds quite like "Peckin'," a song written six years later. The saxophones play the second A section, with muted trumpets replacing them an octave higher on the two-bar extension of *c*.

Ellington opens the A minor section with a rollicking four-bar vamp that alternates two beats each of tonic and dominant seventh, maintaining this pattern for the entire section. Bigard, coming in so late in the fifth bar as to make one think four more bars of vamp are in the offing, performs a sixteen-bar clarinet solo that is a joy to hear and is as cheerful as one can be in minor. Careful listening to Bigard will show the debt clarinetists of the swing era owe to this short solo. Without losing a beat, Ellington, at this point, modulates to C major and repeats his opening four bars, but instead of continuing on to the *abc* of the opening section he reverses himself to give Tricky Sam

Nanton a chance to present his version of *d*, or what had previously been Williams' trumpet solo. But the difference is in the best interests of variety and balance. The saxophones soli repeat the background they offered Williams, but, whereas Williams' solo was bustling and rifflike, Nanton's solo is an extravagantly sustained variation mainly on two tones; the effect is one of fresh material, but one cannot miss the saxophones' offbeat pushes every two measures. Nanton's solo is followed by a literal repetition of the *abc*, and, with Williams' humorous two-bar tag, on "Taps," the piece ends on an imperfect cadence.

Ellington's melodic inventiveness had to be at a peak in "Rockin' in Rhythm," mainly because the harmonic basis is static so much of the time. The principal strain is based essentially on a C major chord, and more than half of the composition's 134 measures are fundamentally the tonic chord. If we include the A minor section, the proportion is even greater. By judiciously alternating and contrasting diatonic and chromatic scale figures with arpeggio figures, Ellington and his men have created in "Rockin' in Rhythm" a significant jazz structure that stands as a landmark in the preswing era.

While Ellington's work has continued to develop and expand through the thirties and up to the present, the same cannot be said of other important preswing figures. Armstrong, as has already been pointed out, reached a self-imposed impasse somewhere in the thirties and has since continued to remain a great jazz figure—but of the past. His occasional appearances on television or as an American representative abroad have too often produced euphuistic interpretations of jazz unbecoming to the most significant of all jazzmen. At any rate, Armstrong and Ellington have both reaped the financial rewards of successful pioneers, and in this respect they are more fortunate than Fletcher Henderson, who received little popular acclaim and less fortune. Henderson's decline somewhat resembles King Oliver's. After innumerable attempts at band leading, in 1939 he finally turned to full-time arranging for Benny Goodman, whose Henderson arrangements had a large part in his early successes. But this brought Henderson no further toward his goal. In 1950 he suffered a stroke and died two years later. His wife, Leora, tries to tell in a few sentences what Henderson apparently endured for a great many years. She says: "The last job that Fletcher had before the stroke was in the *Jazz Train* show that played in that place on Broadway, Bop City. He worked so hard on that. He was really trying to make a comeback—workin' days and nights on arrangements and rehearsals, but all of it was for nothing." [18]

On October 24, 1934, Hugues Panassié completed his book *Le Jazz Hot,* the first attempt at an extensive, serious jazz study. The date of completion may well mark the end of an era. It is also significant that in the spring of the same year Benny Goodman organized his first big band.

chapter 8

SWING

Toward the end of September, 1934," Benny Goodman says in his autobiography, "the word got around that the National Biscuit Company was planning to put on a big program at NBC, starting around December. They were going to have three bands playing alternate sets from about eleven o'clock until two in the morning, every Saturday night. The set-up called for a rhumba band, a sweet orchestra, and a hot band." [1] In December the Xavier Cugat rumba band, the Kel Murray orchestra, and the Benny Goodman orchestra became the representatives of Ritz crackers, a product sufficiently important to the National Biscuit Company and the National Broadcasting Company to cause them to impose a three-hour program, "Let's Dance"—the longest sponsored radio program up to that time—upon fifty-three stations, coast to coast. Goodman had the last hour to himself, and

223

it is likely that the "Let's Dance" program contributed as much as anything else to the unprecedented success the Goodman band enjoyed until the sound of swing was overwhelmed by the portentous explosion at Pearl Harbor.

Why, after so many years of being relegated to the fringes of social acceptance, jazz should have achieved the wide popularity it did is not easy to say. New York, Kansas City, Chicago, and other jazz centers, like the rest of the country, were in the midst of a great depression. Banking and finance had sunk to a low level, industry was being bolstered by government intercession, and breadlines were a common sight in the big cities. The year before Goodman made his NBC debut, Prohibition was repealed, an event that made public drinking as easy as public dining and dancing. Hotels and nightclubs providing public eating, drinking, and dancing were assured almost instantaneous success, and following close on the heels of these establishments were the public dance halls, which were now able to install bars to keep the thirsty crowds wetted down, and bouncers to keep the soaks off the floor. Furthermore, musicians came cheap (several months before the "Let's Dance" program Goodman and an orchestra worked at Billy Rose's Music Hall for less than the union wage scale), and any club, hotel, or ballroom worthy of the name was able to afford a big band. Working almost as if by plan, the national broadcasters piped hotel music to hundreds of thousands of people who would then flock to dance halls and theaters to hear these same bands on tour, after which the broadcasters could sell the bands to sponsors who wished their products to be associated with these by now "name bands."

The combined efforts of the national broadcasters, the hotel industry with its allied service industries, the recording industry, the advertising business, and the entertainment industries in general made band leaders as well known as major-league baseball players and Hollywood movie stars. The end result was an endless multiplication of big bands. As Goodman told Gilbert Millstein:

> The thing got to be an industry. I never considered it one. Others did. I considered it an individual enterprise with each orchestra based upon the qualities of its men. Our band happened to be a pretty good loud band. They never had that kind of music in hotels before. We made good and then the industry came in and said, "We'll have a band like this, too. It doesn't have to be good, just so long as it's loud." [2]

There were undoubtedly enough "loud bands" to satisfy everyone, for by 1938 swing was the country's popular music. On May 29, 1938, a "Carnival of Swing" was held at Randall's Island Stadium in New York, where Artie Shaw, Count Basie, Jimmie Lunceford, and at least twenty other swing groups played for more than twenty-three thousand dancers. In the same stadium three months later, seven thousand so-called jitterbugs and alligators turned up for the first of four swing benefits conducted by Larry Clinton, Richard Himber, George Olsen, and a number of others, who obviously must have been a large segment of the "industry" mentioned above by Goodman. The general public considered, and still does, popular music to be jazz;

in the swing era, however, there *was* little distinction because the best swing of the time was popular not only with
jitterbugs and hip kids but among the educated and mon-
eyed people as well. Goodman told Richard Gehman:

> . . . the literary set took us up. Clifton Fadiman, the distin-
> guished book critic, did two scripts for our "Caravan" radio
> show. He was succeeded by Robert Paul Smith, the novelist.
> Robert Benchley appeared with us on the program, and he in-
> troduced the band to a group of writers for *The New Yorker*,
> including S. J. Perelman and E. B. White. They used to show
> up at the Madhattan Room of the Hotel Pennsylvania in New
> York every Saturday night.[3]

And readers of a *New York Times* item of October 30,
1938, about the fall opening of Goodman's band at the
Empire Room of the Waldorf Astoria learned that "Goodman's welcome at the swank hostelry is being closely gauged
by the trend-watchers, and if early indications mean anything, one might say that the jitterbug mania is now assured
of the blessing of the more polite folk." In short, men,
women, and children on all levels of society accepted and,
in some instances, embraced swing as the popular music
of their time. We have passed lightly over the forces responsible for the promotion and dissemination of swing;
let us now look briefly at the men directly responsible for
making the music.

Never before had there been as much jazz activity or as
many jazzmen as there were in the swing era. Besides the
hundreds of dance bands and the hundreds of white and

Negro musicians who sought easy fame and fortune in the swing surge, there were those preswing bands and musicians who had laid the foundations of swing and continued to work through most of the period. Of the preswing bands that played significant roles during this time, some of the most important were those of Duke Ellington, Fletcher Henderson, Don Redman, Earl Hines, Chick Webb, Andy Kirk, and Jimmie Lunceford. While there was much activity among Dixieland and sweet bands in the preswing era, only a handful contributed to the formulation of swing, and these only through individual jazzmen who gave up the Dixieland and sweet music and went on to become significant swing figures—men from the bands of Ben Pollack, Isham Jones, and Paul Whiteman, to mention a few. The most noteworthy of the white preswing bands were the Dorsey Brothers orchestra and the Casa Loma orchestra. Because of the uniqueness of the Casa Loma's early position, it is interesting to compare its qualities with those that later brought success to the swing band "industry." Wilder Hobson tells us:

> There were various reasons for the Casa Loma's success. The band was young and physically attractive, with none of those gargoyle types which sometimes appear in musicians' tuxedos. Also, a good deal more than it played jazz, it played the sentimental melodies of the day, orchestrated simply and with finish, featuring the sentimental singing of a handsome young saxophonist, Kenny Sargent. And when jazz was played, it was presented in a way in which it might be easily received. There was no improvised "counterpoint," chaos to unfamiliar ears. There was no exotic coloring, such as the Negro bands fre-

quently offered, nor was there much orchestral elaboration. The band's guitarist and arranger, Gene Gifford, wrote scores which allowed for solo improvising in a setting of very simple rhythmic phrases, often with repetitions of the same phrase; and the band played these scores with clean precision. The improvisers, of course, played as they wished, and often not only with the Negro spirit but also with considerable "dirtiness." . . . But such improvising was at its most intelligible against the Casa Loma's orderly, rather mechanical backgrounds. Thousands of ears which would have been confused by the Chicagoans' "counterpoint" or Ellington's coloration responded easily to the Casa Loma's neat exercises. Here was a form in which certain elements of the jazz language, at least the urgency of its rhythms, reached a huge public, and other musicians began to get the idea. The "swing" fad shortly followed.[4]

It may be significant that in 1958, after twenty years of little activity, Glen Gray formed another Casa Loma orchestra to record the arrangements played by his original group in the thirties, presumably in the belief that there are still many people who would remember them. And a great many people undoubtedly did; however, their remembrances are more likely to be tinged with nostalgia for the time than with any feeling that here was jazz. The fact is that, while the period between 1934 and 1945 abounded in good jazzmen, the real success—that is, the popular and financial success—went to the comparative few who were handled properly by the music business interests. For every Goodman, Shaw, Dorsey, Miller, James, and Ellington, to name only the most famous, there were thousands of mediocre bands and musicians whose names came before the public only slightly less frequently than those just mentioned. Toward the end of the swing era Paul Bowles wrote:

> The cascade of hyperbolical praise in the form of ecstatic magazine articles and books which appeared about the time commercial "swing" took the public's fancy, was certainly not designed to keep jazz pure and humble. On the contrary, every performer whose talent ranged from mediocre up was encouraged to think of himself as possessed of a truly personal style.[5]

Close study shows that with few exceptions the character and individuality of the best swing bands depended more on their arrangers than on their soloists. It was the work of the section men that gave a band its quality; soloists provided bravura and dash. This becomes evident when one studies the seeming itinerancy of any number of first-rate soloists during this period. The impression is that of a circulatory system in which from time to time objects (that is, soloists) swirl around and pass each other, and then go on to the next point (or band). The function of the band leader seems to have been to watch the circulation closely and to capture the proper combination of soloists as they passed through his group. A few examples should make the point clear. Between 1935 and 1939, in addition to a continual round of journeyman saxophone players, these reedmen passed through the Bunny Berigan band: Eddie Miller, Hymie Schertzer, Edgar Sampson, Georgie Auld, Bud Freeman, Artie Shaw, Toots Mondello, and Babe Russin, while the drums were manned by Ray Bauduc, Dave Tough, Cozy Cole, George Wettling, and Buddy Rich. Between 1936 and 1945 Cab Calloway managed to get hold of reedmen Ben Webster, Chu Berry, Ike Quebec, and Hilton Jefferson—Jefferson being the only standby. Dave Dexter, Jr., tells us that "Goodman's managers in 1942 admitted that more than 150 musicians had been affiliated with the Goodman band in its eight years of existence!" [6]

In *The Book of Jazz*, Leonard Feather has done a much-needed piece of work by listing most of the important swing soloists, as well as jazzmen of other periods, according to their instruments, and a number of the 150 Goodman alumni may be found there. For our purposes, however, we need only pinpoint the personnel of the Goodman band (and later the Basie band) about whom Goodman said:

> . . . but the band I think of as the best and the one that stayed together longest during the time when the country was really swinging, lined up like this:
> Gordon (Chris) Griffin, Harry James and Ziggy Elman, trumpets; Murray McEachern (or Vernon Brown) and Red Ballard, trombones; Hymie Schertzer, Vido Musso (or Dick Clark), Toots Mondello, George Koenig (or Bill DePew) and Art Rollini, saxophones; Jess Stacy, piano; Harry Goodman, bass; Allan Reuss, guitar; Gene Krupa, drums; Helen Ward (later, Martha Tilton), vocals.[7]

This was the 1937 band that alternated between the Madhattan Room of the Hotel Pennsylvania and the Paramount Theater where, during the first week of March, the band smashed all boxoffice records (first day's attendance: 21,000) and then went on to their important "Camel Caravan" radio show and afterward to Hollywood. Goodman's special feeling of warmth for this group is therefore understandable. In the dazzle of their overwhelming success, however, it is easy to lose sight of their generally undistinguished backgrounds. As for Red Ballard, Dick Clark, Bill DePew, Hymie Schertzer, and Harry Goodman, little is known of their work before they joined Goodman. Vernon Brown came to the band with a Dixieland background, having played with Frankie Trumbauer in 1925 and with Goldkette in 1928, but his primary quality, like that of Chris Griffin, seems to have been that he was capable and steady. Ziggy Elman's principal experience was gained with local bands in Atlantic City, where from 1930 to 1936 he played mostly trombone. Toots Mondello's experience was mainly with sweet bands, and Allan Reuss had apparently had almost no dance band experience. Murray McEachern, before joining Goodman, did a one-man band act, and Art Rollini had played with the Whiteman band. (As a possible insight into the essential quality of the men so far named, it may be worth while to point out that, once the swing era had begun to wane, Elman, Mondello, Reuss, McEachern, and Rollini avoided the competition and relative insecurity of jazz by entering the more stable field of commercial music: Elman, McEachern, and Reuss became Hollywood studio musicians; Mondello went into commercial radio work; and Rollini became a staff musician for the American Broadcasting Company.)

Of the remaining members—Vido Musso, Harry James, Gene Krupa, and Jess Stacy—Krupa and Stacy had by far the most experience. Stacy had worked the Mississippi riverboats in 1925 and had played with Dixieland bands in

Chicago and later with commercial dance bands before joining Goodman in 1935. Krupa's training had been with such Dixieland and sweet groups as the McKenzie-Condon Chicagoans, Red Nichols, Irving Aaronson, and Buddy Rogers. James's early training was legitimate; he had played with Ben Pollack and commercial groups for about a year before joining Goodman in 1936. Musso had little experience, but is bracketed with the others because the members of this quartet showed a degree of individuality by indicating a desire to go it alone. Musso attempted band leading several times but was never quite successful and finally gave it up to freelance in California. Stacy, too, tried his hand at it in 1944. The most successful were the bands of Krupa, started in 1938, and of James, started in 1939. (In recent years Krupa has operated a drum school in New York, and James, after a period of semiretirement, has recently formed a new band in California and is attempting a comeback.) The total experience of Goodman's important 1937 band is not particularly distinguished, as we have seen. What, then, accounts for the acknowledged success of the band? In order to answer this question we must first know something about the band's principal soloist and featured attraction.

Goodman was born in Chicago in 1909, the eighth of twelve children. At the age of ten he was already able to play some clarinet, and at twelve he was alternating professional imitations of Ted Lewis, the then-current popular success, with the scales and arpeggios forced upon him by his teacher, Franz Schoeppe, clarinetist with the Chicago

Symphony. Between the ages of fourteen and eighteen he
played with local Chicago bands, where he was undoubtedly influenced by the Dixieland music all about him. During this period he is said to have been particularly influenced by Leon Rapollo, a New Orleans jazzman then
working with the New Orleans Rhythm Kings. By 1927 he
was well known to local musicians, and during the next
few years he worked with Ben Pollack, Isham Jones, and
various small recording groups.

In 1929 Goodman left Pollack, with whom he had come
to New York, to become a freelance. The desire to be a
leader was upon him, however, and in 1931 he led a pit
band in a revue called *Fun for All*. That enterprise was
unfortunately shortlived; after fifteen performances the
revue closed and Goodman was once more—literally—out
in the street. In 1933 he met John Hammond, an enthusiastic jazz fan and entrepreneur, who asked him to organize
a group for the purpose of making eight records for two
English recording companies, and it was this substantial
offer plus the unabating encouragement of Hammond that
resulted in Goodman's first important band. Robert Goffin
has suggested what may have been in Goodman's mind in
1933:

> . . . he realized the trend jazz was taking; he witnessed the
> rise and success of Fletcher Henderson, Duke Ellington, and the
> Casa Loma band. Big band jazz was the thing; small Dixieland
> outfits were out. If you put the emphasis on orchestration but
> left spots for instrumental solos, you might be able to produce
> good commercial jazz, or swing. Benny laid his plans.[8]

The following year the "Let's Dance" radio show materialized, and the success that followed has already been recounted many times. Goodman's method of combining his legitimate playing technique with jazz ideas proved so successful that even legitimate music interests found reason to jump on the Goodman bandwagon. As a final note to understanding Goodman's seemingly universal appeal, here are two items from the *New York Times* music page of August 14, 1938:

> The Budapest String Quartet will present a series of five late afternoon concerts next season at Town Hall under the auspices of the League of Music Lovers, to take place on Nov. 5, 12, 19, Dec. 26 and Jan. 2. Benny Goodman, the swingmaster, will assist at two of these concerts. In the first he will make his public debut in classical music by playing the Mozart clarinet quintet. On Jan. 2 he will play the Brahms quintet.

> And now we hear that Béla Bartók, the Hungarian composer, is at work on a new concerto for violin, clarinet and orchestra. Joseph Szigeti is the violinist who has suggested the project to Bartók, and he would naturally be the string soloist. His colleague would be Mr. Goodman. [On September 26, 1938, Béla Bartók completed this work, *Three Contrasts* for violin, clarinet, and piano, in Budapest.]

In addition to his faultless musicianship, Goodman's dress was impeccable and the general impression he gave was one of wholesomeness and studious respectability, and to the public mind these were no small matter; it is certainly more than coincidence that the popular leaders of the swing era—Goodman, Tommy Dorsey, Artie Shaw, Glenn Miller, and others—all publicly emanated a distinctive, salubrious air. At a time when jazz was fighting to come up out of the cellar, so to speak, and into the open, Goodman's healthy appearance unquestionably worked to his advantage. This sort of advantage belongs, of course, in a category of intangibles. More concretely, the success of the Goodman entourage can be traced to his organizational and disciplinary ability, the work of his arrangers, and the featuring of his small ensembles—not losing sight for one moment of the influence and direction of John Hammond and Goodman's business representative, Willard Alexander.

Goodman had a firm idea of what he wanted from his bandmen, and, unlike so many other leaders—Fletcher Henderson, for example, or Bunny Berigan—he was more concerned with getting what he wanted from them than with being considered a good fellow. Popsie Randolph, once Goodman's bandboy, tells us something of Goodman's methods:

> Benny wanted what he wanted, that's all. If a guy worked for him, he had to do the job right. Sure, he was changeable, all right, like the weather—a little fickle you might say. But man, he was a perfectionist. A guy would come into the band one day and two days later Benny'd say he was no good—and out he'd go.[9]

In 1937 the Goodman band earned $350,000, with each player receiving about $10,000. For that kind of money Goodman could have had a merry-go-round of the biggest names in jazz, yet he continued to choose his men for their steadiness, reliability, and ability to assume an unassuming

position; exuberance was permissible, but a boyish diffi-
dence was more likely to bring a steady paycheck. Goodman has said: ". . . there was the collective feeling we
had. We knew we were doing something nobody else had
done. We were all bound and determined to show the public that jazz was a healthy form of expression, not just a
passing fancy on the part of some kids. We were dedi-
cated; that's the only word for it." [10]

In the swing era big bands achieved distinction by own-
ing distinctive arrangements, and few band leaders knew
this fact as well as Goodman. For the public, arrangements
and the ensuing Goodman sound were taken for granted;
Goodman, however, realized quite early that his band
would go nowhere without the best arrangers, and the arrangers he employed included the best available: Horace
Henderson ("Big John Special"), Edgar Sampson
("Stompin' at the Savoy"), Fud Livingston ("Alexander's
Ragtime Band"), Spud Murphy ("Get Happy"), Gordon
Jenkins (Goodman's closing theme, "Goodbye"), Dean
Kincaide, Bennie Carter, Jimmy Mundy, and the redoubt-
able Fletcher Henderson. Goodman, in discussing the prob-
lem of initiating the "Let's Dance" program, said:

> Now there was a series of hasty conferences. The first prob-
> lem was to get some arrangements. The great Negro leader
> Fletcher Henderson had more or less broken up his band the
> year before. He was looking for work, and was only too happy
> to begin developing a book for our band. He charged us only
> $37.50 per arrangement! As I recall, the first things he did were
> "Sometimes I'm Happy" and "King Porter Stomp." We also

got some other arrangements, but Fletcher was the man who really made our band, by arranging popular tunes in the same style he used for hot numbers, which we called killer-dillers.[11]

Henderson's arrangements of the popular tunes did not, however, come until the program was well along. In his autobiography, Goodman tells us how it came about, and points up the significance of Henderson's work to the band:

As we went along playing the "Let's Dance" program we began to get some good reactions around the country, and especially in New York. But while it was grand having such material as "Stompin' at the Savoy" (which we got from Edgar Sampson for the first program) and "King Porter" to wind up a set with, we knew that the band didn't have the right material for the regular sequence of numbers. Sometimes they got off well, and sometimes they didn't.

It was then that we made one of the most important discoveries of all—that Fletcher Henderson, in addition to writing big arrangements such as the ones I have mentioned, could also do a wonderful job on melodic tunes such as "Can't We Be Friends," "Sleepy Time Down South," "Blue Skies," "I Can't Give You Anything But Love," and above all "Sometimes I'm Happy." He had to be convinced of it himself, but once he started he did marvelous work. These were the things, with their wonderful easy style and great background figures, that really set the style of the band.[12]

By the end of the program's twenty-six-week run, Henderson had contributed thirty-six arrangements to the band's book, and, despite the fact that the National Biscuit Company did not pick up its option to renew, the band's style was established. Henderson continued, on and off, to do arrangements for Goodman until the end of the swing period, and together with Jimmy Mundy, who turned out about four hundred arrangements for Goodman between 1936 and 1939, created the Goodman big-band sound. As Marshall Stearns put it, "The Negro supplied the fire and feeling, the white supplied the polish and packaging." [13]

In 1935 Goodman initiated the Benny Goodman Trio, the first of his several small groups. With Teddy Wilson on piano and Krupa on drums, Goodman was able to attract the favorable attention of jazz enthusiasts who had had reservations about big-band jazz, and, while their opinions of big-band jazz were not altered to any great degree, their opinion of Goodman was. Furthermore, the addition of a Negro to his unit further strengthened Goodman's connection with jazz, for some fundamentalists at least. The following year the trio was expanded to include Lionel Hampton on vibraphone, and still later various other jazzmen, including the important guitarist Charlie Christian. The jazz treatment of such tunes as "Moonglow," "I Know That You Know," "Rose Room," and "Flying Home," helping to make up sets of such big-band arrangements as "Is That the Way to Treat a Sweetheart," "A Little Kiss at Twilight," "Bob White," and "You're a Sweet Little Headache," spiced by "Don't Be That Way" and "Jam Session," or "Down South Camp Meeting," was calculated to appeal to just about everyone, and the record shows it did.

For some time the Goodman band had the field to itself, but not for long. The success of the Goodman band and the ready acceptance of swing by the public engendered hundreds of big bands, each seeking its share of popularity.

Although most of the big bands that achieved success in the swing era came after Goodman's initial success and were undoubtedly on the scene at the right time, a number of bands that had been organized before the Goodman band, and were doing only moderately well, could now reach the spotlight far more easily than they would have otherwise. Significant among these, for example, is the band of Tommy Dorsey, who with his brother Jimmy led the Dorsey Brothers orchestra in 1933; in 1935 Tommy began on his own the climb that eventually made him as popular as Goodman. Charlie Barnet was another who had started early; after having inched along since 1932, he finally vaulted into popularity in 1939 with his recording of "Cherokee." Woody Herman tried leading a band in 1933 with no success; he finally got under way in 1936 and by 1939 had established himself. Artie Shaw made several unsuccessful starts, but in 1937, after the engaging truculence of "Chant" and other numbers, it became apparent that he was a palpable threat to Goodman's position. Glenn Miller, who had been playing and arranging for many groups, made a number of false starts but by 1939 was also to be reckoned among the most popular leaders. Bob Crosby and a Dixieland group from the Ben Pollack band caught the public fancy shortly after Goodman's initial success and continued to promote Dixieland music through the entire period. Of the men from Goodman's original band who formed bands of their own, Gene Krupa and his 1938 band, and Harry James and his 1939 band, have already been mentioned. Teddy Wilson organized a band in 1939, and a year later Lionel Hampton tried his hand with considerably more success than Wilson.

Barry Ulanov reminds us that "the white bands got the first swing customers; the Negro outfits followed close behind." [14] The bands of Chick Webb, Erskine Hawkins, Cab Calloway, and Andy Kirk are several that come to mind. Two outfits that did not reach the popular heights of Ellington or Basie, but are nevertheless worth mentioning, were directed by Bennie Carter and Jimmie Lunceford. Bennie Carter, who played alto saxophone and arranged for Fletcher Henderson in 1930, started a band of his own in 1933, and after spending some time performing in Europe (1936-38) returned to the United States to continue, if not with great commercial success, at least to provide first-rate jazz. Jimmie Lunceford, a Fisk University graduate, joined the list of important swing band leaders in 1935 and during the next few years recorded such swing classics as Sy Oliver's "For Dancers Only" and "White Heat." Leonard Feather writes:

> By 1939 the market was flooded with swing bands. Many of them, like Harry James', came to rely more on insipid commercial performances than on real swinging jazz for their success. Even a second-rate band could by now give a passable imitation of the Goodman or Lunceford ensembles. The only unique sounds and the only completely inimitable orchestral units in jazz seemed to be those of Duke Ellington and Count Basie. Jazz, to some extent, had reached a stalemate as the 1930s drew to a close. [15]

The Ellington band needs no further discussion here, since it simply rolled along the same original and inventive track it started out upon in the preswing era. We shall, however, briefly survey the Basie band of 1938-42, which, if not as popular as the Goodman band, was actually more responsible for the musical character of swing. It is significant that Goodman, at the pinnacle of his success, found it necessary to adopt many of Basie's numbers, including "One o'Clock Jump."

William "Count" Basie was born in Red Bank, New Jersey, August 21, 1904, and received his early influence from the jazzmen of New York. In the late twenties, while playing piano with a road show, he was stranded in Kansas City, Missouri, where in 1929 he joined Walter Page's Blue Devils which included Dan Minor on trombone, Walter Page on bass, and Jimmy Rushing on vocals—men who, together with Jo Jones, the drummer, were to be his close associates until well after the end of the swing era. About a year later Bennie Moten became the nominal leader of the Blue Devils, and when he died in 1935 the band broke up. Shortly after, Basie and a band that included several members of the Moten band were heard over the radio by Goodman and John Hammond, and in 1936—after Goodman and Hammond had persuaded Willard Alexander, of the Music Corporation of America, to handle Basie's bookings—Basie left Kansas City under a contract to record twenty-four sides for Decca for $750 and no royalties. ("One o'Clock Jump" and "Jumpin' at the Woodside" were included.)

Unlike numerous bands of the swing era, the Basie band remained fairly stable. The band's personnel included, at various times, Ed Lewis, Harry Edison, Buck Clayton, Shad Collins, and Al Killian on trumpet; Dan Minor, Bennie Morton, Dickie Wells, and Ed Cuffey on trombone; Herschel Evans, Earl Warren, Jack Washington, Chu Berry, Lester Young, Buddy Tate, Tab Smith, and Don Byas on saxophones; and the solidly steadfast rhythm of Walter Page on bass, Freddie Green on guitar, Jo Jones on drums, and Basie on piano.

With Goodman's and Hammond's encouragement and numerous arrangements lent him by Fletcher Henderson (Basie has often acknowledged that Henderson was largely responsible for his success), Basie opened at the Grand Terrace in Chicago and shortly after in New York's Roseland Ballroom. "When we first started out," said Buck Clayton, who was with Basie in 1936, "we didn't have good arrangers writing just for the band. We used heads we made up on the job for the first four years or so, and then we began to get arrangements, too." [16] The "heads" were conceived to a large extent in rehearsal; the band had three three-hour rehearsals each week, and during these sessions they worked out many riffs that were afterward picked up and passed around by other bands as common currency. Sidney Finkelstein summed it up when he said, "The riffs of 'One o'Clock Jump,' 'Jump for Me,' 'Swinging the Blues,' have become part of the folk lore of swing music." [17]

In its early period the Basie band exhibited all the best qualities of the small swinging group: first-rate improvisation against provocative riffs, and a vibrant, pulsating, rhythmic background. In the hands of Lester Young, Herschel Evans, and Buddy Tate, the tenor saxophone became the prince of solo instruments. Because of Basie's self-imposed subordinate role—he thought of himself primarily as one of the rhythm section—his piano solo work has not yet been given its proper study. His practice of playing isolated chords for the purpose of pushing his soloists is too well known to need recounting here. Freddie Green tells us:

> . . . he contributes the missing things. I feel very comfortable with him because he always seems to know the right thing to play for rhythm. Count is also just about the best piano player I know for pushing a band and for comping soloists. I mean the way he makes different preparations for each soloist and the way, at the end of one of *his* solos, he prepares an entrance for the next man. He leaves the way open.[18]

Another Basie veteran, less articulate perhaps but as much to the point, once told Barry Ulanov, "I don't know what it is. Count don't play nothing but it sure sounds good." [19]

The principal characteristics of swing were already well established in the preswing era. The instrumentation of the big band included five to seven brasses, four or five reeds, and three or four rhythm instruments. The combinations of sound remained much the same except for more frequent use of section unisons and octaves. Arrangements included a minimum of one solo, but most big-band jazz included several solos. Preference in solos was usually given to the tenor saxophone, clarinet, trumpet, piano, trombone, alto saxophone, bass, and drums, approximately in that order; this order and frequency were of course affected by the leader's solo instrument.

The most usual combinations of instruments and the various types of background against which solos were heard have been discussed in the chapter on preswing. While the types of backgrounds were substantially the same for both periods, swing made more frequent use of a combination of two independent, rifflike lines. The following example illustrates the use of this device. Frequently the upper line was played by the saxophones in octaves, the lower by trumpets in unison, while a muted trumpet or clarinet played a solo above the two lines.

The forms of swing show a marked increase in the use of the thirty-two-bar AABA popular song form; the twelve-bar blues continues to be an important small form; and, by the end of the period, stomps, marches, and rags become increasingly rare. Standard tunes such as "Once in a While" and "Avalon" continue to provide the jazzman's thematic material, along with a seemingly never-ending supply of tunes based on two-bar instrumental riffs. Tonality remains firmly established, of course; however, modulations to next-related keys become a commonplace, usually in the last section of big-band arrangements—although many arrangements maintain the same tonality throughout, particularly in head arrangements of both big and small bands.

In the swing era there is a greater impression of melodic organization simply because the riff repetition lends a more coherent, if somewhat simplified, arrangement to the tones. The riff serves as a motive which, in many works, may be repeated as many as twenty or thirty times, and it is truly an insensitive listener who is not able to understand what the jazzmen are driving at. Riffs at their best are driving, pushing, rocking forces that move the soloist to exceed his limitations; too often, however, the riff becomes an end in itself and the arrangement degenerates into a monotonous repetition of a figure something less than stimulating to either the soloist or the listener. The difficulty is the result of the jazzman's overdependence, in the swing period, on harmony. This is not to say that the problem did not exist in the preswing era. It did. In the swing period, however, chords with added notes and chord progressions themselves dominated the jazzman's thought. One could no longer "feel" every progression, so to speak, the way one "felt" the blues progression; one had to learn the progressions of a hundred or more standards, and the jazzman did. The chords that were fresh for Ellington in the earlier period were, by the end of the thirties, the property of the least jazzman. Although there were countless blues played on slightly modified traditional progressions, the following progression, taken from Basie's "Volcano"

(1939), will serve as an example of the kind of blues progression that was to be taken up by the so-called "progressives" at the end of the period. It may be of interest to compare it with the progression in his 1938 version of "Sent for You Yesterday."

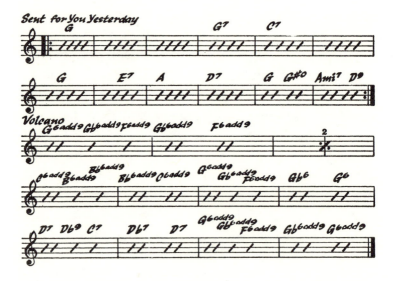

Irving Kolodin, in an interpolation in *The Kingdom of Swing,* writes:

As the distinction between the two kinds of jazz playing became more pronounced—the aspiration, on the one hand, of some bands to a style that refined away the crudities of early jazz, and the concentration, by others, on combining improvisation and arrangement in a single structure—it became apparent that there was an element in the playing of the best Negro bands (such as Fletcher Henderson's, Louis Armstrong's, and Duke Ellington's) that could not be identified as an expression of any-

246

thing in the written parts they were using. It was a style of performance, an interrelation of rhythms, *a product of a mere enthusiasm for the act of playing, a freshness and spontaneity that could not be indicated by accents, note-values or other written symbols.*[20]

It seems hardly necessary to point out once more the inefficiency of our traditional system of notation; one has only to hear the patterns shown below performed by different performers to recognize this. In the late thirties these rhythms could be heard from the sixteen-piece band on the stage of the New York Paramount or from the four-piece band in a St. Louis cellar club. The rhythms of swing are much the same as those of the preswing era, and it seems necessary to add only those which became the property of all. Examples *c, d,* and *e* need special mention, since they are brass rhythms effected by placing a hat or plunger over the bell of the horn (+) and then removing it (0). The sound is sometimes described as "du-wah," the "du" being the closed sound and the "wah," the open sound.

In 1942, at a time when the swing era had nearly run its course, the Basie band recorded "It's Sand, Man," a jump tune that is not only characteristic of the period but also shows what arranger Buck Clayton was able to do with a minimum of material. The thematic material was provided by Ed Lewis, and the band's personnel included Lewis, Clayton, Al Killian, and Harry Edison on trumpet; Dickie Wells, Robert Scott, and Eli Robinson on trombone; Earl Warren, Jack Washington, Buddy Tate, Don Byas, and Caughey Roberts on saxophones; and, of course, the Basie rhythm section. The work is essentially a large ternary form with the tutti ensemble enclosing the solo improvisations of the tenor saxophone and the piano. The three large sections may be shown in brief as

Introduction
A (*aaba*)
B {
  ensemble episode
  piano solo
  ensemble bridge
  tenor solo
}
A final section
coda

After the ensemble eight-bar introduction, which is built on the three-note upbeat to the principal theme followed by a descending semichromatic scale, the saxophones soli have the first sixteen bars (*aa*), with low brass filling in the one-and-a-half-beat rests that come about every two bars. A wonderfully effective device occurs in bars 7 and 8 of the principal theme: the first two tones of the theme itself, after the upbeat, are B-flat and G; bars 15 and 16 are a rhythmic variation of these two tones which then continues relentlessly into a repetition of *a*, the device serving to hide the seam where the two phrases are joined. The brass section takes the eight-bar release (*b*), with the saxophones filling in, and closes the A section with a repetition of the first eight bars (*a*). In the episode that follows, the trumpets play a unison lead consisting basically of consecutive eighth-note scales against an independent line of eighth-note arpeggio figures in the saxophones soli, and slow-moving melodic chords in the trombones. This episode, as well as the one later on, is cleverly constructed to serve not only as a transition to the improvised solo, but as an introduction to the solo as well. This is effected by the further rhythmic development of B-flat and G in the second half of the episode's twenty-four bars (at measure 53); the episode, starting in the full ensemble as outlined above, gains momentum by a steady rise up the scale and reaches its climax at the halfway point, where the saxophones, as we have just mentioned, rhythmically develop the B-flat and G, while a solo trumpet continues the flight upward; the rest of the ensemble joins the saxophones in developing the two-note figure, and the cessation of the solo trumpet, plus the driving, pushing, repetition of the B-flat, signifies an introduction to Basie's solo.

The eight-bar piano solo, hard and lean, pits a striding left hand against a rippling, reiterated, chromatic triplet figure in the right. It leads into a ten-bar bridge that in-

cludes three descending whole-tone scales of two bars each
in the saxophones soli against sustained chords in the brass
—each version a half-tone higher than the last—and four
bars [21] of what has turned out to be the swing soloist's
sursum corda:

The tenor solo, which is. harmonically at least, a thirty-
two-bar *aaba* form (the harmonic bases of all the solos are
distinct from each other as well as from the other sections),
is heard for the most part against "du-wah" ensemble fill-
ins in the last two bars of each phrase of the *aa* (at measure
97). Driving into the release (*b*), the high brass scrabble
at the piece's two-note motive above the aggressively as-
sertive tenor, who then blows his way exultantly and unaccompanied through the last eight. The full ensemble then
returns to extend the phrase two bars. In the final section
the full ensemble plays a sixteen-bar truncated version of

the principal theme, derived mainly from the *b* and two-note motive preceding it (at measure 117); the sparse, isolated chords of the piano solo that follows the ensemble serve momentarily to relax the tension. The eight-bar coda, however, which is derived from the principal theme's three-note upbeat (as well as the introductory upbeat), goes out in a storm of lightning and thunder that includes a two-bar break in the drums and a roaring, high, sustained chord in the full band.

As an indication of Clayton's rhythmic ingenuity and further to illustrate the essential character of "It's Sand, Man," the following example offers several interesting vari-

ations on the two-note motive, B-flat and G. Particularly noteworthy is the interesting harmonic augmentation apparent when one compares examples *a* and *b* (the arabic numerals refer to measure numbers).

"It's Sand, Man" is a fair example of the kind of jazz that kept Basie popular toward the end of the swing era. Swing, however, could not cope with the tribulations of the second World War, and sometime during the early forties its popularity gave way to other, more important things. Although a good many swing musicians entered the armed forces, many were above the military age limit and, with most of the top jazz groups disbanded, were forced to take musical potluck, so to speak. *Esquire's 1945 Jazz Book* had the following to say about the activities of Benny Goodman:

> This past year Benny Goodman disbanded his orchestra, appeared with a quartet at a jazz concert in New Orleans, made numerous radio guest appearances and formed a quintet including Red Norvo, Teddy Wilson and Sid Weiss, which is featured in the Billy Rose musical, The Seven Lively Arts. Now in his eleventh year as a national jazz figure he again received a strong majority approval (16 experts out of 22) from Esquire's Board as the greatest clarinetist, maintaining the wide margin he held in 1944.[22]

Despite the awards Goodman has received for his matchless musicianship, his influence on jazzmen has been small. Refusing to become interested in the various jazz styles that began to manifest themselves in the forties and fifties, he went into a semiretirement that seemed permanent until the spring of 1958, when the Westinghouse Broadcasting

Company undertook to promote and sponsor a band led by Goodman as part of the United States cultural program at the Brussels World's Fair. The general public therefore continues to look upon Goodman as the leader of a famous dance band. Count Basie, on the other hand, kept a band going all through the forties and, except for a brief period in the early fifties, has managed to continue playing the music he knows best right up to the present time. In 1954 he made a successful European tour, and in 1958 he recorded two albums—"Basie," for Roulette, and "The Sound of Jazz," for Columbia. About "Basie" John S. Wilson said, "Here is a roaring reaffirmation of the old Basie fire along with a renewal of the warm probing of the blues that was once a Basie trademark." [23] Apparently Basie will continue to provide first-rate jazz for some time to come.

chapter **9**

THE MODERN ERA

BY 1945 MANY FACTORS OP-
erated together to bring the swing era and its big-band jazz
to an end. The strongest was, without doubt, the second
World War with its effect on big-band personnel. Although
many of the name bands were forced to dissolve, a good
many managed to hang on in one way or another; Tommy
Dorsey and Harry James, for example, added strings to
their bands, while Gene Krupa, Sonny Dunham, Les
Brown, and innumerable others turned to out-and-out commercial arrangements of commercial music. Even the re-
doubtable Earl Hines found reason to outfit himself with a
vocal quartet, a string quartet, and a harpist. Almost as
strong a factor as the war in bringing the period to a close,
however, was the slow rise of a new jazz style variously
called rebop, bebop, and, eventually, simply bop, the
invention of a group of Negro jazzmen in revolt against

commercialism and Jim Crowism in jazz as well as discrimination in general. In 1948 Richard Boyer wrote:

> Bebop, according to its pioneer practitioners, is a manifestation of revolt. Eight or ten years ago, many Negro jazz musicians, particularly the younger ones, who were sometimes graduates of music conservatories, began to feel, rightly or wrongly, that the white world wanted them to keep to the old-time jazz. They held the opinion that the old jazz, which they called "Uncle Tom music," was an art form representative of a meeker generation than theirs. They said that it did not express the modern American Negro and they resented the apostrophes of critics who referred to them, with the most complimentary intent, as modern primitives playing an almost instinctive music.[1]

The musicians were not involved in the new movement in a formal way, of course. Their problem was primarily one of self-expression, and, while in the beginning there may not have been an organized movement with banners and slogans, the goal was nonetheless clear, at any rate to those who helped create the new style. Ralph Ellison tells us that the desire of early bop musicians "to master the classical technique was linked with the struggle for recognition in the larger society, and with a desire to throw off those nonmusical features which came into jazz from the minstrel tradition."[2] The musicians were particularly grieved with what they considered to be the defection of such jazzmen as Louis Armstrong. As late as 1949 Dizzy Gillespie, who may be considered a spokesman for many of his colleagues, told a reporter that "Louis is the plantation character that so many of us . . . younger men . . . resent."[3] To still another reporter he

255

said: "Nowadays we try to work out different rhythms and things that they didn't think about when Louis Armstrong blew. In his day all he did was play strictly from the soul —just strictly from his heart. You got to go forward and progress. We study." [4] Nat Hentoff sums up this important aspect of the problem:

> Jazz, after all, is a medium for urgent self-expression, and the young insurgents of the 1940's could no longer feel—let alone speak—in the language of Armstrong. Aside from musical needs, the young Negro jazzmen, who at first formed the majority of the modernists, felt more assertively combative about many issues apart from music than did Armstrong and most other Negro jazzmen of earlier generations; and this change in attitude to their social context came out in their music.[5]

Ross Russell sums up another aspect of the problem when he says, "Bebop is music of revolt: revolt against big bands, arrangers, vertical harmonies, soggy rhythms, non-playing orchestra leaders, Tin Pan Alley—against commercialized music in general." [6] It may be of interest to observe specifically the kind of commercial music the early bop musicians were in revolt against. On October 1, 1942 —about ten months after Pearl Harbor—the ten most-played records on the nation's jukeboxes, according to the Chicago Automatic Hostess Co., were: (1) Bing Crosby's "Be Careful, It's My Heart," (2) Kay Kyser's "Jingle, Jangle, Jingle," (3) Glenn Miller's "Gal in Kalamazoo," (4) Kay Kyser's "He Wears a Pair of Silver Wings," (5) Benny Goodman's "Take Me," (6) Harry James's "Strictly Instrumental," (7) Woody Herman's "Amen," (8) Charlie

Spivak's "Stage Door Canteen," (9) Benny Goodman's "Idaho," (10) Charlie Spivak's "My Devotion."

Even more significant was the "Victory Parade of Spotlight Bands," a coast-to-coast radio program sponsored by Coca-Cola and featuring a band a night, six nights a week. In the fall of 1942, while a handful of jazzmen in New York's Harlem were probing, among other technical devices, the use of the augmented fourth, the rest of the nation could have their choice of listening to Jan Savitt, Ted Lewis, Dick Jurgens, Jan Garber, and Sammy Kaye, from October 1 to 7; and Herbie Kay, Russ Morgan, Harry James, Lionel Hampton, Sammy Kaye, Charlie Spivak, and Horace Heidt, from October 7 to 16. It is plain that the "Victory Parade" was mainly concerned with bands that played dance music, groups that for various reasons preferred to provide the open, steady, two-, three-, or four-four beat necessary to dancers who grew up in the swing and preswing eras. This beat became, in fact, the *bête noire* of the bopsters. As John Mehegan tells us:

> The revolution centered about the very core of jazz—the beat. The musicians associated with this movement felt that the time-honored "dance beat" of jazz with the accented second and fourth beats which gave a dancer a "lift" was too restrictive; it prevented the free-flowing expression of melodic ideas these musicians were more and more coming to hear not only in Stravinsky, but even in Bach. In other words, the musician declared his freedom from the dancer and at this point jazz ceased to be folk music and became a struggling art form.[7]

The seeds of the "struggling art form" had been planted in the middle and late thirties, but it was not until the opening of Minton's Playhouse in New York's Harlem that the seeds could make the most of the cultivated ground, the warm encouraging air, so necessary to their later flowering. Around October, 1940, Henry Minton, a former bandleader and the first Harlem delegate to Local 802 of the Musicians' Union, opened a room next door to the Hotel Cecil on West 118th Street and installed Teddy Hill, another former bandleader, as manager. Hill hired a quartet that included Thelonious Monk on piano, Kenny Clarke on drums, Nick Fenton on bass, and Joe Guy on trumpet. Before long, Minton's policy of allowing jazzmen to spend their free time there eating, drinking, and sitting in with the house band made his place a haven for all the early bop innovators. Minton's principal attraction was what might be called freedom of the bandstand, and it was here that the bop principals gathered nightly to work out the plans for their revolution. Monk and Clarke were soon in association with such early experimentalists as Charlie Christian, Dizzy Gillespie, Charlie Parker, Tadd Dameron, Bud Powell, and dozens of less talented well-wishers, all unknowingly working toward a common goal. Minton's, it should be recognized, was unique only in that it happened to be the place where, at the time, jazzmen were able to focus their attention on each other's experiments; the probing and experimenting had been going on for some time before Minton's opened. Ralph Ellison cautions us to remember:

> We know much of jazz as entertainment, but a mere handful of clichés constitutes our knowledge of jazz as experience.

Worst, it is this which is frequently taken for all there is, and we get the impression that jazz styles are created in some club on some particular occasion and there and then codified according to the preconceptions of the jazz publicists in an atmosphere as grave and traditional, say, as that attending the deliberations of the Academie Française.[8]

Minton's was a vortex that drew jazzmen who had previously found some encouragement in such places as Monroe's Uptown House and other less-known rooms and clubs. Orrin Keepnews tells us that

. . . the precise beginning of the music first known as "bebop" will most probably always be shrouded in confusion, contradiction and double-talk. It was not necessarily recognized by the participants as a glamorous period of creativity: pianist Thelonious Monk says, "Nobody was sitting there trying to make up something new on purpose. The job at Minton's was a job we were playing, that's all." [9]

At the outset almost all jazzmen, of whatever school, could mount the Minton bandstand and be accommodated, but as time went on it became obvious that those whose roots were too firmly set in swing would receive little notice. For one thing, not many jazzmen could improvise on the chord changes being punched out by the pianist Monk. It was not that the chords themselves were particularly unusual, although there was certainly a greater frequency of augmented chords; the strangeness to swing jazzmen grew rather out of the fact that the chord progressions of such traditional jamming tunes as "Rose Room" and "Ain't Misbehavin' " were being passed over in favor of such newcomers as "All the Things You Are" and "Lover Come

Back to Me." And almost all the old standards yielded to "How High the Moon," a popular song written by Morgan Lewis in 1939 for the musical *Two for the Show* and later fashioned into a bop standard by Dizzy Gillespie. Furthermore, the chord progressions of such standards as "I Got Rhythm" and "Just You, Just Me" were treated in much the same manner as the traditional twelve-bar blues progression, that is, as a series of chords not identified with a particular melody. For swing musicians, an improvisation on "I Got Rhythm" meant a creation based on the melody as well as the harmonic foundation; when a bop musician said "Rhythm"—an abbreviation—he spoke only of the harmonic foundation, a foundation that could serve for any number of original compositions. In Charlie Parker's recordings of "Bird Lore" and "Ornithology," for example, both numbers have their harmonic basis in "How High the Moon"; Monk's "Evidence" is based on "Just You, Just Me," and Dameron's "Hot House" is based on "What Is This Thing Called Love." (Leonard Feather's *Inside Bebop*, 1949, reissued in 1955 as *Inside Jazz*, lists a full page of bop compositions based on the chord progressions in standard tunes.)

Besides finding the changes difficult, those with an ear for the Gene Krupa-George Wettling-Ray McKinley school of drumming soon discovered that the drumming of Kenny Clarke and Max Roach (discussed more fully later on) provided them with little rhythmic support. Clarke recalls how the early bopmen rid themselves of unwanted jazzmen:

260

We often talked in the afternoon. That's how we came to write different chord progressions and the like. We did that to discourage the sitters-in at night we didn't want. Monk, Joe Guy, Dizzy, and I would work them out. We often did it on the job, too. Even during the course of the night at Minton's. We usually did what we pleased on stand. Teddy Hill, the manager of Minton's, turned the whole back room over to us. As for those sitters-in that we didn't want, when we started playing these different changes we'd made up, they'd become discouraged after the first chorus and they'd slowly walk away and leave the professional musicians on stand.[10]

There is little question that the intellectual leader of the early bop musicians was Thelonious Monk, born in New York in 1920; it is also likely that, despite the public relations work done in behalf of Dizzy Gillespie, he and other members of the group were not persuaded by it to overlook Monk's position. In a group of eccentrics, Monk was the archeccentric. Largely self-taught, he played, and still does, with a curious combination of classical and jazz styles calculated to estrange him from the middling performers in each of these classifications. Most of his colleagues—and no doubt Monk himself—realized that his technical proficiency at the keyboard could hardly keep pace with his harmonic, melodic, and rhythmic ruminations. His playing is perhaps best described, in a word, as undisciplined. It is likely that the difficulty he encountered in relating his musical thoughts to his technique kept him, for the most part, off the big-band scene. Except for a brief stint with the Lucky Millinder band in 1942—Gillespie was with the band that year and may have been indirectly responsible for Monk's being there—Monk has continued to perform with small groups. In 1944 he worked with the Coleman Hawkins Quartet, and in 1958 he recorded for Riverside with a septet that performed five original Monk compositions. While Monk's improvising is dark and scraggy, his notated music generally has been flowing and sometimes, as in his ballad " 'Round About Midnight," even moving. His position in modern jazz continues to expand, and if his work—"Thelonious Himself," "Monk's Music," "Brilliant Corners," "Thelonious Monk Plays Duke Ellington," and others, all on Riverside—is indicative of what he will continue to do, then it seems certain that, along with John Lewis, Jimmy Giuffre, and a few others, he will remain one of the acknowledged leaders of modern jazz.

The strength of Charlie Christian's influence and direction during the short time he reigned at Minton's Playhouse indicates that, had he lived, he, too, would have been among the jazz leaders of the future. In 1939, when Mary Lou Williams suggested to John Hammond that he go hear a guitar player she had heard in Oklahoma City, Charlie Christian was twenty and untried; on the strength of a brief audition, Hammond arranged for Christian to join the Goodman band. Upon his arrival in New York the young jazzman was introduced to the group at Minton's Playhouse by Mel Powell, the Goodman pianist. The Mintonites, impressed by the freshness of Christian's amplified single-string style and the uniqueness of his invention, quickly gave him a place of honor and enjoined all other guitarists from sitting in. Jerry Newman, a jazz fan, recorded some of the 1941 Minton sessions, which were released in a Vox album in 1947 and later on two records for Esoteric. These records, made by a quintet that included the Minton quartet mentioned above, consisted of a long treatment of "Stompin' at the Savoy" and an original composition known variously as "Swing to Bop" and "Charlie's Choice." With the Goodman band Christian is heard to good advantage in "Honeysuckle Rose," recorded at the end of 1939, and "Solo Flight," recorded early in 1941 by Columbia. He may also be heard in nine selections—some with Goodman, some with Basie—in "Spirituals to Swing," John Hammond's records of 1938-39 Carnegie Hall concerts released by Vanguard in 1959.

Bill Simon writes, "The guitar had some history in jazz before Charlie Christian, but there's little evidence, if any, that Charlie was particularly aware of it." [11] Christian may not have been influenced by guitarists—only the French guitarist Django Reinhardt played in a style comparable to his—but he must certainly have been strongly influenced by the bounteous jazz harvest reaped around Oklahoma City in the early and middle thirties. Ralph Ellison, who knew Christian as a boy, tells us:

> . . . perhaps the most stimulating influence upon Christian, and one with whom he was later to be identified, was that of a tall, intense young musician who arrived in Oklahoma City sometime in 1929 and who, with his heavy white sweater, blue stocking cap, and up-and-out-thrust silver saxophone, left absolutely no reed player and few young players of any instrument unstirred by the wild, excitingly original flights of his imagination. Who

else but Lester Young, who with his battered horn upset the entire Negro section of the town.[12]

When Lester Young arrived in Oklahoma City, Christian was ten years old, and, while he may have been stimulated by Young's presence, it does not seem likely that there could have been, at that time, much transference of technique. However, Young, as we shall see further on, influenced an entire generation of young jazzmen, and perhaps his presence in Oklahoma City was itself sufficient to create a desire in young Christian for the technical perfection that was later his.

Christian helped free the guitar from its traditional confining position as a rhythm instrument. He combined the sound of his single-string work with wind instruments as if he were part of the wind section, and he inspired the rest of the rhythm section to do likewise. In short, he was responsible for the emergence of the rhythm section as a group able to think and play as individuals. As Morgan and Horrocks put it, "He had the whole section swinging, thinking individually but merging collectively into a cohesive, pliable unit."[13] In the spring of 1941, after two years of New York's excitement—some of it artificially stimulated—Christian was taken to a sanitarium for tubercular patients where, the following winter, he died. Bill Simon has composed a somewhat effusive but nonetheless sincere tribute:

Charlie Christian probably is the only jazz figure who would have been able to serve as the model stylist on his chosen instrument as long as fifteen years after his disappearance from the scene. There isn't an important guitarist playing today [1957] who does not recognize him as the all-time best, and who does not credit him as a prime influence. In most of the better modernists, the strain has crossed with that of a saxophonist, Charlie Parker. But basically, it's Charlie Christian. The best thing anybody can say about a guitarist today is that he could be "the closest thing to Christian." [14]

John Birks "Dizzy" Gillespie, while contributing as much technically to the new jazz movement as Monk and Christian did, has had the additional distinction of being a personality to bring bop to the attention of the critics and the public. The antics of Gillespie in the early forties were recorded by the press with a fervor and delight they had previously shown only toward the most idiosyncratic Hollywood stars. Gillespie has matured considerably since those early days and therefore no longer inspires the press he once had; however, his musical contributions to modern jazz have remained, along with Charlie Parker's, the dominating influence on contemporary jazz.

Gillespie was born in Cheraw, South Carolina, in 1917. By the time he was fifteen he was studying trombone and trumpet and, at the Laurinburg Institute, an industrial school in North Carolina, the elements of harmony. Three years later he moved to Philadelphia, where, when he was not studying and imitating the florid trumpet style of Roy Eldridge, he was playing with local bands. In 1937, when Eldridge left Teddy Hill's band, Gillespie was asked to join the trumpet section his idol had dominated, and in

May of that year he participated in the recording of six sides for Bluebird, including an Eldridge-like solo in "King Porter Stomp." Between 1939 and 1941 Gillespie worked with the Cab Calloway band; then he tried his hand at arranging, placing arrangements with Woody Herman, Earl Hines, and Jimmy Dorsey. Morgan and Horrocks point up Gillespie's importance at this time to jazzmen in general, and in particular to those who were not members of the Minton group:

> Though not so much an imaginative composer as a careful arranger, Gillespie's writing was important to musicians at the time. Many of the ideas which he would hear tossed about between musicians at the improvised sessions in New York, he would stabilize on paper, later spreading the doctrine amongst other musicians, showing the source of the latent power in the crude conception of a new movement.[15]

Between 1941 and the time he organized his own big band in 1945, Gillespie played with the bands of Benny Carter, Charlie Barnet, Earl Hines, Lucky Millinder, Duke Ellington, and Billy Eckstine, to mention some of the best known. Then there were, of course, the nights at Minton's, where he continued to work out with his colleagues the melodic, rhythmic, and harmonic ideas that were to become the characteristics of bop, the musical ideas that he was even then using freely in his solos with the big bands. These were the years of experimenting, analyzing, editing, and codifying, the years that saw the death of Charlie Christian and the fading of the Minton sessions, the years when Gillespie learned of Charlie Parker's ability (when

266

Parker played in Jay McShann's band and Gillespie and Parker played in Earl Hines's 1943 band), the years of the rise and decline of Parker. Leonard Feather writes:

> The year of Gillespie's heroic accolade is generally placed at 1945, though it is a fact that even in 1943 he was the subject of much excited conversation among fellow musicians and was well on the way to becoming a cult.
>
> The year 1945, though, was the most significant in that it brought to records the first evidence of bop's most fruitful partnership, that of Gillespie with the alto saxophonist Charlie Parker, who was to Dizzy what Wilbur Wright was to Orville.[16]

In 1945 Gillespie and Parker, with various small groups, made a number of first-rate sides for Musicraft (originally Guild) including "Dizzy Atmosphere," "All the Things You Are," "Lover Man," "Salt Peanuts," and "Hot House." The growing popularity of Gillespie with modern jazz fans led to the formation of his first big band, which, after one unsuccessful tour in combination with a revue called *Hep-Sations of 1945*, was disbanded. He tried another band the following year, and this, after a slow start, achieved sufficient success to be featured in a concert at Carnegie Hall. A European tour followed in 1948, again with varying degrees of success (Gillespie had to wire his agent for money to bring the band back to the United States), and in 1950 the group was once more disbanded. Shortly before this, Aaron Copland wrote:

> It is interesting to note in this connection that bebop, the latest jazz manifestation, has been introducing more and more dissonant harmonic textures into popular music, thereby arous-

ing some of the same resistance from the mass public as was encountered by the serious composers in their field.[17]

For Gillespie and the bop musicians, however, the problem was an old one: where to put the explicit beat. For the paying customers, the dancers, that is, the answer was of course a simple one. In the fall of 1950 Gillespie told a reporter his side of the story. "It really broke my heart to break up that band," Gillespie said. "But there wasn't any work for us. Right now it's rough. Everybody wants you to play what they call dance music. What they mean is that ticky-ticky-tick stuff. Man, that ain't dance music!" [18] In recent years Gillespie has emerged as a serious jazz musician with serious intentions. Representing the United States on State Department tours to the Middle East and South America, he has proved that it is not always necessary for a jazzman to be a tragic figure in order to be significant.

Perhaps the most tragic figure in modern jazz is Charlie Parker. In a business where superlatives are a commonplace, few are able to express what Parker was about. His unbelievable technique and improvisational ability, like much of his disorganized, hapless existence, seemed rootless and, for the most part, inexplicable. As Orrin Keepnews said:

> He lacked any sort of formative jazz background: he had heard little if anything of the music of early jazz greats; it seems clear that the swing of the mid-'thirties meant little to him musically; and his immediate reaction to the heavily vibrato-filled style of just about all jazz saxophonists of the time was simply, "I didn't like it." [19]

Listening to certain of Parker's improvisations, one has the impression that he finds little to approve of even in his own work. His dominant attitude seems to be one of chill, corrosive bitterness and intentional cruelty; his playing, the outraged cry of a man at the end of his endurance. There are many lyrical passages in his work, and buoyant ones, too, and, on occasion, tender ones, but inevitably he returns to the anguish, the violent convulsion. It is plain that in the thirty-five years of his life Parker had little to be tender about. He was born in 1920 in Kansas City, Kansas. At the age of eleven he acquired a saxophone; at fifteen he was through with school and trying to jam his way into the jazz business by sitting in with any outfit that would have him, and, when it seemed that few would have him, he found comfort in the heroin some less exacting individuals taught him how to use.

At the age of seventeen Parker evidently played well enough to join the Jay McShann band, a rough and ready group specializing in the blues. Because of his newly acquired habits, however, he was in and out of the band, and during the next few years he found his way to Chicago and then to New York, where he worked briefly at Monroe's Uptown House. In 1939 and 1940—the period of Parker's first prolonged contact with Harlem and its jazzmen—he apparently began finding himself, musically speaking. He rejoined McShann and made his first records with the band in 1941 for Decca. And again he gave up McShann for the sessions at Minton's. Between this time and 1946, the year he had a breakdown and was taken to Camarillo State

Hospital, his technical proficiency and his musicianship expanded despite the self-imposed hardships he endured playing with the Noble Sissle band ("Sissle hated me") and the Earl Hines band, where he had to play tenor. He played irregularly with bands led by Cootie Williams, Andy Kirk, and Billy Eckstine, as well as in numerous small groups. By 1945, when he recorded for Savoy (with Miles Davis on trumpet, Curley Russell on bass, Max Roach on drums, and Dizzy Gillespie on piano) a group of engaging compositions—"Billie's Bounce," "Now's the Time," "Thriving from a Riff," and "Ko-Ko" with a muted trumpet solo by Gillespie—his manner of playing was well established. Whitney Balliett tells us:

> The heart of Parker's style was its unceasing and uncanny projection of surprise. It was composed, principally, of long and short melodic lines, legato and staccato phrases, simple one-two-three rhythms and intense Stravinsky-like rhythms, a sometimes whiney tone and a rich, full-blooded sound, as well as that rare thing among jazz musicians, an acute grasp of dynamics.
>
> The magic, however, was the stomach-punching combinations that Parker could, at lightning speed or in the languor of a slow blues, manipulate these contradictory bits and pieces into.[20]

To illustrate the point one need only listen to Parker's twelve-bar chorus in "Slam Slam Blues," made with Red Norvo in 1945 for Comet and later reissued by the Jazztone Society, with Norvo on vibraphone, Flip Phillips on tenor, Teddy Wilson on piano, Slam Stewart on bass, and either J. C. Heard or Specs Powell on drums, in which first Parker and then Gillespie show the wide contrast between their modern styles and the solid, on-the-beat style of the others. After Wilson's four-bar introduction, and coming hard on Stewart's dark, slogging bowed-bass solo, Parker's searing alto splits the darkness with a savage forward thrust, moving ineluctably into a fluid, undulating exhortation exceeded in invention only by the stunning fantasy of the last six bars. The impression is not of a twelve-bar chorus, but rather of an ingeniously worked out composition—short, but superbly complete.

After his release from Camarillo State Hospital, Parker enjoyed a period of comparative well-being and success. He worked with many small groups, including those of Norman Granz's Jazz at the Philharmonic; he went to Europe in 1949 and again in 1950, and his playing, when he was not fighting his affliction, became singularly distinguished and celebrated among his contemporaries. Morgan and Horrocks help describe the Parker phenomenon:

> The tone itself, acrid and bitter, piercing, yet singularly clean and beautiful, was a unique thing. . . . The remarkable dexterity of fingering, this, too, was the man's inherent possession. So also was the babbling fountain of ideas, each complete and glittering in itself, presented with the remarkable transition between mind and fingers. For these things Parker would look to no one.[21]

Before he died in March, 1955, Parker left an abundance of music on records, not all of it first-rate, but enough of it to show the power of his work when he was in control of his remarkable faculties. An album recorded for Verve, in which Parker is accompanied by strings, shows him ill at ease with the pretentiousness of the backgrounds for

"April in Paris," "I'm in the Mood for Love," and others; he nevertheless manages to take the measure of "Just Friends." He overcomes the pomposity of Machito's bongo rumba group to bring off "Mango Mangue" and "Okiedoke," and, pitted against a cloying vocal group, he manages to overpower them with "Old Folks." These last were, of course, attempts by the music business to capitalize on Parker's growing reputation. His best recorded work continued to be done in small groups, some of the most noteworthy being the sides he made for Verve with Al Haig on piano, Percy Heath on bass, and Max Roach on drums, released under the title "Now's the Time." Yet in spite of his remarkable powers he was not accepted or even understood by certain jazzmen and the general public. Many jazzmen were more widely known to the public in the late forties and fifties, and certainly many enjoyed greater personal satisfaction and financial success, but no one, except Louis Armstrong in his time, had as much influence on jazz as Parker did. The reasons for his bitter disappointment, which led to frustration, outrage, and, finally, torment and defeat, are set forth with great perception by Wilder Hobson:

> The fact is that any genuinely creative artist—one who is breaking esthetic ground in an inevitably uncomprehending world—must carry a certain baggage of bewilderment as part of his standard gear. And his unease and his experiment, his imbalance as he works toward balance, his disorder as he works toward order, are apt, if they are not definitely bound, to result in a more or less chaotic personal life. This is in the nature of the contract. And if this be true of major creative figures

think of the confusions and complexes of the second and third rate and of the pathetic, self-deluded sixth raters who can merely attitudinize on the fringes of the arts. The jazz world, like every other field, is full of these.[22]

Of the jazzmen that surrounded Monk, Christian, Gillespie, and Parker, a number have become significant in their own right. The scope of this work forbids any wide-scale effort to include all those who are responsible for the rise and development of modern jazz; we may, however, mention a number of those who gained some special notice. Kenny Clarke was one of the pioneers; a member of the first Minton band, he, along with Christian, helped create the new concept of the rhythm section. "Around 1940," Clarke said, "I was playing with Roy Eldridge and it was chiefly through Roy that I began to play the top cymbal—superimposing rhythms with the left hand—and that helped me develop my ideas all the more." Earlier, when Clarke and Gillespie were in Teddy Hill's band, they were both working toward the new style. Clarke said: "It was the turning point of the whole business, because I could feel Dizzy changing his way—he used to play like Roy— and he dug my way. Later, every drummer who worked with him, Dizzy taught to play like me. He really taught Max Roach and Art Blakey how to play their particular ways." [23] After Kenny Clarke, the most important early modern jazz drummers are Max Roach, Art Blakey, and Stan Levey.

Tadd Dameron, a pianist-arranger and intimate of Monk (in the early forties he was called "The Disciple"), helped move bop out of the small band into the larger ensemble. A swing arranger, Dameron was concerned with adapting the new musical ideas of the Minton improvisers in order to create a new big-band sound. Although he wrote many arrangements and original works for Count Basie, Jimmie Lunceford, Gillespie, and many others, his most personal work, as of 1957, can be heard to excellent advantage on the Prestige recording "A Study in Dameronia." Bud Powell is one of the early Minton pianists whose technical capacity could at once match the difficulties of the new style. Owner of a facile technique that has been compared to Art Tatum's, Powell has a vigor and lyricism matched by few. What Parker brought to the alto saxophone, Powell brought to the piano. A fine example of his exceptional drive and apparently limitless virtuosity is on Clef's "Bud Powell's Moods," and, for a show of his lyrical sense, one can turn to his "Bud!" on Blue Note. Other significant early bop pianists are Al Haig and George Wallington.

As for the remaining instruments, the bass was represented by such jazzmen as Oscar Pettiford, George Duvivier, Ray Brown, and Percy Heath; the vibraphone by Milt Jackson, and by Terry Gibbs of the Woody Herman band; the clarinet was being transformed by Buddy DeFranco, of the Charlie Barnet band; but the saxophones—alto, tenor, and baritone—like the trombone, were not to come into their own until the later, cool period. While Charlie Parker's sound may have overawed alto saxophonists during the early days of bop, Gillespie's trumpet, on the other hand, had many disciples. Among the best known of these are Benny Harris, Howard McGhee, Fats Navarro, Kenny Dorham, Red Rodney, and Miles Davis; of these, Davis deserves closer attention as one of the founders, in the late forties, of the new cool jazz. But before we discuss this, it is necessary to consider briefly the state of the phenomenon usually referred to as "progressive jazz."

For the general public the bands of Stan Kenton, Woody Herman, Boyd Raeburn, and other so-called progressive jazz groups constituted the logical extension of swing as exemplified by Goodman, Shaw, and the bands that had apparently run their course by the mid-forties. The Kenton band, which got its start in California in 1940, first came to the special attention of the public in 1946 with a number of recordings arranged mainly by Pete Rugolo, who helped determine the band's principal style, described by Whitney Balliett as "a big reed section securely rooted with a baritone saxophone, a metallic-sounding, inflexible rhythm section, and driving, ear-rending brass teams, all of which are piled up, block by block, into granitic masses of sound." [24] On the other hand, Leonard Feather, writing about Kenton in 1945, said, "Stan Kenton, a pianist whose style is strongly akin to Hines' and whose orchestrations have highly individual characteristics, was one of the few admirable leaders of big bands who preferred losing commercial opportunities to sacrificing good jazz." [25] The fact is that Kenton's big-band style was certainly one of the most popular in the middle forties. Some characteristic Kenton records made between 1945 and 1947, at the peak of his popularity, are "Artistry Jumps," "Artistry in Bolero," "Opus in Pastels," "Machito," and "Theme to the West." From 1950 on he tried without success to recapture his popularity; his attempts have included organizing a forty-piece touring orchestra and other smaller groups in order to produce such expansive works as are included in "City of Glass," "Innovations in Modern Music," "Contemporary Concepts," and a number of others, all to be heard on Capitol recordings. Although the Kenton band has included, from time to time, important soloists (Eddie Safranski, Shelly Manne, Kai Winding, Art Pepper, and Lee Konitz), its mainstay was elaborately arranged ensemble work by highly competent jazz arrangers and composers more concerned with orchestration and the creation of sounds per se than with creating backgrounds for improvising soloists. Kenton's arrangers (perhaps arrangers writing for the Kenton band would be more nearly correct) have shown a tendency to give more independence to the sections of the band, and even to instruments within the sections; the simpler rhythms of Stravinsky and Bartók were discovered, and Ravel reigned harmonically.

In 1945 Woody Herman had a band that included trumpeter Neil Hefti and pianist Ralph Burns, both journeyman performers but exceptionally gifted arrangers. Hefti and Burns were cognizant not only of the current jazz scene but also of a large body of contemporary music, and they have not hesitated to draw from both. Herman gave his arrangers complete license, and the results have justified his confidence. "Caldonia," "Northwest Passage," "The Good

Earth," and "Bijou," all recorded by Columbia in 1945, reflect the spirit of the new jazz as much as a big band could at the time. Characteristic bop treatments of engaging subject matter were much in evidence, and, as in the work of other "progressive" groups, Stravinsky and Ravel received their due; Stravinsky's influence was, in fact, acknowledged in the Herman band's recording of "Igor." The progressives' enthusiasm for contemporary music may have been dashed by Stravinsky's "Ebony Concerto," written for the Herman band and recorded by them in 1946—a composition that probably produced more publicity than it did jazz. But, like Kenton's band, the Herman band was playing big-band jazz, and, though Herman attempted some pretentious, overblown works, on the whole he concentrated on his imposing soloists. Many of these became leaders in the jazz of the fifties: Billy Bauer, John LaPorta, Shorty Rogers, Bill Harris, Stan Getz, Al Cohn, Jimmy Giuffre, and Milt Jackson.

Of the several progressive big bands in the late forties, Boyd Raeburn's achieved some special distinction. Better known to jazzmen than to the public, he mixed—with the help of his arrangers George Handy and Eddie Finckle—a dash of bop with a touch of Debussy and a large helping of Stravinsky to produce an occasional *pièce de resistance.* Like Herman, Raeburn had many exceptional soloists with whom to work; among the best known are Dizzy Gillespie, Benny Harris, Trummy Young, Johnny Bothwell, Al Cohn, Oscar Pettiford, Shelly Manne, and Dodo Marmarosa. Dave Dexter, Jr., in what seems now an imprudent prophecy, wrote in 1946: "Boyd Raeburn's incredibly cubistic, imaginative experiments are most comparable to some of Stravinsky and Milhaud's works. The public is yet to hail Raeburn, a saxophonist, but in all probability his magnificent music will some day be acclaimed by other than musicians." [26] Raeburn's most characteristic sounds may be found on the Guild recordings—also reissued on other labels—"Interlude," "March of the Boyds," "Boyd's Nest"; and on Jewel, "Yerxa," "Boyd Meets Stravinsky," and the overexpansive but nevertheless good-humored "Dalvatore Sali."

As one studies the development of jazz in the forties and fifties, the problems of jazz seem often to be as much semantic as they are musical. The term "progressive jazz" implies that other, unprogressive kinds of jazz were also current; this, of course, is absurd when one studies the work of the Mintonites or Ellington, for example. The "progressives" could not expect to rally strong support among those serious jazzmen who happened to be working in another direction. Furthermore, seeking musical materials in Stravinsky, Debussy, Ravel, Bartók, and Schoenberg is in itself neither progressive nor regressive. What is important is the manner in which such material is used. When devices from classical music are simply superimposed upon a jazz background, the result is at best a clever sham and at worst clumsy and inept. In the past jazzmen of Ellington's caliber, for example, have found a way of assimilating classical techniques without obtruding their progressiveness upon the listener. Despite the favorable connotation of "progressive," the label was doomed to the same limbo as "bop." The terms "rebop," "bebop," and "bop" are not the kind that inspire confidence; their very sounds suggest ephemera. Bop's life was nonetheless a long one as those things go; unnamed at the beginning of the forties, it reached the peak of its popularity about 1947 and by the early fifties had been absorbed by cool jazz—a category not so much substantially different as more felicitously entitled; but in the late fifties a school of "hard" bop appeared as a contender for recognition.

The trumpeter Miles Davis, with the eight-piece ensemble he organized in 1949, is generally considered the founder of cool jazz. According to Barry Ulanov:

> Bop lengthened melodic lines, weakened the grip of the two- and four-bar riff, gave jazz a rhythmic lift and fresh melodic and harmonic inspiration. Freshness was the key element in bop; when bop musicians could no longer recognize staleness and themselves became susceptible to stereotypes and clichés, they were finished as a cohesive group.[27]

This is not to say that the music itself was finished; what was finished was the "togetherness" of the early bop musicians, and the exclusion of jazzmen who had not been a part of the Harlem-Minton milieu. The Miles Davis group was formed as a result of Davis' desire to create an ensemble sound that would not only be unique in jazz but would, at the same time, provide stimulating support for soloists. Together with Gerry Mulligan and Gil Evans, arrangers sympathetic to his plan, Davis worked out an instrumentation consisting of a trumpet, trombone, French horn, tuba, alto saxophone, baritone saxophone, piano, bass, and drums. In January, 1949, with the additional help of arrangements by John Lewis, the group recorded four compositions for Capitol—"Godchild," "Budo," "Geru," and "Move." The ensemble sound was indeed new to jazz. The scoring for the brass instruments—horn and tuba particularly—lent roundness and depth to the group and provided an admirable richness of texture that was immediately distinctive, and a voicing of the entire ensemble that was imaginative and compelling. After two more recording sessions, in April, 1949, and March, 1950, the group was disbanded because it showed little promise of commercial success. However, its relaxed sound, the careful scoring of its arrangements, its spirit—in short, its entire approach to jazz—could not be dispelled as easily as its organization. The sound of the Davis group may be heard in "Birth of the Cool," on Capitol.

The Davis group may have gone unnoticed by the public, but its special quality was not lost on serious jazzmen. In its three sessions the group included, besides Davis on trumpet, J. J. Johnson or Kai Winding on trombone; Sandy Siegelstein, Addison Collins, or Gunther Schuller on French horn; John Barber on tuba; Lee Konitz on alto saxophone; Gerry Mulligan on baritone saxophone; Al Haig or John Lewis on piano; Nelson Boyd, Joe Schulman, or Al McKibbon on bass; and Max Roach or Kenny Clarke on drums. Many of these expert jazzmen have gone on to become the center of their own little groups. Some, like

Konitz and Mulligan, have become formidable soloists, while the technical facility of others, Johnson and Winding, for example, is incomparable. (The Dixielandish trumpeter Ruby Braff, in reviewing a recording made by the two trombonists, wrote, in the *Saturday Review* of January 11, 1957, "J. J. Johnson and Kai Winding are two instrumentalists who have more technical facility than anyone needs in jazz.") Of the group's longtime jazzmen, only Davis lacked the technique to express intelligibly all his musical thoughts; however, continued practice and study have removed many of his earlier technical impediments, and a first-rate representation of his later work may be heard on the 1954 Prestige recording "Bags' Groove: Miles Davis and the Modern Jazz Giants." The Columbia recording "Kind of Blue" is representative of Davis' work in 1959.

Orrin Keepnews, in his notes to Riverside's "Mulligan Meets Monk," wrote, "You would be fairly safe, even in so argumentative a field as jazz, in reducing matters to the simplest terms and saying that bop begins with Monk and cool jazz begins with Mulligan." Whether or not one would be "fairly safe" in saying this, the name of Gerry Mulligan ranks high as an advocate and performer of cool jazz. In 1952 he moved from the East to California where he organized a jazz quartet that excluded the piano. Working at various times with a trumpet or trombone against bass and drums, Mulligan soon became an important and highly influential figure on the West Coast jazz scene. His arranging, even though it is sparse and features much octave

281

doubling as well as simple two-part counterpoint, is extremely effective mainly because he has a simple melodic and harmonic sense; rhythmically, his approach to jazz may be briefly summed up as sprightly. With the death of Serge Chaloff in 1957, Mulligan became the most important baritone saxophonist on either coast. The baritone in Mulligan's hands loses its grotesqueness and becomes an instrument capable of producing a multiplicity of tone qualities at a rate of speed that used to be associated only with the smaller saxophones.

With the rise of cool jazz, saxophonists seem to have worked their way from under Charlie Parker's green thumb and are found in profusion everywhere. This renaissance is certainly due in part to the reaffirmation of Lester Young's influence. Technically, Young was no Parker, and he contributed nothing to the harmonic and rhythmic style of the fifties; nevertheless he exerted a strong influence in the forties on many young jazzmen, saxophonists particularly. As Ross Russell writes:

> What they admired in Lester Young was his lighter and purer tone, his broader harmonic concepts, his greater extension of the solo line—with the resultant freedom from its bar divisions —his dreamier and more lyrical style. And of course, like all who appreciate great jazz of any kind, they recognized his transcendent qualities: his melodic gift, inventiveness and, above all, his tremendous swing.[28]

In short, they admired Young's "coolness." For the new jazzmen who felt hampered by swing—by what they perhaps thought of as its sentimentality—Young's soft, flat, relaxed delivery and tone were the welcome antithesis of the driving, dramatic approach affected by most swing tenor players and exemplified by Coleman Hawkins. Of Young's disciples, Stan Getz, Al Cohn, and Zoot Sims merit special notice, and of these Getz has worked hard to establish himself as an individual stylist. His recording, "Stan Getz and J. J. Johnson at the Opera House" (Verve), illustrates what may well be the foremost examples of cool tenor and trombone playing.

On the other hand, examples of modern-era saxophone playing inspired by Coleman Hawkins—frequently found in the "hard bop" category—are certainly not wanting. Sonny Rollins, who may be the hardest-working practitioner of the hard bop tenor school, illustrates the style to good advantage in "Way Out West" (Contemporary), and "Freedom Suite" (Riverside). In 1958 some critics referred to cool jazz, as exemplified in the work of Miles Davis, Getz, and others, as "soft bop" to distinguish it from "hard bop." We need only remember that the distinction is one of approach rather than of musical materials, and the same is true when questions arise about distinctions between so-called West Coast and East Coast jazz.

Of the cool brassmen, trumpeter Shorty Rogers, formerly of the Woody Herman and Stan Kenton bands, shows the influence of Miles Davis; Rogers, however, is rapidly achieving the distinction of being the most prolific arranger in jazz. His ultimate position may very well be determined by his big-band arrangements, which almost always include a touch of what less commercial jazzmen are experimenting with; and since Rogers' work is highly popular he is, by this means, introducing ideas and devices to a public that otherwise would never hear them. Rogers has done innumerable arrangements for others, but he appears on his own in a number of recordings, and a fair sample of his work can be heard in the Victor recording, "Shorty Rogers and His Giants." In addition to the trombonists already mentioned, one who should be considered is Bob Brookmeyer, who specializes in valve trombone and plays with the ease and facility of the top trumpeters. His versatility and technical facility become apparent in "Traditionalism Revisited" (World Pacific Jazz), "The Modernity of Bob Brookmeyer" (Verve), and "Storyville Presents Brookmeyer" (Storyville).

On clarinet, Tony Scott came into the cool spotlight in the middle fifties with a bop-oriented style and a technique that has practically nudged all others aside; "The Complete Tony Scott" (Victor), shows him to good advantage. Jimmy Giuffre, with little real technical facility, has distinguished himself nonetheless by exploiting the clarinet's chalumeau register and by almost making up in musical idea and content what he lacks in technique. It is likely, however, that his reputation as a jazz composer and arranger will ultimately determine his position. The quality of his playing and composing is clearly evident in "The Jimmy Giuffre Three" and "The Jimmy Giuffre Clarinet" (Atlantic), and "Tangents in Jazz" and "Jimmy Giuffre" (Capitol).

In a 1957 survey of jazz pianists, John S. Wilson listed sixty-five as "modern." [29] It is possible, however, to make this formidable number manageable by considering only the fairly well established of these. In addition to Thelonious Monk, John Lewis, Al Haig, and others mentioned earlier, the following have distinguished themselves: Erroll Garner, Hank Jones, Dodo Marmarosa, Phineas Newborn, Bernard Peiffer, Oscar Peterson, George Shearing, Horace Silver, Billy Taylor, and Lennie Tristano. Of this group Lennie Tristano, who comes last because of the alphabetic arrangement of the list, is probably the most significant. Analyzing Tristano's position, Leonard Feather writes:

> Lennie Tristano is the complete heretic of modern jazz piano. Where Brubeck has catapulted an intellectual approach into aggressive musical statement and limitless commercial success, Tristano has preferred to withdraw from jazz society. Limiting his audience to students, patrons of the New York studio that has been his bastion since 1951, he has been to the introvert of jazz what Brubeck is to the extrovert, drawing long, lean, horizontal lines from the harmonic experimentation that has lent a quiet, cerebral originality to his work. . . . Tristano, in a sense, is a composer and generic influence rather than a pianist, for saxophonists and even drummers have benefited from an examination of his rhythmic and harmonic ideation. [30]

A fair sampling of Tristano's work can be heard in "Lennie Tristano and Lee Konitz" (Prestige), "Tristano" (Mercury), and "Lennie Tristano" (Atlantic).

The pianist John Lewis, whose position matches Tristano's in many respects, is often judged by his work with the Modern Jazz Quartet, probably the best known of the small jazz units. The group was organized by Lewis in 1952 and included Lewis on piano, Milt Jackson on vibraphone, Percy Heath on bass, and Kenny Clarke on drums; except for Clarke, who was replaced by Connie Kay in February, 1955, the personnel has remained unchanged. With Lewis doing the arranging, the quartet manages to achieve a small-ensemble sound as distinctive as that of the Miles Davis ensemble of 1949. The quartet emphasizes a delicate, intimate, *sotto voce* style that, particularly when the performers are not improvising, suggests great cohesion by occasional simple imitative and contrapuntal devices. The faintly baroque feeling of the music is frequently offset by a swinging blues, often modal in quality, which is at once crafty and charming—if one may use these words to describe the blues; "Ralph's New Blues" included in the Prestige recording of "Concorde," is a typical example of the quartet's handling of such material. The work of the quartet has been variously described as "cerebral," "intellectual," and the like. Much of their quality is difficult to discern through the clink of glasses and the buzz of small talk, but the fact is that their music is quite direct and unassuming, particularly when heard in the quiet of one's study. A broad view of the quartet's contribution to jazz can be found in "Django" (Prestige), and "Fontessa" and "The Modern Jazz Quartet at Music Inn" (Atlantic).

It is likely that history will eventually show the modern jazz era as the period in which the big band declined and

the small ensemble dominated the field. In 1948 Ross
Russell wrote:

> We can most easily visualize the beginnings of bebop as a
> simplification of big band instrumentation. Indeed the new
> music can best be understood as a revolt against a large, com-
> plicated music that reached its peak with Lunceford. The bebop
> insurgents were invariably frustrated orchestra sidemen (Gil-
> lespie, Parker, Christian, Clarke). For them free expression
> meant playing in a small combination. . . .[31]

Russell goes on to point out that, because experimentation
required a minimum number of voices, the trumpet had to
serve as the entire brass section and the alto saxophone
as the reed section; to these were added the three-piece
rhythm section. When Charlie Christian was available, the
early rhythm section had four pieces; after Christian's
death the guitar was not generally considered an essential
part of the section.

Occasionally the tenor saxophone was used instead of the
alto. In the fifties the clarinet and trombone attained recognition as "legitimate" small-group instruments, but by
that time, although the instrumentation of the big bands
still extant was substantially that of the big swing bands
(seven or eight brass, five reeds, and rhythm), the combinations of instruments in the small groups were being
multiplied beyond anything the swing jazzman could imagine. Tenor saxophonist Charlie Ventura, for example, had
a small group that included a vocalist who sang in unison
with his saxophone; Gerry Mulligan often used his baritone saxophone without piano and in combination with

trumpet, trombone, or whatever was handy; the Miles Davis group, as mentioned previously, made use of the French horn and tuba; Dave Brubeck teamed up with the alto saxophonist Paul Desmond; and drummer Chico Hamilton organized a group that included guitar, bass, cello, and flute. (The flute has made remarkable progress in the modern period toward becoming a major jazz instrument, especially in the hands of such players as Frank Wess, Bud Shank, and Herbie Mann.) Again, while such instruments as the accordion and Hammond organ could in earlier periods be found only in sweet swing salons, they are now to be found in the hands of such serious jazz musicians as Mat Matthews (accordion) and Jimmy Smith (organ). The ten sides of "Critics' Choice" (Dawn), offer typical examples of the various small instrumental combinations to be found in the middle fifties. Two of the selections are played by piano, bass, and drums; two are played by tenor, trombone, piano, bass, and drums. The others are alto, piano, bass, and drums; clarinet, guitar, bass, and drums; French horn, tenor, harp, soprano voice, piano, bass, and drums; accordion, French horn, guitar, bass, and drums; guitar, accordion, bass; and a band consisting of a tenor and a baritone saxophone, three trumpets, trombone, piano, bass, and drums.

There is little difference between the functions of big-band sections in this period and in the two preceding periods. Backgrounds are essentially of the same type, and riffs are still very much in evidence, as are the saxophone soli chorus and the brass ensemble punctuation and reinforcement. It is in the small group that one must look for differences. While the small swing group functioned primarily as a group of soloists against a rhythm background, the modern small group tends to think of itself as a unified whole. The individual members improvise solos, of course, but, where the swing soloist merely waited his turn, so to speak, the best modern soloists are concerned with the over-all structure of the work; that is, the soloist makes an effort to relate his work to that of the entire ensemble. Because of this attitude on the part of all the players, it would not be correct to say that the function of the trumpet, for example, is to play the lead, or that the piano plays rhythm. (The piano does provide a rhythmic foundation most frequently; it is, however, calculated to "fit" a particular soloist's work, not merely to provide a four-to-the-bar, left-hand-right-hand accompaniment.) The so-called solo instruments in the small ensemble are equal in function: all are required to play, usually in unison or octaves, composed lines; all are required to improvise solos; and all are required either to read or to improvise secondary melodic lines against an improvised solo. The greatest change in the function of instruments, however, has occurred in the rhythm section.

The pianist, whose function in the thirties was to provide a steady four-four, discovered in this period that the strong, steady beat of the plucked bass made the work he was doing with his left hand redundant. More and more he came to rely on the beat of the bass and to concentrate on the single notes he could play with his right hand. He kept his left free to punch out a chord whenever it seemed necessary to reinforce something his right hand was doing, provide an especially strong up- and downbeat punctuation for the soloist, or occasionally to remind himself and the others of a particular chord progression or cadence— to play what some jazzmen call "feed" chords. A characteristic piano accompaniment for a soloist may be illustrated in brief as follows:

The most revolutionary change, however, has come about in the function of the drummer. His aim, like that of the swing pianist, had previously been to maintain a straightforward four-beats-to-the-bar, which he accomplished by tapping his foot on the bass drum pedal; meanwhile he created a variety of rhythms with the sticks in his hands, frequently using the high hat (foot cymbal) for afterbeats and the suspended cymbals for occasional crashes. The modern drummer attempts to create a sustained legato effect by setting the suspended cymbals to vibrating in order to produce a fluid, unaccented four-four beat; the bass drum is used to punctuate or reinforce the rhythm with soft explosions intended to stimulate the soloist. The use of the fingers, sticks, and brushes on various-sized cymbals has opened new and delicate tonal variations to the modern drummer. (A particularly fine display of the use of these devices can be found in any of the Modern Jazz Quartet's recordings.)

Probably in no technical jazz area has there been so little progress as in structure. Whatever formal changes have come, have generally appeared internally; the mileposts and guidelines of the thirty-two-bar popular song form and the twelve-bar blues dominate structure as they did in previous periods. The typical small ensemble form consists of an introduction, in which arrangers seem to extend themselves most; an ensemble unison or octave presentation of the first sixteen bars; a solo during the eight-bar bridge; and an ensemble return to the last eight, followed by an agreed number of improvised solos, after which the original chorus is repeated, sometimes followed by a short coda. Modern compositions based on the blues are generally handled much as they have been since the twenties, that is, by twelve-bar choruses, occasionally broken by eight- or sixteen-bar episodes. John Lewis, whose work with the

Modern Jazz Quartet shows a rare concern with form, tells us:

> The audience for jazz can be widened if we strengthen our work with structure. If there is more of a reason for what's going on, there'll be more overall sense, and therefore, more interest for the listener. I do not think, however, that the sections in this "structured jazz"—both the improvised and written sections—should take on too much complexity. The total effect must be within the mind's ability to appreciate through the ear.[32]

When Lewis says that structured jazz should not "take on too much complexity," it is apparent that he believes that in some instances at least it has—and he speaks with authority. The complexity however is not, and has not been, the result of the form, or frame; this has not become more complex. What has become more complex is the manner in which the musical material has been stretched over the frame, particularly in improvised music. While notated jazz has continued to remain foursquare, improvised music has developed a technique of what we may call "free phrasing" that is intended to escape the tyranny of the four- and eight-bar phrase.

The improvised phrases of swing and previous periods were, as we have shown earlier, quite simply cast in some multiple of two bars and invariably coincided with the cadential formulas peculiar to the pre-established harmonic basis of whatever was being improvised upon. Usually the chord progressions of the thirty-two-bar AABA structure called for half or full cadences every four or eight bars, and the soloist, regardless of how free his flight, managed to come down solidly in these places. Among modern jazz-men, however, this practice is now held in low esteem. For example, against a simple sixteen-bar theme, with a traditional cadence every four bars, the modern improviser is capable of constructing a five-bar statement followed by a four-bar statement followed by a seven-bar statement. Even separated from their harmonic context, the improvised statements look like phrases because the tones at the end of the statements tend to have a longer duration than the others; the improviser has also developed highly the art of placing rests. It takes patience and repeated hearings to follow the changes in certain twelve-bar blues structures when a performer like Charlie Parker used them as a basis for improvisation. One must forget, or at least not expect to hear, the usual cadences between measures 4 and 5, 6 and 7, and 10 and 11. If one concentrates on the harmonic background the progressions can be easily distinguished, but concentration on the solo line instead brings to the listener's ears a new composition, seemingly unbalanced at first, but fanciful and, above all, fresh. Lee Konitz, the alto saxophonist, is quoted by Barry Ulanov:

> Let's say we change the punctuation of the thirty-two bar structure, like carrying the second eight bars over into the bridge, making our breaks sometime within the second eight and in the middle of the bridge instead of at the conventional points. We reparagraph the chorus. Or better, since we have already altered the construction of the line, we reparagraph a paraphrase. And that leads to the next logical point, to continuity and development. Because you've got to think in terms of

both, so that everything holds together, so that you get not four choruses but a four-chorus statement.[33]

The use of classical forms does not appear to satisfy the jazzman's need; neither does the "extended form" promulgated by Charlie Mingus in his "Pithecanthropus Erectus" and "Love Chant" (Atlantic). Mingus' use of extended form is by harmonic repetition or augmentation. The soloist "stays" with a chord until he feels he has explored it sufficiently, after which he moves on to the next chord or measure; this practice may be viewed as a variant of the contemporary composer's use of continuous development. It should be pointed out that what Konitz outlines above is what many advanced modern jazzmen are striving to do. In practice their improvised solos frequently fit a category somewhere between the free phrasing just mentioned and the square phrasing of earlier periods; I believe that the end result is more satisfactory from a structural standpoint than the completely free phrasing that is occasionally effected. This combination of both kinds of phrasing may be what Lewis meant when he said, "The total effect must be within the mind's ability to appreciate through the ear." It also seems to be the answer to the problem as summarized by Gunther Schuller:

Experience, moreover, has shown us that the borrowing of a baroque form such as the fugue—the most widely used non-jazz form at the moment—very rarely produces the happiest results. Even when successful, it is certainly not the ultimate solution to the problem of evolving new forms in jazz, mainly because jazz is a player's art, and the old classical and baroque forms are definitely related to the art of composing. (Bach's ability to improvise complete fugues notwithstanding.) Used in jazz these classic forms can, at best, produce only specific and limited results, but cannot open the way to a new musical order. Jazz, it seems to me, is strong and rich enough to find within its own domain forms much more indigenous to its own essential nature.[34]

As time goes on, the question of form will undoubtedly become increasingly important to the avant-garde jazzman, if only because he has begun to explore the possibilities of modal, twelve-tone, and atonal composition. At the present time, none of these techniques is in the mainstream; modal composition, however, appears to be making the greatest headway. Minor blues, for example, while not yet common, appear with consistently greater frequency, and the continued interchange of the major and minor seventh resulting in the whole step between the seventh and eighth scale degrees is only a slight remove from the declared use of the Dorian, Phrygian, Aeolian, and Locrian modes.

Since the mainstream jazzman has no more compunction about using a pre-established chord progression as a basis for original composition than the classical composer has in borrowing a theme for a set of variations, the basic harmonies of modern jazz composition must be sought in the progressions of such tunes as "Just You, Just Me," "Cherokee," "Idaho," and a number of similar standards, in addition to variants of the twelve-bar blues. Since the most popular progressions, particularly in the forties, were those of "I Got Rhythm" (which still has currency) and

"How High the Moon" (which seems to have run its course), these are shown here:

Two typical blues progressions are the following:

The above examples help to illustrate various character-istic harmonic patterns that occur throughout the period. As has been pointed out many times before, the modern era shows a harmonic development not unlike the one that followed Wagner and Debussy in the nineteenth century. Major and minor sevenths, ninths, added-note chords, and augmented chords are frequent, although the augmented interval is more likely to be heard in the practice of the performer than it is to be seen in the chord symbol. On the other hand, while triads appear with great frequency as chord symbols, they are seldom used without some additional tone, most frequently the added sixth. When it comes to showing so-called original progressions, the language of the symbol is at the whim of the arranger or composer, and, while some will show a symbol for a simple

297

version of a chord, others will try to have the symbol show a chord of great complexity.

As in previous periods, consecutive secondary dominants continue to be greatly favored by modern jazzmen, and the progression of secondary dominants in the bridge of "I Got Rhythm" is a characteristic one. Another favorite in this period is a long line of consecutive minor sevenths, as shown in measures 7, 8, and 9 of the first blues above. (Four- and eight-bar introductions to head arrangements in this period often consist entirely of ascending or descending stepwise progressions of minor seventh chords landing on the dominant.) Another harmonic characteristic initiated early in the period, and still current, is the Neapolitan sixth, that is, the major triad built on the minor second degree of the scale, thought by some to be derived from the Phrygian mode. Its substitution for a secondary dominant may be seen in the first blues shown above, in measure 4, where the D-flat^9, acting as a substitute for V of IV, resolves to the IV in measure 5. As a dominant substitute its use is made clear in the second blues, measure 10, where the A^9 resolves to the tonic in measure 11.

In discussing modern jazz rhythm we must distinguish between the rhythms of arranged ensemble music and those of improvised music. The arranged rhythms are still, to a large extent, swing oriented; the main difference is in the wider use of rests in the lead line. Phrases uninterrupted by rests are likely to consist mainly of consecutive eighth notes or "double-time" sixteenth notes. Triplets of all kinds are common in this period; the middle note is most frequently an upper auxiliary, this embellishment being a most common figure in the period. An important aspect of the practice of performance during this time is the slight stress placed on the weak part of the beat in consecutive eighth-note patterns; in the forties, these stresses were shown in arranged rhythms by various artificial accent symbols in the proper places, as in the first example below. By the fifties, however, the practice was so common it was not considered necessary to show the accents. The following examples are typical rhythmic patterns of the period; they are not, however, riff patterns.

As an example of masterful handling of rhythm, and for a study of individual technique, we have chosen to dwell upon Dizzy Gillespie's extended solo in "Tour de Force," an original work found in "Dizzy Gillespie, World Statesman" (Verve). The work, arranged by Gillespie in Athens while he was on a tour for the State Department, is quite simple in form and serves mainly as a showcase for Gillespie's brilliantly conceived forty measures of trumpet solo. A four-bar introduction by the full ensemble is followed

by the standard thirty-two-bar AABA with the reeds taking
the first sixteen, the brass the bridge, and the reeds the
last eight. A ten-bar transition by the ensemble leads to a
sixteen-bar piano solo (AA), followed by four in the band
and four by Gillespie on what is substantially the bridge
harmony (B), and a closing statement of A by Gillespie.
Without pause, he continues to the main part of his solo—
thirty-two bars based on the harmonies of the opening
AABA. Four bars of ensemble then lead to a tenor saxophone alternating four-bar solos with four bars of ensemble for a total of sixteen bars. A *da capo* returns the group
to the opening sixteen, followed by a four-bar coda. The
thematic material is quite ordinary and rifflike in character; the harmonic foundation, for all its simplicity, is interesting; and during Gillespie's solo the musical transformation is extraordinary. The harmonies are as follows:

The Fmi^6 opening chord is of course a substitute for the tonic chord, and it is worth noting that nowhere does the tonic chord appear in its pure state. Although there are strong cadences at the end of each eight bars, in his solo Gillespie creates a somewhat different effect. In the first eight of his complete chorus, with the reeds softly blowing the tune underneath, he enters on the third beat of bar 2, but finishes the phrase traditionally in bar 8. The second eight he divides into a two-bar statement and a six-bar statement; he ends the bridge on the seventh bar, and divides the last eight into two fours. The total effect is not as square as the description would seem to imply, mainly because he enters on the last four of the bridge following the piano solo and continues through the last eight of the piano chorus, ending by overlapping the first bar of his own full chorus. The structure of the work is plainly perceived on two or three hearings. On the other hand, Gillespie's treatment of the melody over the harmonic foundation is more complex.

An analysis of his nonharmonic tones indicates that Gillespie's use of them is essentially traditional. There are, however, places in the music that need further explication. There is, for example, Gillespie's device of anticipating chords by improvising on them a beat before they are due, so to speak. This device may be observed in measures 3 and 4, 4 and 5, and 6 and 7 of the first eight bars, as well as in other places in Jerome Richardson's first-rate transcription: [35]

Ninths and elevenths abound in Gillespie's melodic line, and, since the approach is harmonically a late nineteenth-century one, there would be little point in attempting to analyze a large number of these as resolved or unresolved appoggiaturas. It is more than likely that the ninths, elevenths, and thirteenths are considered to be essential parts of the chord, and as such need no resolution. Other tones may be seen as simple nonharmonic tones, including traditional *cambiatas, échappées,* and escape tones; a particularly felicitous use of the ornamental resolution of what may be considered a suspension appears in measures 1 and 2 of the eight bars preceding Gillespie's full chorus, where G resolves to G-flat. Notice, again, the anticipation of the C minor chord on the fourth beat of measure 1:

The process of improvising rapidly must, of necessity, lead to the playing of a great many figures and lines that lie in the hand, and mediocre improvisers often rely on these devices even in a slow tempo. However, Gillespie's ingenuity in handling these devices is most remarkable. A study of his work shows that he has learned to organize the ascending and descending diatonic, chromatic, and whole-tone scale patterns, and arpeggio patterns, in such a way as to make them seem at once both calculated and reckless. His solo in this work shows an exceptional concern for the proper balance between tension and release; the impression he creates by contrasting passages of little intervallic motion with rapidly moving jagged lines is not unlike a panoramic view of mountain peaks descending to plains

and valleys. Gillespie's most brilliant work in "Tour de Force" is unquestionably the seven-bar phrase that constitutes the bridge of his solo. It is worth showing as an example both of his exhilarating rhythmic and harmonic sense and of his apparently irrepressible imagination.

chapter **10**

TOWARD THE FUTURE

IT SEEMS REASONABLE TO AS-
sume that the direction jazz will take in the next twenty-
five years or so will depend in large part on contributions
from three sources: jazzmen with formal academic training, jazzmen without academic training, and contemporary
nonjazz composers. To take the last category first, let us
immediately distinguish between composers whose work
may influence jazz and those who, because they have borrowed from jazz, have in some curious way come to be
identified with jazz. For example, we are certain to find
references to the borrowings of such minor composers as
Kurt Weill, John Alden Carpenter, and Louis Gruenberg.
But the future of jazz is not likely to be influenced by the
work of contemporary composers whose position in classical music is not of the highest major rank, and at the present time few contemporary nonjazz composers hold this

305

distinction. The few about whom there seems to be no question are Stravinsky, Bartók, Hindemith, Schoenberg, and perhaps Milhaud; and if we are to include possible influences from older music we must include J. S. Bach. According to John Mehegan, East Coast jazzmen prefer Stravinsky and Bartók while West Coast jazzmen prefer Hindemith, with both groups "adapting Bachian bass-lines and superimposing modern mannerisms above them." [1]

The question of what constitutes influence is as difficult to resolve in jazz as it is in politics. In spite of Mehegan's statement, one who is familiar with the work of Bach and the major contemporary figures will see only the most superficial signs of their influence on jazz—a harmonic characteristic or two, an intervallic trick, a rhythmic device, a typical sonority. Whether these constitute influence is, of course, the question, and many qualified writers apparently have been so delighted to have jazz receive outside (and respectable) influences that they count a little Schoenberg or Bach as going a long way. This sort of encouragement may yet be a good thing. Mehegan points out, correctly I believe, that jazz has not yet penetrated Bartók and Schoenberg. He writes:

> Whether jazz will be able to absorb these new materials is a critical question since jazz has always been and still is a music rooted in tonality (a definite key feeling).
> The utilization of these atonal (no key feeling) materials will constantly occur in the next few years and may very well be the determining factor in the future of jazz.[2]

Mehegaṅ knows, of course, that if his statement is true it belies what a number of serious musicians and thinkers have postulated. As recently as 1946, when swing was apparently breathing its last and bop was surging forward, Winthrop Sargeant summed up what many thought then and still think:

> One of the most striking features of jazz as compared with art music is its lack of evolutionary development. Aside from a few minor changes of fashion, its history shows no technical evolution whatever. The formulas of the jazz musical language that we have analyzed were nearly all used in the earliest of jazz and still constitute, with minor modifications, the basis of jazz technique.[3]

The arguments in favor of this statement are the common property of all traditionalists—those whose arguments are based on the unshakable premise that once evolution and change occur the result no longer fits the "true" definition of jazz and therefore there is no evolution. For the progressives this is a difficult premise to accept, and we shall explore this question later. For the present it is only necessary to point out that the traditionalists have a great deal of weight on their side, as well as the authority of no less a figure than Stravinsky, who has himself been both a borrower from and a lender to jazz. As for his borrowings, Gene Krupa's statement characterizes the opinion many have of such works of Stravinsky's as "Ragtime," for eleven instruments, "Piano-Rag Music," and "Ebony Concerto." In an article entitled "Has Jazz Influenced the Symphony?" Krupa said:

Stravinsky did evince preoccupation with jazz music. He talked about it. He wrote a series of compositions with titles referring to "ragtime" but no evidence of that preoccupation appears in the actual music, honestly examined, honestly listened to. That preoccupation was purely verbal. Although apparently able to sense, to feel the jazz tempo, he has been unable to express it. For all his tremendous musical vitality, that vitality did not encompass the peculiar rhythmic, driving, let us say American quality which is the essence of jazz.[4]

While I do not believe that the rhythmic, driving quality Krupa speaks of is necessarily peculiarly American, he does seem to have stated clearly what one hears in Stravinsky's jazz-inspired compositions. Stravinsky, however, has stated his own case. On being asked by Robert Craft what his attitude toward jazz is, Stravinsky said:

Jazz is a different fraternity altogether, a wholly different kind of music-making. It has nothing to do with composed music, and when it seeks to be influenced by contemporary music, it isn't jazz, and it isn't good. Improvisation has its own time-world, necessarily a loose and a large one since only in an imprecisely limited time could real improvisation be worked up to: the stage has to be set, and there must be *heat*. The percussion and bass (not the piano—that instrument is too hybrid, and besides, most of the players have just discovered Debussy) function as a central heating system. The point of interest is instrumental virtuosity, instrumental personality; not melody, not harmony, and certainly not rhythm. Rhythm doesn't really exist because no rhythmic proportion or relaxation exists. Instead of rhythm there is "beat." The players beat all the time merely to keep up and to know which side of the beat they are on.

Has jazz influenced me? Jazz patterns and especially jazz instrumental combinations did influence me forty years ago, of

308

course, but not the idea of jazz. As I say, that is another world. I don't follow it, but I respect it.[5]

Stravinsky's parenthetical expression concerning Debussy shows that he is apparently unaware of the work of pianists and other jazzmen who have long put Debussy's influence behind them. Stravinsky's belief that jazz "has nothing to do with composed music" is, I believe, based on his knowledge of jazz of the past, and not of its possibilities for the future. His position seems to be that, since jazz has shown no technical evolution distinguishable from that already found in contemporary classical music, jazz is therefore somehow diminished. This may have been true for the past thirty years. The evidence in the work of many jazzmen in the late fifties, however, indicates at least a possibility that in the future jazzmen and classical composers will draw their compositional material from the same source, that is, from the sum total of our musical inheritance. If this should turn out to be true—and I believe it will—new jazz will continue to be distinct from new classical music because it cannot, and will not want to, be free of the roots it put down in its first fifty years of trial and error.

Jazz has reached a high point of development. In the late fifties it not only encompasses jazzmen with virtuosity beyond the conception of the pioneers, but it has produced a good number of jazz teachers, historians, theorists, and critics. The group that will help determine the future of jazz will unquestionably include a large number of academically trained jazzmen; this is not a prophecy but a fact. It may be a surprise to those who do not have an acute interest in modern jazz to learn that it is already crowded with academically trained musicians anxious to relate what they have acquired in the classroom to the jazz situation. Of the many institutions that have provided some form of academic study for the jazzman, the Juilliard School of Music in New York is among the leaders; jazzmen who are only now in their early thirties and who have had work at Juilliard include the composer-performers Miles Davis, Teddy Charles, Harvey Leonard, Dick Hyman, and Teo Macero. Older men like George Handy and John Mehegan, both of whom were born in 1920, have accomplished significant work and will probably continue to do so. Mehegan's concentration on teaching will undoubtedly influence and contribute to the broadening of students interested in the future of jazz, and his volume on jazz improvisation will, in the years to come, very likely bring fresh approaches to old techniques. Mel Powell, who is thirty-seven and a first-rate swing pianist and composer, after a stay as theory instructor at Queens College in New York became in 1958 a member of the faculty of the Yale School of Music, where he had previously studied with Hindemith. It seems very likely that his earlier work in jazz will not be forgotten and that his regard for jazz will not go unnoticed among sensitive music students.

Other eastern schools have also contributed a fair share of their atmosphere and seriousness of purpose to jazz. The Manhattan School of Music, for example, has contributed something to the musical dimensions of such promising young jazzmen as Dick Katz, Johnny Mandel, and Julius Watkins; the New England Conservatory helped shape Ralph Burns and Barbara Carroll; and the Boston Conservatory, Gigi Gryce. Perhaps at this point a partial list of young jazzmen and their academic affiliations will help to show the extent to which serious musical study has penetrated the field. I believe that jazzmen will continue to study in such institutions in the future, thus helping to erase the line now separating contemporary jazz from contemporary classical music.

Don Bagley	Los Angeles City College
Chet Baker	El Camino College
John Barber	Juilliard School of Music
Bob Brookmeyer	Kansas City Conservatory
Dave Brubeck	College of the Pacific
Ike Carpenter	Duke University
Dick Collins	San Jose State College
Paul Desmond	San Francisco State College
Don Elliot	Juilliard School of Music
Herb Ellis	North Texas State College
Gil Fuller	New York University
Jimmy Giuffre	North Texas State College
André Hodeir	National Conservatory (France)
Bill Holman	Westlake College
Milt Jackson	Michigan State University
Quincy Jones	Schillinger House, Boston
Lee Konitz	Roosevelt College
Don Lamond	Peabody Conservatory

John Lewis	University of New Mexico
Charles Mariano	Schillinger House, Boston
Marian McPartland	Guildhall School of Music (England)
Jack Montrose	Los Angeles State College
Lennie Niehaus	Los Angeles City College
Hall Overton	Juilliard School of Music
Marty Paich	Los Angeles Conservatory
Bernard Peiffer	Marseilles Conservatory (France)
André Previn	Berlin Royal Conservatory (Germany)
Shorty Rogers	Los Angeles Conservatory
George Russell	Wilberforce University
Billy Taylor	Virginia State College
Cal Tjader	San Francisco State College
Ernie Wilkins	Wilberforce University

Two points need emphasis: first, the ages of those listed fall between those of Gil Fuller, born in 1920, and Quincy Jones, born in 1933; second, while the East and West Coast colleges make up the large majority, midwestern and southern schools are not neglected, and it is possible that the 1954 Supreme Court decision on integration will encourage greater southern participation in the future. The few European schools listed and the steady increase of jazz activity in the major European cities seem to be additional evidence of the breaking down of the jazz-classical music barrier. As a proper expansion of this list we must add the names of such jazzmen as Bill Russo, who has been strong enough intellectually to train himself without formal instruction, and Charlie Mingus, John Graas, Clifford Brown, and a good many other first-rate jazzmen who had private instruction from traditionally trained nonjazz teachers and composers such as Darius Milhaud, Ernst Toch, Stefan Wolpe, Alexei Haieff, and Wesley LaViolette. Lennie Tristano's work as a teacher cannot be overlooked. He has sought to penetrate the far reaches of serious composition with the help of his principal disciples, Lee Konitz, Warne Marsh, and Billy Bauer, who in turn have drawn other students to themselves, young men like Bob Wilber and Phil Woods. In addition, Spud Murphy, a once important swing arranger now turned teacher, has developed a twelve-tone technique that he is engaged in passing on to a number of young jazzmen, including the promising thirty-four-year-old composer Curtis Counce.

Not all the jazzmen in the above list are arrangers and composers. About half of them are; the others are musicians who are capable of arranging or composing an occasional piece but who consider themselves primarily performers. What is important from our view, however, is that players who have had academic training on any level are likely to be susceptible to the academically oriented ideas of their composer-colleagues. And this, I believe, is all to the good. On the other hand, we can be certain that the academic groves will continue to produce their share of musicians who, attracted by the glint of hard money, are likely to seek the comfort of commercial music, and perhaps this, too, is all to the good. If we are able to judge from the past, we may expect a fair amount of this sort of backsliding, but we can find comfort in the numbers of jazzmen who, despite their lack of academic training, continue to support what is new and vital and offers them opportunity for individual growth.

It is certain that for some time to come the unacademically trained jazzmen will continue to dominate the jazz scene. Of these, we can without presumption expect some to seek intellectual and musical expansion; and we can expect some to make out a good case for playing what comes naturally. About a decade ago Ralph De Toledano said: "The eclectics—those now commercial jazzmen who are not interested in theories or in musicological research, but seek to play hot music as they feel it and to the best of their abilities—hold the future of jazz in their hands." [6] It would be lamentable indeed if this statement were fact. Fortunately these past ten years have proved that the future of jazz is in those who are willing to explore what is for them new and unknown, who understand the importance of knowing the history of jazz and of music in general, and who recognize the need for building on the foundation laid by significant jazzmen of the past fifty years instead of viewing the foundation as the structure itself.

The work of Count Basie and Duke Ellington, for example, can provide two of the strongest elements from which the jazz of the future can be made. In Basie the knowledgeable young jazzmen will detect the beginnings of jazz, the essence of swing, and the substructure of modern jazz; and in Ellington he will find perhaps the earliest serious work in harmony, orchestration, and form. The spirit in which these men work can be an incentive, but, we repeat, the young jazzman must avoid the kind of direct imitation that results in barrenness; he must know that popular success often goes hand in hand with an indolent imagination; and, finally, he must know that growth in the face of these difficulties can nevertheless be accomplished. The future of jazz belongs to those who are strong enough to flourish alongside the established jazz properties controlled by sometimes sincere but still commercial interests. A long-established jazz name is an image to value of itself; to the commercial interests in jazz, however, a name is only as valuable as the promotion and public acceptance it receives, and no promoter, manager, or press agent wants to envision a future that brings the depreciation of his property. For this reason he must oppose any change as long as he can, and, with the control he has over our present system of communications, change will be a long time in coming.

Every artistic endeavor goes through legitimately arrived at periods of renaissance, and jazz in the late fifties may be suffering its first pangs. Before the first World War, jazz was almost entirely improvised; as we moved into the twenties and on through the swing era, the notated music began to weigh heavily against improvised music; for long stretches in the forties and early fifties the balance moved once more toward improvised music; and at present it seems as if we are in a full-fledged back-to-the-blues movement. This is not to say that we have ever left the blues; we have not. But for the past ten years the avant-garde jazzmen have moved away from the feeling and atmosphere of the old twelve-bar blues, and it is this aspect of early jazz that many are now in the process of exploring. There are jazzmen who never really left the squareness of the traditional blues, but these jazzmen have little place in the future. The jazzman's return to the spirit of early jazz is not a regression, but an attempt to assimilate all of jazz in the same way classical composers look back and discover, or rediscover, fourteenth-century chansons, fifteenth-century motets, or sixteenth-century counterpoint; and, just as it is not the classical composer's purpose to construct music that could have been composed by Machaut, Dufay, or Josquin, neither is it the jazzman's purpose to reconstruct the solos of Oliver or Armstrong. The return to an older style gives one breadth and depth of perception, provided, of course, that the step backward is followed by two steps forward. Only in this way is progress assured. André Hodeir states the case for the future when he says:

> As far as collective creation is concerned, no future worthy of the name is possible if the improviser is condemned to turning around in circles on ground that his predecessors have broken, cultivated, and worn out. He absolutely must get away from the theme-and-variations form, at least from the way it is still conceived today. New blood will begin to circulate as soon as someone discovers a new method of improvisation that will preserve both the soloist's freedom and the orchestral work's basic unity while establishing between the two a necessary and harmonious relationship.[7]

Toward the Future

Hodeir and many other forward-looking critics and composers believe that improvisation and notated music can be harmoniously related, and that it is not a question of one or the other. If jazz is to progress it will be created in much the same way it is now, that is, by a deep look into and strict evaluation of its past, which should bring about the realization that an art cannot feed entirely upon itself. This in turn should cause jazz to expand its view in order to find forms and materials outside itself. As we have seen, this is the method of those who attempt to draw their musical materials from all of music, those who are prepared to accept the principle that there is no absolute boundary between classical music and jazz, and that notated and improvised music can be joined together. Sidney Finkelstein tells us:

> They are different, but not hermetically sealed from one another. The difference is not between two different worlds of music, but between two different uses of music. . . . Larger forms of music demand composition, the working out of music to embody more complex problems of human conflict and emotion, more subtle portrayals of the processes of human thought. Composed music does not negate improvised. . . . The two can be of the greatest musical assistance. It is when the composed forms are most accessible to people, and advance most freely, that improvisation also advances and spreads enormously.[8]

Improvisation is of course a basic ingredient of jazz, and, if it is to grow along with notated music, jazzmen will have to acquire many more techniques than they are now using. When Leonard Feather says, "If jazz is to remain a separate entity at all, the element of swing, the implied steady beat and tempo, will still be a vital part of every jazz performance, as will the art of improvisation on a given set of chord patterns," [9] he is unquestionably correct. Probably no other single limitation could continue to keep jazz "a separate entity" and hold back its progress so much as requiring improvisation to be on "a given set of chord patterns." There seems little question that harmonically conceived jazz will always be with us just as the harmonically conceived music of previous centuries will always be with us, and, as a constant reminder of our heritage, this is as it should be; however, if jazz is to expand, if improvisation is to keep up with notated music, jazzmen will have to learn to improvise on a series of tones rather than on eighteenth- and nineteenth-century chord structures. Whether the series will contain twelve tones or less, remain tonal or become atonal, remains to be seen; in any event advances seem most likely to come about through the use of some kind of row or serial technique, and forward-looking jazzmen have already been working with all these techniques. The emphasis, however, has been on their use in notated music. Perhaps the time will come when certain tone rows are as familiar to jazzmen as certain chord progressions now are. Undoubtedly a jazzman would have to work with an original row, its retrograde form, and the inversions of these for a considerable time before he owned them, so to speak; but the endless possibilities for free invention that would be sure to follow make the effort seem worthwhile.

Toward the Future

For jazzmen interested in the possibilities of new techniques in jazz, the techniques of twentieth-century classical music are still relatively unexplored, probably because many jazzmen are still probing the possibilities of certain traditional techniques, or, to put it another way, they are still familiarizing themselves with the principles of composition. For example, Jimmy Giuffre, as conscientious and sensitive a jazzman as one is likely to find in the late fifties, talks with the enthusiasm of discovery about the principle of combining independent lines—the basic principle of traditional counterpoint—which he terms "slow-motion counterpoint":

> I have found this technique, used to varying degrees, in the works of Bach, Beethoven, Shostakovitch, LaViolette, John Lewis of the Modern Jazz Quartet, and Jim Hall. The crux of this idea is the marked contrast of the melodies being used against each other. The result is a certain feeling of suspension, of dissonance if it's handled right. In slow-motion counterpoint, for example, if one melody is an eighth-note pattern that is changing notes often, the other melody changes notes much less often, perhaps only every four bars. And for rhythmic interest, the slow-changing line can be broken up by repeated notes and rests. A third line and possibly a fourth could be proceeding at other varying rates of speed simultaneously. In our present trio, while the clarinet is playing eighth notes, the bass might be playing whole notes and the guitar could be in between. They're all co-ordinated so that you can hear every note each man plays.
>
> For the listener . . . the contrast between lines made possible by this approach provides the clarity that is necessary for him to be able to follow all the lines; and to a certain extent, the listener will have more time to absorb each harmonic feeling,

because in my writing, the harmonies are the results of the lines rather than the lines being fitted to the harmonies.[10]

Although Giuffre's combining of lines is presently producing traditional harmonies, the important thing, it seems to me, is his awareness that it is not necessary to start with a "given set of chord patterns," and that harmonies may grow out of the horizontal lines instead of the vertical ones. It is patently difficult to create lines without constantly being aware of their harmonic relationship to each other, and the tendency is to favor those intervallic relationships that sound normal or traditional, unless one is steeped in atonal music. This statement is not intended as a plea for atonality, but rather as a reminder that harmonies conceived horizontally are not created completely free of one's harmonic sense, and, if the resulting harmonies turn out to be eighteenth- and nineteenth-century harmonies, one may just as well—for all the harmonic freshness that will result —start with set traditional patterns.

Traditional patterns will no doubt continue to receive greater immediate acceptance; but it is not immediate acceptance we are concerned with here. We are concerned rather with a method of operation, a means by which young jazzmen will apply to jazz the techniques and principles of composition as practiced by the great classical composers of all periods. The study of style characteristics, as we mentioned earlier, can be of great value; but, if style study is not to be spread too thin and its value diminished, it must be bound up in the principles of composition, that is, what constitutes form, direction, texture, tension, release, and the many other tangible and intangible qualities that produce coherent and significant music. Once the principles are understood and accepted, the young composer's purpose will be to acquire the techniques necessary to express himself, and for the jazz improviser this will mean acquiring compositional devices and techniques as well as an instrumental facility that will enable him to express freely what is in his imagination.

There is little we can say about acquiring instrumental virtuosity that has not been said many times over; it seems plain, however, that the jazzman of the future will be the owner of a considerably larger body of theoretical knowledge than his earlier counterparts. As a means of discussing what theoretical knowledge is presently available to jazzmen, it may be valuable, or at least interesting, to indicate the musical knowledge we believe to be essential to the growth and development of jazz. Since the following survey of the techniques, devices, methods, and systems of composition is intended to serve as a guide to young jazzmen, we shall make no attempt to present the material in any systematic fashion—historical or otherwise. The acquisition of musical knowledge is a lengthy, sometimes tiresome process, and even a random savoring of a variety of musical means may serve a good purpose.

Many young jazzmen are at present concerned with giving some of their work a modal feeling, and we shall therefore start with the question of modal music. While it is not necessary to return to ancient Greek music to use the modes creatively, a knowledge of what Glareanus set out to do in his *Dodecachordon* of 1547 is important background. In the period from 1600 to 1900—the period of tonality and the major-minor system—composers intent on making the shift from modality to tonality were often able to find satisfactory solutions only in compromise. Many of Bach's chorales show this mixed style—*Erbarm dich mein, O Herre Gott, Komm Gott Schöpfer, heiliger Geist,* and *Gelobet seist du Jesu Christ,* to mention only a few. Other later examples of this mixed style are found in Brahms, Ravel, Bartók, and Stravinsky. In some instances the so-called mixed style may be due to the composer's calculated use of an ambiguous third which results in an alternating tonic major and tonic minor, or perhaps in a dominant major or minor. And from this device it is but a step to the combined major-minor approach—the simultaneous use of a major and minor third in an otherwise traditional chord—found frequently in Stravinsky's work, for example, *Les Noces* and *Symphony in Three Movements,* and in the *Third Symphony* of Roy Harris. This ambiguous major-minor approach is seen by some as a smaller device within the larger framework of bitonality or bimodality—the simultaneous use of two tonalities or modes—which, in turn, may be classified under the heading of polytonality or polymodality. The young jazzman will explore the numerous examples of each of these devices to be found in Bartók and in Milhaud, who is perhaps the foremost exponent of this technique.

The subject of tonality in general brings to mind a number of specific devices of tonality that may be of use to jazz in the future. For one thing, even an expanded use of different keys instead of the two related keys usually found in the thirty-two-bar AABA form would provide additional freshness to the music, although change of key is not to be considered a substitute for inventiveness. Rapid and unexpected tonal shifts have already been used in jazz performances, particularly in the standards "Tea for Two" and "How High the Moon," but with compensating shifts that return the listener to home base; perhaps jazzmen would gain further insight into this device by studying the delightfully surprising tonal shifts in most works of Shostakovich and Prokofieff. At the opposite extreme—no shifts —we find pandiatonicism, which is not a device but a system of composing using only the "white keys" and avoiding the traditional use of functional harmonies. The pandiatonic style is, in one sense, the result of polymodal writing—again, using only the "white keys." For jazzmen who feel that the number of consecutive secondary dominants now in use has reached the point of saturation, pandiatonicism may offer a new outlook. Excellent examples of pandiatonic writing can be found in many works of Milhaud, Copland, Stravinsky, and Poulenc.

Up to this point we have been discussing tonality, a phenomenon that to composers means thinking vertically. Although we intend to move on to questions of linear composing—a much more satisfactory approach to the future of music in general, I believe—there are still a few harmonic aspects we wish to reflect upon, some old-fashioned harmonic ideas we hope all future jazzmen will learn about and then put behind them. As a preparation for understanding the serious composer's negation of tonality in the twentieth century, it would be helpful to study the music of Chopin, especially those works that, because of their extreme chromatic character and extended use of dominant-function chords, barely avert atonality; from this standpoint Chopin's "Mazurka," Opus 50, No. 2, may be studied profitably. Certain works of Wagner, too, have long been a resource for students interested in chromatic harmony. His preludes to *Die Meistersinger* and *Tristan,* for example, offer what seems an endless supply of sequential chromatic melodies and their accompanying artificial dominants and altered chord harmonizations. More of the same type of material may be found in the tone poems of Richard Strauss, in many works of César Franck, and in the large works of Rachmaninoff. The extensive use of augmented triads and whole-tone scale harmonies, as well as added-note chords, consecutive major triads in free progression, major sevenths, ninths, elevenths, and thirteenths, may be studied in many works of Debussy. Examples of chords constructed on a nontertian basis are also to be found in profusion in the late nineteenth and early twentieth centuries, most often as vertical structures and later as the frequent result of combined horizontal lines. As vertical structures, chords built in fourths are found in Debussy's *La Cathédrale engloutie,* in Schoenberg's *Pelleas und Melisande,* as well as in Scriabin's "mystic" chord. Chords built in fifths are uncommon if one is searching for examples of their consecutive use; however, in alternation with other chords, they are found in Schoenberg's *Three Piano Pieces,* as well as in Stravinsky's *The Rite of Spring* and *Les Noces.*

The jazzman of the future will know that it is possible to create expressive melodic lines that are not necessarily derived from the traditional major and minor melodic sources. We have already passed lightly over the question of modal resources, and it is only necessary to remind ourselves here that the modes do not have their origin in major and minor scales, that each mode has its characteristic melodic flavor, and that a whole step between the leading tone and the tonic can be made to sound as convincing as a half step. If one's taste does not run to atonality and nonvocal melodic lines, modal melodic resources can offer a stimulating departure from the major and minor system. A still further departure may be effected by a close study of various pentatonic scales, where the tonal center may be freely shifted among any of the tones, and the six-note whole-tone scale is another device for achieving a vagueness of tonal feeling. We must remember, however, that the use of pentatonic and whole-tone scales are devices, not systems or methods of composition, and, while they may be used effectively with discretion, they are likely, if used extensively, to become tedious and prosaic. Finally, there are the ingenious artificially constructed scales that abound in the works of the major contemporary composers, scales constructed to provide the composer with whatever intervallic relationships he feels he needs for his work. The construction of such scales and the derivation of harmonies from these scales are more likely to lead to a system of composing than the random use of an assortment of devices. At any rate, the young jazzman must first be familiar with the musical means at his disposal before he makes his various choices.

The rhythmic freedom of contemporary jazz is not far removed from that of contemporary classical music. The main difference lies in the meter signature and the placement of the bar lines; for the most part jazz still abides by some form of duple meter, at least nominally, and the limitations that result from relating metrical accents to the bar line. However, if jazz should continue to advance rhythmically, as it has, there is good reason to believe it will encompass the rhythmic devices of current classical music and perhaps even provide, as in the period immediately after World War I, new rhythmic ideas for all to draw from. The jazzman of the future will be adept with rhythm whose accents are independent of the meter, a free-flowing force whose vitality is drawn from its own shape and momentum; he will be at home with such asymmetric meters as 7/8 and 10/8 and any number of asymmetric divisions of the meter; he will recognize changing meters—a measure of 2/4 followed by several of 3/4, for example, and one of 3/8, and so forth—as a means of gaining an unaccented rhythmic flow.

Of all the twentieth-century composers, Stravinsky is perhaps the greatest exponent of contemporary harmonic and rhythmic devices *in toto*. Despite his recent attempts at twelve-tone composing, Stravinsky is primarily a harmonically inspired composer, and the jazzman of the future may look to the body of Stravinsky's work to see the many devices manipulated with the highest degree of craftsmanship and creativity. Perhaps none of his other works provides a summary of the composers' craft, as it was practiced through the 1920's at least, so well as his cantata *Les Noces*, for soli, chorus, four pianos, and seventeen percussion instruments. A study of the Philharmonia pocket score of *Les Noces* (1923) reveals significant treatment of the following devices (the numbers in parentheses refer to rehearsal numbers in the score): (1) bitonality, a persistent B-flat pedal against a persistent E in the soprano; (12) displaced scalic patterns; (16) parallelism plus bitonality; (17) bitonality, E major over C major; (21) Aeolian melody against atonal pedal; (23) two-part counterpoint in parallel fourths—one part Aeolian on A, the other part Aeolian on E; (41) pandiatonic parts against chromatic parts in parallel fifths; (59) an ostinato F arpeggio in the tympani against an A major-minor ostinato; (65) parallel major sevenths; (77) superposed triads a minor second apart—A major atop A-flat major; (87) parallel major chords; (91) percussive clusters; (119) combined C pedal, C-sharp pedal, and parallel major chords; (124) pandiatonicism; (125) parallel major ninths. Altogether, *Les Noces* shows examples of nearly every twentieth-century harmonic technique—bitonality, polytonality, parallelism, ambiguity, clusters, pandiaton-icism, displaced scalic patterns, modality, percussive ato-nality, and obscure dominant-tonic relationships—all dis-played in an exuberantly imaginative rhythmic setting.

Of the various systems and methods of composition in the twentieth century, I believe that those encouraging the use of the row technique and the free use of dissonance hold the greatest promise for jazz in the future. Rows may consist of the twelve tones as conceived by Schoenberg and his pupils, or by Wallingford Riegger; or jazzmen may work with a lesser number of tones, derived perhaps from a series of artificially created chords or scales. The goal is a free linear approach to jazz, and it is only through a wide knowledge of contrapuntal techniques that the jazz student will be able to extricate himself from the confines of traditional harmony. He will master the skills of melodic augmentation, diminution, inversion, and the octave dis-placement of notes sometimes called pointillism; he will study the development of chromatic counterpoint as it is found in the Germans Bach, Reger, Mahler, and Schoen-berg, and the ingenious contrapuntal devices of all periods, as represented in the works of Milhaud, Hindemith, and Bartók.

As an introduction to contemporary counterpoint, as well as other contemporary techniques that may have a place in the future of jazz, I can think of no single work that is as useful as Bartók's *Mikrokosmos* (1926-37, Boosey and Hawkes). This six-volume work is a compendium of contemporary devices that illustrates clearly and in a creative context the manner in which these devices can serve the composer. Aside from occasional emphasis on contemporary keyboard techniques, the *Mikrokosmos* contains a masterful exposition of contrapuntal imitation, inversion, augmentation, diminution, retrogression, and canon of all kinds; many ingenious uses of pedals and ostinato figures; many pieces based on artificially constructed scales, changing meter, and asymmetric meter; and a seemingly inexhaustible rhythmic invention throughout, particularly in the "Six Dances in Bulgarian Rhythm" (Vol. VI, p. 35).

For specifics the jazz student may wish to study the following: examples of bitonality (Vol. IV, pp. 11, 18; Vol. III, p. 32; Vol. V, p. 10; Vol. VI, p. 9) which show the opposing of white and black keys; the percussive use of bitonal chords (Vol. IV, p. 27); bimodality (Vol. III, p. 15); the simple opposing of pentatonic scales (Vol. III, p. 22); the less simple opposing of an F-sharp major pentatonic scale and a D minor pentatonic scale (Vol. III, p. 12); the opposing of the two whole-tone scales (Vol. V, p. 32); mixed style (Vol. V, p. 16); the use of consecutive triads in root position (Vol. IV, p. 46); the combining of broken triads to create artificial arpeggios (Vol. VI, p. 13); chords with added seconds (Vol. V, p. 4); chord parallelism (Vol. III, p. 48); the opposing of pairs of fourths (Vol. V, p. 22); the use of tone clusters (Vol. IV, p. 21); the rapid shifting of tonalities (Vol. IV, p. 16); the combining of a melodic subject with its inversion (Vol. VI,

p. 6); the free development of a rhythmic motive (Vol. VI, p. 2); the opposing of atonal patterns (Vol. IV, p. 24); atonal inventions (Vol. III, pp. 39, 40).

Jazz critics who are not at home with current classical music are often quick to point out that atonal music is unintelligible even to the classical music public, and that its use in jazz is therefore pretentious and ludicrous, if not arrogant and boorishly offensive. Some critics solve the problem by implying that atonality has no place in jazz and that its use in jazz therefore relieves them of the responsibility of criticizing and evaluating—a tactic I cannot hold with. What the future of jazz will be and the extent to which it will absorb classical techniques lie, it would seem, within the province of the jazz composer and performer. The critic may not like certain procedures that flout his long-established critical norm, but it is his responsibility to understand how all of music has developed. It is a simple matter to suggest that some pieces—such as certain of the Brandeis University commissions—are not jazz; it is more difficult to suggest that these foreshadow the jazz to come, and as such deserve special attention and critical standards heretofore usually unknown to jazz. If the jazz critic of the future is to serve jazz well, he must possess a wide knowledge of all music. He will, like the jazzman, have to extend the traditional principle of dominant-to-tonic to mean tension-to-release, but in an all-inclusive sense—melodic, rhythmic, directional, and textural, as well as harmonic. He will understand that dominant can mean motion, and tonic, repose; that dominant can mean a thick texture, and tonic, a unison. He will readily understand that melodies may be diatonic, chromatic, static, or jagged, and that harmonic direction may be suggested by the rhythmic emphasis of single tones instead of traditional chords; and, above all, that dissonance is a relative quality. The jazz critic with the capacity and flexibility to make the enormously difficult transition to the new jazz, *during the transition*, can be a broadening, even compelling, influence on the future of jazz.

NOTES

CHAPTER 1

1. Nat Hentoff, "Reading the Blues," *Nation,* CLXXXVI (March 15, 1958), 240.

2. *Down Beat,* XXII (February 9, 1955).

3. *Ibid.,* XXI (February 19, 1954).

4. André Hodeir, *Jazz: Its Evolution and Essence* (New York: Grove Press, 1957), p. 32, translated by David Noakes from Hodeir's *Hommes et problèmes du jazz* (Paris: Au Portulan, chez Flammarion, 1954); Part VI, a section on contemporary jazz, was added for the English version.

5. Winthrop Sargeant, *Jazz: Hot and Hybrid* (New York: E. P. Dutton and Co., 1946), p. 25.

6. Morroe Berger, "Jazz Pre-History, and Bunk Johnson," in *Frontiers of Jazz,* ed. Ralph de Toledano (New York: Oliver Durrell, 1947), p. 103.

7. Orrin Keepnews and Bill Grauer, *A Pictorial History of Jazz* (New York: Crown Publishers, 1955), p. 1.

8. Jacques Barzun, *Music in American Life* (New York: Doubleday and Co., 1956), p. 85.

9. Nat Shapiro and Nat Hentoff (eds.), *The Jazz Makers* (New York: Rinehart and Co., 1957), p. 232.

10. Whitney Balliett, "Jazz Records," *New Yorker*, XXXIV (February 8, 1958), 103.

11. Nicolas Slonimsky, *Music since 1900* (Boston: Coleman-Ross Co., 1949), pp. 170-71.

12. G. H. Knoles, *The Jazz Age Revisited* (Stanford: Stanford University Press, 1955), p. 120.

13. *Ibid.*, p. 102.

14. Aldous Huxley, *Jesting Pilate: An Intellectual Holiday* (New York: George H. Doran and Co., 1926), p. 297.

15. H. O. Osgood, *So This Is Jazz* (Boston: Little, Brown, and Co., 1926), p. 103.

16. P. F. Laubenstein, "Jazz—Debit and Credit," *Musical Quarterly*, XV (October, 1929), 606.

17. Slonimsky, *Music since 1900*, pp. 359, 397.

18. *Ibid.*, p. 449.

CHAPTER 2

1. Sidney Finkelstein, *Jazz: A People's Music* (New York: Citadel Press, 1948), p. 25.

2. André Hodeir, *Jazz: Its Evolution and Essence* (New York: Grove Press, 1957), p. 46.

3. Sam Morgenstern (ed.), *Composers on Music* (New York: Pantheon Books, 1956), pp. 359, 392.

4. Barry Ulanov, *A History of Jazz in America* (New York: Viking Press, 1952), p. 5.

5. Hodeir, *Jazz*, pp. 3, 6.

6. Morgenstern, *Composers on Music*, p. 512.

7. Ulanov, *A History of Jazz in America*, p. 196.

8. Hodeir, *Jazz*, p. 18.

9. Wilder Hobson, *American Jazz Music* (New York: W. W. Norton and Co., 1939), p. 54.

10. Virgil Thomson, "Swing Music," *Modern Music*, XIII (May, 1936), 17.

11. Ulanov, *A History of Jazz in America,* p. 195.

12. Robert Goffin, *Jazz, from the Congo to the Metropolitan* (New York: Doubleday and Co., 1944), p. 243.

13. Paul Eduard Miller, "An Analysis of the Art in Jazz," *Esquire's 1946 Jazz Book* (New York: A. S. Barnes and Co., 1946), pp. 139-40. Italics in original.

14. Ulanov, *A History of Jazz in America,* p. 7.

15. Marshall Stearns, *The Story of Jazz* (New York: Oxford University Press, 1956), pp. 260, 282. Italics in original.

16. Hodeir, *Jazz,* p. 197.

17. Miller, *Esquire's 1946 Jazz Book,* p. 134.

18. Stearns, *The Story of Jazz,* p. 304. Italics in original.

19. Hodeir, *Jazz,* p. 159.

20. *Ibid.,* p. 197.

21. *Ibid.,* p. 205.

22. *Ibid.,* p. 143.

23. *Ibid.*

24. Stearns, *The Story of Jazz,* p. 108.

25. Hodeir, *Jazz,* p. 139.

26. *Ibid.,* p. 240.

CHAPTER 3

1. Morton White, *The Age of Analysis* (New York: New American Library, 1945), p. 225.

2. Barry Ulanov, *A History of Jazz in America* (New York: Viking Press, 1952), p. 239.

3. Béla Bartók, *Hungarian Folk Music,* trans. M. C. Calvocoressi (New York: Oxford University Press, 1931), pp. 2-3.

4. Gustave Reese, *Music in the Middle Ages* (New York: W. W. Norton and Co., 1941), see pp. 48, 263, 353, 401.

5. Gustave Reese, *Music in the Renaissance* (New York: W. W. Norton and Co., 1954), p. 42.

6. *Ibid.,* p. 544.

7. Manfred F. Bukofzer, *Music in the Baroque Era* (New York: W. W. Norton and Co., 1947), p. 371.

8. Paul Henry Lang, *Music in Western Civilization* (New York: W. W. Norton and Co., 1951), pp. 359, 709.

9. Alexander Wheelock Thayer, *The Life of Ludwig van Beethoven* (3 vols.; New York: Beethoven Association, 1921), II, 10.

10. Casimir Wierzynski, *The Life and Death of Chopin*, trans. Norbert Guterman (New York: Simon and Schuster, 1949), pp. 83-84.

11. Nat Shapiro and Nat Hentoff (eds.), *Hear Me Talkin' to Ya* (New York: Rinehart and Co., 1955), p. 19.

12. *Ibid.*, p. 36.

13. *Ibid.*, p. 90.

14. *Ibid.*, p. 22.

15. *Ibid.*, pp. 77, 78.

16. Ernest Borneman, "The Jazz Cult," Part I, *Harper's*, CXCIV (February, 1947), 142.

17. Sidney Finkelstein, *Jazz: A People's Music* (New York: Citadel Press, 1948), p. 25.

18. Leonard Feather, *The Book of Jazz* (New York: Horizon Press, 1957), p. 209.

19. *Ibid.*, p. 214.

20. *Ibid.*

21. André Hodeir, *Jazz: Its Evolution and Essence* (New York: Grove Press, 1956), p. 144.

22. Robert U. Nelson, *The Technique of Variation* (Berkeley: University of California Press, 1948), pp. 31-32.

23. *Ibid.*, pp. 47-48.

24. Bukofzer, *Music in the Baroque Era*, p. 384.

25. Feather, *The Book of Jazz*, p. 215.

26. Winthrop Sargeant, *Jazz: Hot and Hybrid* (New York: E. P. Dutton and Co., 1946), pp. 260-61.

27. Finkelstein, *Jazz: A People's Music*, p. 111.

28. Gilbert Seldes, "No More Swing?" *Scribner's*, C (November, 1936), 70.

29. Shapiro and Hentoff, *Hear Me Talkin' to Ya*, p. 20.

30. *Ibid.*, pp. 46, 47.

31. John Tynan, "Teagarden Talks," *Down Beat,* XXIV (March 6, 1957), 19.

32. Shapiro and Hentoff, *Hear Me Talkin' to Ya,* p. 354.

33. Eric Larrabee, "Jazz Notes," *Harper's,* CCXVI (May, 1958), 96.

34. Ethel Waters and Charles Samuels, *His Eye Is on the Sparrow* (New York: Doubleday and Co., 1951), pp. 146-47.

35. Benny Goodman and Irving Kolodin, *The Kingdom of Swing* (Harrisburg, Pa.: Stackpole Co., 1939), p. 161.

36. *Ibid.,* p. 187.

37. Ralph J. Gleason, "Brubeck," *Down Beat,* XXIV (September 5, 1957), 16.

38. Whitney Balliett, "Jazz Records," *New Yorker,* XXXIV (February 22, 1958), 126.

39. Goodman and Kolodin, *The Kingdom of Swing,* p. 39.

40. Shapiro and Hentoff, *Hear Me Talkin' to Ya,* p. 343.

41. Sam Morgenstern (ed.), *Composers on Music* (New York: Pantheon Books, 1956), p. 554.

CHAPTER 4

1. Willi Apel, *The Notation of Polyphonic Music 900-1600* (4th ed.; Cambridge, Mass.: Mediaeval Academy, 1949), p. viii.

2. A. H. Fox Strangways in *The Oxford History of Music,* Introductory Vol. (New York: Oxford University Press, 1929), p. 179.

3. Béla Bartók, *Hungarian Folk Music,* trans. M. D. Calvocoressi (New York: Oxford University Press, 1931), p. 195.

4. Leonard Feather, *The Encyclopedia of Jazz* (New York: Horizon Press, 1955), p. 59.

5. *Ibid.,* p. 62.

6. Bartók, *Hungarian Folk Music,* p. 9.

7. Walter Piston, *Harmony* (New York: W. W. Norton and Co., 1941; rev. ed., 1948), pp. 52-53.

8. Feather, *The Encyclopedia of Jazz,* pp. 53, 61-62.

9. Marshall Stearns, *The Story of Jazz* (New York: Oxford University Press, 1956), p. 282.

10. *Ibid.*

11. Piston, *Harmony*, p. 227.

12. *Ibid.* For greater detail see the chapter on nonharmonic tones, pp. 102-116.

13. Winthrop Sargeant, *Jazz: Hot and Hybrid* (New York: E. P. Dutton and Co., 1946), pp. 159-60.

14. Stearns, *The Story of Jazz*, p. 8.

15. Piston, *Harmony*, p. 37.

CHAPTER 5

1. Manfred F. Bukofzer, *Music in the Baroque Era* (New York: W. W. Norton and Co., Inc., 1947), p. xiii.

2. André Hodeir, *Jazz: Its Evolution and Essence* (New York: Grove Press, 1956), pp. 35-36.

3. Whitney Balliett, in *Eddie Condon's Treasury of Jazz* (New York: Dial Press, 1956), pp. 310-11.

4. Bukofzer, *Music in the Baroque Era*, p. 391.

5. Aaron Copland, "A Modernist Defends Modern Music," *New York Times*, December 25, 1949.

6. Barry Ulanov, *History of Jazz in America* (New York: Viking Press, 1954), pp. 338-39.

7. Guido Adler, "Style-Criticism," *Musical Quarterly*, XX (April, 1934), 172.

8. *Ibid.*, p. 174.

9. Marshall Stearns, *The Story of Jazz* (New York: Oxford University Press, 1956), p. 67.

10. John S. Wilson, "Forty Years in the Groove," *High Fidelity Magazine*, VII (February, 1957), p. 45.

11. Leonard Feather, "Duke Ellington," in *The Jazz Makers*, ed. Nat Shapiro and Nat Hentoff (New York: Rinehart and Co., 1957), p. 190.

12. Arnold Schoenberg, *Style and Idea* (New York: Philosophical Library, 1950), p. 183.

Notes

CHAPTER 6

1. John Philip Sousa, *Marching Along* (Boston: Hale, Cushman, and Flint, 1941), p. 175.

2. Richard Franko Goldman, *The Concert Band* (New York: Rinehart and Co., 1946), p. 61.

3. *Ibid.*, p. 56.

4. Louis C. Elson, *The History of American Music* (New York: Macmillan Co., 1925), pp. 157-60.

5. Alan Lomax, *Mister Jelly Roll* (New York: Duell, Sloan and Pearce, 1950), p. 72.

6. *Ibid.*, p. 78.

7. Frederic Ramsey, Jr., notes for *Jazz*, Vol. III: *New Orleans* (New York: Folkways Records, 1951).

8. Henderson H. Donald, *The Negro Freedman* (New York: Henry Schuman, 1952), p. 153.

9. *Ibid.*, p. 145.

10. Lomax, *Mister Jelly Roll*, p. 61.

11. Rudi Blesh, *Shining Trumpets* (New York: Alfred A. Knopf, 1946), pp. 156-57.

12. Lomax, *Mister Jelly Roll*, p. 86.

13. Barry Ulanov, *History of Jazz in America* (New York: Viking Press, 1952), pp. 56-57.

14. Frederic Ramsey, Jr., and Charles Edward Smith (eds.), *Jazzmen* (New York: Harcourt, Brace and Company, 1939), p. 70.

15. Sidney Finkelstein, *Jazz: A People's Music* (New York: Citadel Press, 1948), p. 155.

16. Larry Gara, "Baby Dodds," *Jazz Journal*, May-December, 1955.

17. Nat Shapiro and Nat Hentoff (eds.), *Hear Me Talkin' to Ya* (New York: Rinehart and Co., 1955), p. 90.

18. Ernest Borneman, "Jazz Cult," Part II, *Harper's*, CXCIV (March, 1947), p. 262.

19. Blesh, *Shining Trumpets*, pp. 22, 187.

20. W. L. Grossman and J. W. Farrell, *The Heart of Jazz* (New York: New York University Press, 1956), p. 75.

21. Walter Piston, *Counterpoint* (New York: W. W. Norton and Co., 1947), p. 9.

22. Leonard Feather, *The Book of Jazz* (New York: Horizon Press, 1957), p. 79.

23. Charles Delaunay, *New Hot Discography*, ed. Walter E. Schaap and George Avakian (New York: Criterion Music Corp., 1948), pp. 2-3.

CHAPTER 7

1. John S. Wilson, "Fletcher Henderson," in *The Jazz Makers*, ed. Nat Shapiro and Nat Hentoff (New York: Rinehart and Co., 1957), p. 230.

2. *Ibid.*, p. 224.

3. Charles Edward Smith, *New Republic*, XCIV (February 16, 1938), p. 39.

4. Nat Shapiro and Nat Hentoff (eds.), *Hear Me Talkin' to Ya* (New York: Rinehart and Co., 1955), p. 203.

5. George Hoefer, "Bix Beiderbecke," in *The Jazz Makers*, p. 98.

6. Barry Ulanov, "The Jukes Take Over Swing," *American Mercury*, LI (October, 1940), 172.

7. Marshall Stearns, *The Story of Jazz* (New York: Oxford University Press, 1956), p. 187.

8. Shapiro and Hentoff, *Hear Me Talkin' to Ya*, p. 220.

9. Barry Ulanov, *History of Jazz in America* (New York: Viking Press, 1952), p. 148.

10. Shapiro and Hentoff, *Hear Me Talkin' to Ya*, p. 225.

11. Sidney Finkelstein, *Jazz: A People's Music* (New York: Citadel Press, 1948), pp. 204-5.

12. Leonard Feather, "Duke Ellington," in *The Jazz Makers*, p. 189.

13. Whitney Balliett, "Celebration for the Duke," *Saturday Review*, XXXIX (May 12, 1956), 30.

14. Orrin Keepnews and Bill Grauer, *A Pictorial History of Jazz* (New York: Crown Publishers, 1955), p. 103.

15. Leonard Feather, *The Book of Jazz* (New York: Horizon Press, 1957), p. 195.

16. Barry Ulanov, *History of Jazz in America* (New York: Viking Press, 1952), p. 163.

17. Stearns, *The Story of Jazz*, p. 199.

18. Shapiro and Hentoff, *Hear Me Talkin' to Ya*, p. 223.

CHAPTER 8

1. Benny Goodman and Irving Kolodin, *The Kingdom of Swing* (Harrisburg, Pa.: Stackpole Co., 1939), p. 146.

2. Gilbert Millstein, "Apostle of Swing," *New York Times Magazine*, April 19, 1953.

3. Eddie Condon and Richard Gehman (eds.), *Eddie Condon's Treasury of Jazz* (New York: Dial Press, 1956), p. 272.

4. Wilder Hobson, *American Jazz Music* (New York: W. W. Norton and Company, 1939), pp. 150-51.

5. Paul Bowles, "Once Again, le Jazz Hot," *Modern Music*, XX (January, 1943), 140.

6. Dave Dexter, Jr., *Jazz Cavalcade* (New York: Criterion Music Corp., 1946), p. 91.

7. Condon and Gehman, *Eddie Condon's Treasury of Jazz*, p. 260.

8. Robert Goffin, *Jazz from the Congo to the Metropolitan* (New York: Doubleday and Co., 1944), p. 161.

9. Nat Shapiro and Nat Hentoff (eds.), *Hear Me Talkin' to Ya* (New York: Rinehart and Co., 1955), p. 322.

10. Condon and Gehman, *Eddie Condon's Treasury of Jazz*, pp. 273-74.

11. *Ibid.*, p. 263.

12. Goodman and Kolodin, *The Kingdom of Swing*, p. 161.

13. Marshall Stearns, *The Story of Jazz* (New York: Oxford University Press, 1956), p. 191.

14. Barry Ulanov, *A History of Jazz in America* (New York: Viking Press, 1952), p. 193.

15. Leonard Feather, *The Encyclopedia of Jazz* (New York: Horizon Press, 1955), p. 26.

16. Shapiro and Hentoff, *Hear Me Talkin' to Ya*, p. 303.

17. Sidney Finkelstein, *Jazz: A People's Music* (New York: Citadel Press, 1948), p. 210.

18. Shapiro and Hentoff, *Hear Me Talkin' to Ya*, p. 305.

19. Ulanov, *A History of Jazz in America*, p. 190.

20. Goodman and Kolodin, *The Kingdom of Swing*, p. 173.

21. Adapted from Buck Clayton's arrangement of *It's Sand, Man* (New York: Bregman, Vocco and Conn, 1943).

22. Paul Eduard Miller (ed.), *Esquire's 1945 Jazz Book* (New York: A. S. Barnes and Co., 1945), caption opposite p. 50.

23. John S. Wilson, *New York Times*, March 30, 1958.

CHAPTER 9

1. Richard Boyer, "Bebop," *New Yorker*, XXIV (July 3, 1948), 28.

2. Ralph Ellison, "The Charlie Christian Story," *Saturday Review*, XLI (May 17, 1958), 43.

3. Ted Hallock, *Down Beat*, XVI (July 1, 1949), 13.

4. "Louie the First," *Time*, LIII (February 21, 1949), 52.

5. Nat Hentoff, "The Post-bop Legitimacy of Modern Jazz," *Reporter*, XVIII (February 6, 1958), 39.

6. Ross Russell, "Be-bop Instrumentation," *Record Changer*, VII (November, 1948), 23.

7. John Mehegan, "The ABC of the New Jazz," *Saturday Review*, XXXIX (November 10, 1956), 34.

8. Ellison, "The Charlie Christian Story," p. 43.

9. Orrin Keepnews, "Charlie Parker," in *The Jazz Makers*, ed. Nat Shapiro and Nat Hentoff (Rinehart and Co., 1957), pp. 209-10.

10. Nat Shapiro and Nat Hentoff (eds.), *Hear Me Talkin' to Ya* (New York: Rinehart and Co., 1955), p. 337.

11. Bill Simon, "Charlie Christian," in *The Jazz Makers*, p. 316.

12. Ellison, "The Charlie Christian Story," p. 42.

13. Alun Morgan and Raymond Horricks, *Modern Jazz* (London: Victor Gollancz, 1956), p. 38.

14. Simon, "Charlie Christian," p. 331.

15. Morgan and Horricks, *Modern Jazz*, p. 55.

16. Leonard Feather, "John 'Dizzy' Gillespie," in *The Jazz Makers*, pp. 332-33.

17. Aaron Copland, "A Modernist Defends Modern Music," *New York Times*, December 25, 1949.

18. *Newsweek*, XXXVI (September 4, 1950), 76.

19. Keepnews, "Charlie Parker," p. 207.

20. Whitney Balliett, "The Measure of 'Bird,'" *Saturday Review*, XXXIX (March 17, 1956), 34.

21. Morgan and Horricks, *Modern Jazz*, p. 47.

22. Wilder Hobson, "The Amen Corner," *Saturday Review*, XLI (January 25, 1958), 59.

23. Shapiro and Hentoff, *Hear Me Talkin' to Ya*, pp. 348-49.

24. Whitney Balliett, "Kenton: Artistry in Limbo," *Saturday Review*, XXXVIII (April 30, 1955), 56.

25. Leonard Feather, in *Esquire's 1945 Jazz Book*, ed. Paul Eduard Miller (New York: A. S. Barnes and Co., 1945), p. 21.

26. Dave Dexter, Jr., *Jazz Cavalcade* (New York: Criterion Music Corp., 1946), p. 233.

27. Barry Ulanov, *A History of Jazz in America* (New York: Viking Press, 1952), p. 288.

28. Ross Russell, "Be-bop," *Record Changer*, VIII (April, 1949), 20.

29. John S. Wilson, *High Fidelity Magazine*, VII (August, 1957), 70.

30. Leonard Feather, *The Book of Jazz* (New York: Horizon Press, 1957), p. 70.

31. Ross Russell, "Be-bop Instrumentation," *Record Changer*, VII (November, 1948), 12.

32. John Lewis, *The World of Music* (Information Bulletin No. 4 of the International Music Council, Unesco House, Paris, May, 1958).

33. Ulanov, *A History of Jazz in America*, p. 329.

34. Gunther Schuller, "The Future of Form in Jazz," *Saturday Review*, XL (January 12, 1957), 62.

35. Quincy Jones (ed.), *Dizzy Gillespie, World Statesman—Trumpet Solos* (New York: Silhouette Music Corp., 1957), p. 12.

CHAPTER 10

1. John Mehegan, "The ABC of the New Jazz," *Saturday Review*, XXXIX (November 10, 1956), 35.

2. *Ibid.*

3. Winthrop Sargeant, *Jazz: Hot and Hybrid* (New York: E. P. Dutton and Co., 1946), p. 259.

4. Gene Krupa, "Has Jazz Influenced the Symphony?" in *Esquire's 1947 Jazzbook* (New York: Smith and Durrell, 1947), p. 6.

5. Igor Stravinsky and Robert Craft, "Conversations with Stravinsky," *Horizon*, September, 1958, p. 132, an excerpt from *Conversations with Igor Stravinsky* (New York: Doubleday and Co., 1959).

6. Ralph De Toledano, "Directions in Jazz," in *Frontiers of Jazz*, ed. De Toledano (New York: Oliver Durrell, 1947), p. 71.

7. André Hodeir, *Jazz: Its Evolution and Essence* (New York: Grove Press, 1956), pp. 279-80.

8. Sidney Finkelstein, *Jazz: A People's Music* (New York: Citadel Press, 1948), pp. 236-37.

9. Leonard Feather, *Inside Bebop* (New York: J. J. Robbins and Co., 1949), p. 45.

10. Nat Hentoff, "Jimmy Giuffre: Blues in Counterpoint," *Saturday Review*, XL (July 13, 1957), 37.

A SELECTED
JAZZ BIBLIOGRAPHY

BOOKS

Allen, Walter C., and Brian A. L. Rust. *King Joe Oliver.* Belleville, N. J.: Allen and Rust, 1955. Reprinted in London: Sidgwick and Jackson, 1958.

American Society of Composers, Authors and Publishers. *The ASCAP Biographical Dictionary.* New York: Crowell Publishers, 1952.

Armitage, Merle. *George Gershwin.* New York: Longmans, Green, 1938.

Armstrong, Louis. *Satchmo.* New York: Prentice-Hall, 1954. Paperback ed., New York: Signet Books, 1955.

————. *Swing That Music.* New York: Longmans, Green, 1936.

Back, Jack. *Triumph des Jazz.* Vienna: Alfa-Edition, 1949.

Balliett, Whitney. *The Sound of Surprise.* New York: E. P. Dutton and Co., 1959.

Baresel, Alfred, *Das neue Jazzbuch.* Leipzig: Zimmermann, 1929.

Berendt, Joachim E. *Das Jazzbuch.* Frankfurt: Fischer Bücherei, 1953.

A Selected Jazz Bibliography

————. *Jazz optisch.* Munich: Nymphenburger Verlagshandlung, 1945.

————. *Das neue Jazzbuch; Entwickelung und Bedeutung der Jazzmusik.* Frankfurt: Fischer, 1959.

Bernhard, Edmond, and Jacques de Vergnies. *Apologie du jazz.* Brussels: Les Presses de Belgiques, 1945.

Biamonte, S. G., and E. Micocci. *Il libro del jazz.* Bologna: Cappelli, 1958.

Blackstone, Orin. *Index to Jazz.* 4 vols. New Orleans: Gordon Gullickson, 1947.

Blesh, Rudi. *Shining Trumpets: A History of Jazz.* New York: Alfred A. Knopf, 1946. Revised ed., 1958.

Blesh, Rudi, and Harriet Janis. *They All Played Ragtime.* New York: Alfred A. Knopf, 1950. Reprinted in London: Sidgwick and Jackson, 1958. Reprinted in New York: Grove Press, 1959.

Boulton, David. *Jazz in Britain.* London: W. H. Allen, 1958.

Broonzy, William, as told to Yannick Bruynoghe. *Big Bill Blues.* London: Cassell, 1955.

Burley, Dan. *Dan Burley's Original Handbook of Harlem.* New York, 1944.

Carey, Dave, and Albert McCarthy. *The Directory of Recorded Jazz and Swing Music.* 6 vols. Fordingsbridge, Hampshire, Eng.: Delphic Press, 1949.

Carmichael, Hoagy. *The Stardust Road.* New York: Rinehart and Co., 1946.

Cerri, Livio. *Antologia del jazz.* Pisa: Nistri-Lischi, 1955.

————. *Il mondo del jazz.* Pisa: Nistri-Lischi, 1958.

Cerulli, Dom, Burt Korall, and Mort Nasatir. *The Jazz Word.* New York: Ballantine Books, 1960.

Charters, Samuel B. *Jazz: New Orleans, 1885-1957.* Belleville, N. J., and London: Walter C. Allen, 1958.

————. *The Country Blues.* New York: Rinehart and Co., 1959.

Cœuroy, André. *Histoire générale du jazz: Strette, hot, swing.* Paris: Éditions Denoël, 1942.

Condon, Eddie, and Richard Gehman (eds.). *Eddie Condon's Treasury of Jazz.* New York: Dial Press, 1956.

Condon, Eddie, as told to Thomas Sugrue. *We Called It Music.* New York: Henry Holt and Co., 1947.

Connor, Donald Russell. *B.G.—Off the Record.* Fairless Hills, Pa.: Gaildonna Publishers, 1958.

D.J.L. *Introducing Jazz; Talks to a Catholic Youth Club.* Toronto: St. Paul Publications, 1959.

Dauer, Alfons M., and Stephen Longstreet. *Knaur's Jazz Lexikon.* Munich and Zurich: Knaur, 1957.

Delaunay, Charles, with Kurt Mohr. *Hot discographie encyclopédique.* 3 vols. Paris: Éditions Jazz Disques, 1952——.

Delaunay, Charles, and eds. Walter E. Schaap and George Avakian. *New Hot Discography.* New York: Criterion Music Publishers, 1948.

De Toledano, Ralph (ed.). *Frontiers of Jazz.* New York: Oliver Durrell, 1947.

Dexter, Dave, Jr. *Jazz Cavalcade.* New York: Criterion Music Corp., 1946.

Dodds, Warren, as told to Larry Gara. *The Baby Dodds Story.* Los Angeles: Contemporary Press, 1959.

Donati, William. *Jazz americano del dopoguerra.* Milan: Schearz, 1958.

Esquire's Jazz Book. New York: Smith and Durrell, 1944-47.

Ewen, David. *Panorama of American Popular Music.* New York: Prentice-Hall, 1957.

Feather, Leonard. *The Book of Jazz.* New York: Horizon Press, 1957. Paperback ed., New York: Meridian Books, 1959.

——. *The Encyclopedia of Jazz.* New York: Horizon Press, 1955.

——. *The Encyclopedia Yearbook of Jazz.* New York: Horizon Press, 1957.

——. *Inside Be-bop.* New York: J. J. Robbins, 1949. Reissued as *Inside Jazz.* New York: Consolidated Music, 1955.

——. *Jazz; An Exciting Story.* . . . Los Angeles: Trend Books, 1959.

A Selected Jazz Bibliography

————. *The New Yearbook of Jazz.* New York: Horizon Press, 1957.

Finkelstein, Sidney. *Jazz: A People's Music.* New York: Citadel Press, 1948. German ed., *Jazz.* Stuttgart: G. Hatje, 1951.

Frankenstein, Alfred. *Syncopating Saxophones.* Chicago: R. O. Ballou, 1925.

Gammond, Peter (ed.). *The Decca Book of Jazz.* London: Mueller, 1958.

————— (ed.). *Duke Ellington: His Life and Music.* London: Phoenix House, 1958.

————— (ed.). *Duke Ellington: His Life and Music.* New York: Roy Publishers, 1960.

Garfield, Jane. *Books and Periodicals on Jazz from 1926 to 1932.* New York: Columbia University School of Library Science, June, 1933.

Gleason, Ralph (ed.). *Jam Session, an Anthology of Jazz.* New York: G. P. Putnam, 1958.

Goffin, Robert. *Aux frontières du jazz.* Paris: Éditions du Sagittaire, 1932.

————. *Horn of Plenty: The Story of Louis Armstrong.* New York: Allen, Towne and Heath, 1947. French ed., *Louis Armstrong: Le roi du jazz.* Paris: Seghers, 1947.

————. *Jazz, from the Congo to the Metropolitan.* New York: Doubleday and Co., 1944. French ed., *Histoire du jazz.* Montreal: Parizeau, 1945.

————. *Nouvelle histoire du jazz.* Brussels: L'Écran du monde, 1948.

————. *La Nouvelle-Orléans, capitale du jazz.* New York: Éditions de la Maison française, 1946.

Goldberg, Isaac. *George Gershwin: A Study in American Music.* New York: Simon and Schuster, 1931.

Goodman, Benny, and Irving Kolodin. *The Kingdom of Swing.* Harrisburg, Pa.: Stackpole and Co., 1939.

Grossman, William, and Jack W. Farrell. *The Heart of Jazz.* New York: New York University Press, 1955. Reprinted in London: Vision Press, 1958.

348

A Selected Jazz Bibliography

Guinle, Jorge. *Jazz Panorama*. Rio de Janeiro: Livraria Agir Editôra, 1953.

Handy, William C. *Father of the Blues: An Autobiography*. New York: Macmillan Co., 1941.

————, and Abbe Niles. *A Treasury of the Blues*. New York: C. Boni, 1949. First issued as *Blues: An Anthology*, in 1926. Reprinted in London: Sidgwick and Jackson, 1957.

Harris, Rex. *Jazz*. Marmondsworth, Middlesex: Penguin Books, 1952. Reprinted in New York: Grosset and Dunlap, 1955.

————, and Brian Rust. *Recorded Jazz: A Critical Guide*. Baltimore: Penguin Books, 1958.

Helander, Olle. *Jazzens väg en bok om blues och stomps*. . . . Stockholm: Nordiska musikförlaget, 1947.

Hendrikse, Dick. *Twintig Reuzen van de Jazz*. Haarlem: De Spaarnestad, 1959.

Hentoff, Nat, and Albert McCarthy (eds.). *Jazz*. New York: Rinehart and Co., 1959.

Heuvelmans, Bernard. *De la Bamboula au be-bop*. . . . Paris: Éditions de la main jetée, 1951.

Hobson, Wilder. *American Jazz Music*. New York: W. W. Norton and Co., 1939.

Hodeir, André. *Hommes et problèmes du jazz*. Paris: Au Portulan, chez Flammarion, 1954. English ed., *Jazz: Its Evolution and Essence*. New York: Grove Press, 1956. Paperback ed., 1957.

————. *Introduction à la musique de jazz*. Paris: Libraire Larousse, 1948.

————. *Le jazz, cet inconnu*. Paris: Collection harmoniques, 1945.

Holliday, Billie, as told to Bill Dufty. *Lady Sings the Blues*. New York: Doubleday and Co., 1956. London: Barrie Books, 1958. Paperback ed., New York: Popular Library, 1958.

Horricks, Raymond. *Count Basie and His Orchestra*. London: Victor Gollancz, 1957. Reprinted in New York: Citadel Press, 1958.

349

————, and others. *These Jazzmen of Our Time*. London: Victor Gollancz, 1959.

Hughes, Langston. *The First Book of Jazz*. New York: F. Watts, 1955.

Keepnews, Orrin, and Bill Grauer. *A Pictorial History of Jazz*. New York: Crown Publishers, 1955.

Kristensen, Sven Møller, John Jørgensen, Erik Wiedemann, and Børge Roger Henrichsen. *Jazzens Evem, Evad, Hvor: Politikens Jazzleksikon*. Copenhagen: Politikens forlag, 1953.

Lange, Horst H. *Die deutsche Jazz-Discgraphie*. Berlin: Ed. Bote und Bock, 1955.

Legrand, Gérard. *Puissances du jazz*. Paris: Arcanes, 1953.

Lomax, Alan. *Mister Jelly Roll*. New York: Duell, Sloan and Pearce, 1950. Paperback ed., New York: Grove Press, 1956. Reprinted in New York: Grosset and Dunlap, 1959. Reprinted in London: Pan Books, 1959.

Longstreet, Stephen. *The Real Jazz Old and New*. Baton Rouge: Louisiana State University Press, 1956.

McCarthy, Albert. *The Trumpet in Jazz*. London: Citizen Press, 1945.

Manone, Wingy, as told to Paul Vandervoort. *Trumpet on the Wing*. New York: Doubleday and Co., 1948.

Mehegan, John. *Jazz Improvisation*. New York: Watson-Guptill Publications, 1959.

Mendl, Robert W. S. *The Appeal of Jazz*. London: P. Allan, 1927.

Merriam, Alan P., with Robert J. Banford. *A Bibliography of Jazz*. Philadelphia: American Folklore Society, 1954.

Mezzrow, Milton, as told to Bernard Wolfe. *Really the Blues*. New York: Random House, 1946. French ed., *La Rage de Vivre*. Paris: Éditions Corrêa, 1951. Reprinted in Paris: Buchet-Chastel-Corrêa. 1957.

Morgan, Alun, and Raymond Horricks. *Modern Jazz*. London: Victor Gollancz, 1956.

Newton, Francis. *The Jazz Scene*. London: Macgibbon and Kee, 1959.

Ortiz, Oderigo N. R. *Estética del jazz*. Buenos Aires: Ricordi Americana, 1951.

――――. *Historia del jazz*. Buenos Aires: Ricordi Americana, 1952.

――――. *Perfiles del jazz*. Buenos Aires: Ricordi Americana, 1955.

Osgood, Henry. *So This Is Jazz*. Boston: Little, Brown and Co., 1926.

Panassié, Hugues. *Discographie critique des meilleurs disques de jazz*. 1920-51. Paris: Éditions Corrêa, 1951. New ed., Paris: R. Laffont, 1958.

――――. *Histoire des disques swing*. Geneva: Charles Grasset, 1944.

――――. *Le jazz hot*. Paris: Éditions Corrêa, 1934. English ed., *Hot Jazz*. New York: Witmark Music Publishers, 1936.

――――. *Petit guide pour une discothèque de jazz*. Paris: R. Laffont, 1955.

――――. *The Real Jazz*. New York: Smith and Durrell, 1942. Condensed French ed., *La musique de jazz et le swing*. Paris: Éditions Corrêa, 1945. Reprinted as *La veritable musique de jazz*. Paris: R. Laffont, 1946.

――――. *Les rois du jazz*. . . . 2 vols. Geneva: C. Grasset, 1944.

Panassié, Hugues, and Madeleine Gautier. *Dictionnaire du jazz*. Paris: R. Laffont, 1954. English ed., *Guide to Jazz*. Boston: Houghton Mifflin, 1956.

Patane, Giuseppe. *Be-bop ou pas be-bop? Ou, À la découverte du jazz*. Geneva: Editions Sabaudia, 1951.

Paul, Elliot H. *That Crazy American Music*. New York: Bobbs-Merrill, 1957. London: F. Muller, 1957.

Polillo, Arrigo. *Il jazz moderno: Musica del dopoguerra*. Milan: G. Ricordi Co., 1958.

Ramsey, Frederic, Jr. *A Guide to Longplay Jazz Records*. New York: Long Player Publications, 1954.

――――, and Charles Edward Smith (eds.). *Jazzmen*. New York: Harcourt, Brace and Co., 1939. Paperback ed., 1959.

Reisner, Robert George. *The Literature of Jazz: A Preliminary Bibliography.* New York: New York Public Library, 1954. Revised ed., 1959.

Sargeant, Winthrop. *Jazz: Hot and Hybrid.* New York: Arrow Editions, 1938. Revised ed., New York: E. P. Dutton and Co., 1946.

Schwerké, Irving. *Kings Jazz and David (Jazz et David rois).* Paris: Les Presses Modernes, 1927.

Shapiro, Nat, and Nat Hentoff (eds.). *Hear Me Talkin' to Ya.* New York: Rinehart and Co., 1955.

————. *The Jazz Makers.* New York: Rinehart and Co., 1957. Paperback ed., New York: Grove Press, 1958.

Shaw, Artie. *The Trouble with Cinderella.* New York: Farrar, Straus and Young, 1952.

Smith, Charles Edward, Frederic Ramsey, Jr., and others. *The Jazz Record Book.* New York: Smith and Durrell, 1942.

Spaeth, Sigmund. *A History of Popular Music in America.* New York: Random House, 1948.

Stearns, Marshall. *The Story of Jazz.* New York: Oxford University Press, 1956. Paperback ed., New York: New American Library, 1958.

Terkel, Studs. *Giants of Jazz.* New York: Crowell Publishers, 1957.

Testoni, Gian Carlo, Arrigo Polillo, Giuseppe Barazzetta, Roberto Leydi, and Pino Maffei. *Enciclopedia del jazz.* Milan: Messaggerie musicali, 1953.

Traill, Sinclair (ed.). *Concerning Jazz.* London: Faber and Faber, 1957. Reprinted in Philadelphia: Dufour Editions, 1958.

————. *Play That Music.* London: Faber and Faber, 1956.

Traill, Sinclair, and Gerald Lascelles (eds.). *Just Jazz.* London: Press Davies, 1957.

Twittenhoff, Wilhelm. *Jugend und Jazz: Ein Beitrag zur Klärung.* Mainz: Verlag Junge Musik, 1953.

Tyrmand, Leopold. *U Brzegów jazzu.* Cracow: Polskie Wydawnictwo Muzyczne, 1957.

A Selected Jazz Bibliography

Ulanov, Barry. *Duke Ellington.* New York: Creative Age, 1946. Spanish ed., Buenos Aires: Editorial Estuardo, 1946.

———. *Handbook of Jazz.* New York: Viking Press, 1957. Paperback ed., New York: Viking Press, 1959.

———. *A History of Jazz in America.* New York: Viking Press, 1952.

Vallee, Rudy. *Vagabond Dreams Come True.* New York: E. P. Dutton and Co., 1930.

Wareing, Charles H., and George Barlick. *Bugles for Beiderbecke.* London: Sidgwick and Jackson, 1958.

Waters, Ethel, as told to Charles Samuels. *His Eye Is on the Sparrow.* New York: Doubleday and Co., 1951. Paperback ed., New York: Bantam Books, 1952.

Whiteman, Paul, and Mary Margaret McBride. *Jazz.* New York: J. H. Sears, 1926.

Williams, Martin (ed.). *The Art of Jazz; Essays on the Nature and Development of Jazz.* New York: Oxford University Press, 1959.

Wilson, John S. *The Collector's Jazz: Traditional and Swing.* New York: J. B. Lippincott Co., 1958.

———. *The Collectors Jazz: Modern.* New York: J. B. Lippincott Co., 1959.

ARTICLES CITED

Adler, Guido. "Style-Criticism," *Musical Quarterly,* XX (April, 1934), 172.

Balliett, Whitney. "Celebration for the Duke," *Saturday Review,* XXXIX (May 12, 1956), 30.

———. "Kenton: Artistry in Limbo," *Saturday Review,* XXXVIII (April 30, 1955), 56.

———. "The Measure of 'Bird,'" *Saturday Review,* XXXIX (March 17, 1956), 34.

Borneman, Ernest. "The Jazz Cult," in two parts, *Harper's,* CXCIV (February-March, 1947), 142, 261.

Bowles, Paul. "Once Again, le Jazz Hot," *Modern Music*, XX (January, 1943), 140.

Boyer, Richard. "Bebop," *New Yorker*, XXIV (July 3, 1948), 28.

Copland, Aaron. "A Modernist Defends Modern Music," *New York Times*, December 25, 1949.

Ellison, Ralph. "The Charlie Christian Story," *Saturday Review*, XLI (May 17, 1958), 43.

Gara, Larry. "Baby Dodds," *Jazz Journal*, May-December, 1955.

Gleason, Ralph J. "Brubeck," *Down Beat*, XXIV (September 5, 1957), 16.

Hallock, Ted. "Report," *Down Beat*, XVI (July 1, 1949), 13.

Hentoff, Nat. "Jimmy Giuffre: Blues in Counterpoint," *Saturday Review*, XL (July 13, 1957), 37.

———. "The Post-bop Legitimacy of Modern Jazz," *Reporter*, XVIII (February 6, 1958), 39.

———. "Reading the Blues," *Nation*, CLXXXVI (March 15, 1958), 240.

Hobson, Wilder. "The Amen Corner," *Saturday Review*, XLI (January 25, 1958), 59.

Larrabee, Eric. "Jazz Notes," *Harper's*, CCXVI (May, 1958), 96.

Laubenstein, P. F. "Jazz—Debit and Credit," *Musical Quarterly*, XV (October, 1929), 606.

Mehegan, John. "The ABC of the New Jazz," *Saturday Review*, XXXIX (November 10, 1956), 34.

Millstein, Gilbert. "Apostle of Swing," *New York Times Magazine*, April 19, 1953.

Russell, Ross. "Bebop," *Record Changer*, VIII (April, 1949), 20.

———. "Be-bop Instrumentation," *Record Changer*, VII (November, 1948), 23.

Schuller, Gunther. "The Future of Form in Jazz," *Saturday Review*, XL (January 12, 1957), 62.

Seldes, Gilbert. "No More Swing?" *Scribner's*, C (November, 1936), 70.

A Selected Jazz Bibliography

Smith, Charles E. "Review," *New Republic*, XCIV (February 16, 1938), 39.

Thomson, Virgil. "Swing Music," *Modern Music*, XIII (May, 1936), 17.

Tynan, John. "Teagarden Talks," *Down Beat*, XXIV (March 6, 1957), 19.

Ulanov, Barry. "The Jukes Take Over Swing," *American Mercury*, LI (October, 1940), 172.

Wilson, John S. "Forty Years in the Groove," *High Fidelity Magazine*, VII (February, 1957), 45.

―――. "Record Review," *New York Times*, March 30, 1958.

―――. "Record Review," *High Fidelity Magazine*, VII (August, 1957), 70.

PERIODICALS

Australian Jazz Quarterly (Melbourne)
Bulletin du Hot Club de France (Toulouse)
Bulletin du Hot Club de Genève (Geneva)
Coda (Toronto)
Der Drummer (Frankfort am Main)
Disc (London)
Down Beat (Chicago)
Drum (Johannesburg)
Estrad (Stockholm)
Goodchild's Jazz Bulletin (Nottingham)
Hot Club of Japan Bulletin (Tokyo)
International Discophile (Los Angeles)
Jazz (Marseilles)
Jazz (Waly Jagiellonskie, Poland)
Jazz: A Quarterly of American Music (San Francisco)
Jazzbladid (Reykjavik)
Jazz-Bulletin (Basel)
Jazz di Ieri e di Oggi (Florence)
Jazz-Echo (Hamburg)
Jazz Hot (Paris)

A Selected Jazz Bibliography

Jazz Journal (London)
Jazz Magazine (Buenos Aires)
Jazz Magazine (Paris)
Jazzmania (Buenos Aires)
Jazz Monthly (Cornwall, Eng.)
Jazz Music (Union, N. J.)
Jazz Musik (Bremen)
Jazz News (London)
Jazz Notes (Indianapolis)
Jazz Podium (Stuttgart)
Jazz Review (New York)
Jazz Report (St. Louis)
Jazz Statistics (Los Angeles)
Matrix (London)
Melody Maker (London)
Metronome (New York)
Musica Jazz (Milan)
Musikrevue (Copenhagen)
New Musical Express (London)
Orkester Journalen (Stockholm)
Record Changer (New York)
Record Mirror (London)
Record Research (Brooklyn)
Rhythme (Eindhoven, Holland)
Rytmia (Helsinki)
Schlagzeug (Berlin)
Second Line (New Orleans)
Theme (Hollywood)

INDEX

Aaronson, Irving, 232
African rhythm, 34, 37
Alexander, Van, 108
Alexander, Willard, 235, 241
Armstrong, Lil Hardin, 158, 159, 181, 183, 186, 187, 214
Armstrong, Louis, 72, 78, 79, 80, 126, 127, 130, 138, 140, 158-65 *passim*, 176, 179-84 *passim*, 185-88, 190-93, 207-8, 217-18, 221-22, 255-56
Auld, Georgie, 229
Austin High School, 143, 192, 193

Bagley, Don, 311
Bailey, Buster, 58, 187, 188, 197
Baker, Chet, 311
Ballard, Red, 230, 231
Barber, John, 280, 311
Barnet, Charlie, 206, 239, 266
Bartók, Béla, 50, 92, 93, 94
Basie, William "Count," 126, 140, 141, 195, 225, 240-43, 245, 248-53 *passim*, 314
Bauduc, Ray, 229
Bauer, Billy, 277, 313
Bebop. *See* Bop
Bechet, Sidney, 156, 157, 163, 182
Beiderbecke, Bix, 82, 193, 214
Berigan, Bunny, 229
Berlin, Irving, 14, 16
Berry, Chu, 137, 197, 229, 242
Bigard, Barney, 199, 219, 220
Big bands, 224-29, 236, 238-39, 254,

256-57, 275-78, 284
Blakey, Art, 273
Blue Devils, 241
Blues, 158, 170-71, 172, 176-77, 180-82, 209, 215-16, 245-46, 260, 286, 295, 297, 315-16; form of, 41, 60; harmony of, 73, 98
Blues scale, 118-19, 120, 121
Blue tonality, 119
Bolden, Buddy, 57, 139, 156, 157
Bolden's Ragtime Band, 156, 157
Bop: characteristics of, 109; evolution of, 254-61; rhythm in, 257, 273, 289, 298-99; harmony in, 260, 267, 295, 297-98, 302; instrumentation of, 287; melody in, 289, 302-3; form in, 291-95, 299-304
Bothwell, Johnny, 277
Boyd, Nelson, 280
Brass bands, 57, 58. *See also under individual names*
Braud, Wellman, 199, 219
Brookmeyer, Bob, 284, 311
Brown, Clifford, 313
Brown, Les, 254
Brown, Ray, 274
Brown, Tom, 163, 165
Brown, Vernon, 230, 231
Brown's Dixieland Jass Band, 164
Brubeck, Dave, 80, 129, 285, 288, 311
Burns, Ralph, 276, 311
Burton, Vic, 194
Byas, Don, 242, 248

357

Index

Calloway, Cab, 229, 240, 266
Carey, Mutt "Papa," 72, 156
Carney, Harry, 199, 203, 219
Carpenter, Ike, 311
Carroll, Barbara, 311
Carter, Bennie, 195, 197, 236, 240, 266
Casa Loma, 227-28
Chaloff, Serge, 282
Chambers, Elmer, 187
Charles, Teddy, 310
Chicago style, 125-26, 143, 192. See also New Orleans style
Chord symbols, 111
Christian, Buddy, 160
Christian, Charlie, 238, 258, 262-65, 273
Clark, Dick, 230, 231
Clarke, Kenny, 258, 260, 273, 280, 286
Clayton, Buck, 242, 248, 251
Clinton, Larry, 225
Club Alabam Orchestra, 187, 204
Cohn, Al, 277, 283
Cole, Cozy, 229
Coles, June, 197
Collins, Addison, 280
Collins, Dick, 311
Collins, Shad, 242
Collins, Wallace, 157
Columbus Brass Band, 155
Condon, Eddie, 193
Cook's Dreamland Orchestra, 164, 204, 210
Cool jazz, 275; evolution of, 279-86; instrumentation of, 280, 286-91. See also Bop
Cotton Club Orchestra, 199
Cotton Pickers, 195
Counce, Curtis, 313
Creole, 151-52, 156, 157
Creole Jazz Band, 125, 158-65, 179-84 passim, 186, 187, 190. See also Oliver, Joseph "King"
Criticism. See Jazz criticism
Crosby, Bob, 239
Cuffey, Ed, 242
Cugat, Xavier, 223

Dameron, Tadd, 258, 260, 273
Damrosch, Walter, 19
Davis, Miles, 73, 126, 140, 270, 275, 279-81, 310
Davison, Wild Bill, 183
DeFranco, Buddy, 274
DeParis, Wilbur, 183

DePew, Bill, 230, 231
Desmond, Paul, 43, 287, 311
Diamond Stone Brass Band, 155
Dickerson, Carroll, 192
Dixieland, 125, 165, 192, 209, 227, 231, 232, 233, 239; resurgence of, 75. See also New Orleans style
Dixon, Charlie, 187, 188
Dodds, Johnny, 38, 158, 159, 160, 179, 181-82, 183, 192
Dodds, Warren "Baby," 158, 159, 162, 163, 181, 183
Dominguez, Paul, 157
Dorham, Kenny, 275
Dorsey, Jimmy, 194, 239, 266
Dorsey, Tommy, 195, 239, 254
Dorsey Brothers, 227, 239
Down Beat: jazz writing in, 4-6
Duhé, Lawrence, 161
Duncan, Isadora, 18
Dunham, Sonny, 254
Dutrey, Honore, 158, 182, 183
Duvivier, George, 274

Eagle Band, 150, 156, 160
Eckstine, Billy, 266, 270
Edison, Harry, 242, 248
Edwards, Eddie, 164
Eldridge, Roy, 48, 265, 273
Ellington, Edward Kennedy "Duke," 126, 140, 144-45, 179, 185, 198-202, 227, 240, 266, 314
Elliot, Don, 311
Ellis, Herb, 311
Elman, Ziggy, 230, 231
Escudero, Bobbie, 187
Evans, Gil, 279
Evans, Herschel, 242, 243
Excelsior Band, 155, 156

Fenton, Nick, 258
Finckle, Eddie, 277
Ford, Henry, 18
Form, 41, 42, 61, 65, 67, 69. See also Blues, form of
Freeman, Bud, 192, 229
Friars Society Orchestra, 164
Fuller, Gil, 311, 312

Garner, Erroll, 141
Gershwin, George, 14, 26, 27
Getz, Stan, 43, 277, 283
Gibbs, Terry, 274
Gifford, Gene, 228

Index

Gillespie, Dizzy, 21, 43, 82, 126, 130, 140, 255, 258, 260, 261, 265-68, 270, 273, 274, 277, 299-304
Gilmore, Patrick, 149-50
Giuffre, Jimmy, 37, 262, 277, 284, 311, 319-20
Goffin, Robert, 29, 30
Goldkette, Jean, 231
Goodie, Frank "Big Boy," 127
Goodman, Benny, 21, 43, 78, 79, 80, 82, 126, 127, 129, 140, 193, 195, 198, 206, 222, 223-42 passim, 252-53
Goodman, Harry, 230, 231
Graas, John, 313
Gray, Glen, 228
Green, Charlie "Big," 187
Green, Freddie, 242, 243
Greer, Sonny, 198, 199, 219
Griffin, Gordon "Chris," 230, 231
Gryce, Gigi, 311
Guy, Freddy, 199, 200, 219
Guy, Joe, 258

Haig, Al, 272, 274, 280
Hall, Edmond, 58
Hamilton, Chico, 287
Hammond, John, 233, 241, 242, 262, 263
Hampton, Lionel, 238, 240
Handy, George, 277, 310
Handy, W. C., 189
Hard bop, 279, 283
Hardwick, Toby, 198
Harmonic rhythm, 97-99, 100, 101
Harmony, 85, 106, 107-21 passim; evolution of, 102-6. See also individual periods
Harris, Benny, 275, 277
Harris, Bill, 277
Harrison, Jimmy, 197
Hart, Clyde, 48
Hawkins, Coleman, 140, 187, 188, 196, 197, 203, 262, 283
Hawkins, Erskine, 240
Heard, J. C., 270
Heath, Percy, 272, 274, 286
Hefti, Neal, 276
Henderson, Fletcher, 27, 78, 126, 140, 185-91, 196-98, 204-6, 222, 227, 236-37, 240, 242
Henderson, Horace, 199, 236
Henderson, Leora, 197, 222
Herman, Woody, 239, 266, 275-77

Heterophony, 166-70
Higgenbotham, J. C., 197
Hill, Teddy, 258, 265, 273
Himber, Richard, 225
Hines, Earl, 192, 203, 227, 254, 266, 267, 270
Hinton, Milt, 82
Hodeir, André, 311
Hodges, Johnny, 199, 219
Holman, Bill, 311
Hyman, Dick, 310

Imperial Band, 150, 155
Improvisation: collective, 30-45 passim, 47, 74, 75, 76, 131, 186, 315, 316-18; free and controlled, 47, 48, 49; solo, 47, 75, 131, 140, 186, 289, 292-94, 303; origins of, 50-51; development of, 51-53, 54-56; background for, 77, 78, 79
Indian Brass Band, 155
Intonation, 92, 93. See also Pitch

Jackson, Milt, 274, 277, 286, 311
James, Harry, 230, 231, 232, 239, 254
Jazz: linguistic origin of, 10-11; definition of, 11, 24, 25, 26-29, 31-45; harmonic aspects of, 33-45 passim, 60, 61; melodic aspects of, 33-45 passim; rhythmic aspects of, 33-45 passim; evolution of, 157
Jazz Age, 14, 126, 203
Jazz: A Quarterly of American Music, 141
Jazz criticism: problems of, 8, 9, 17; in nonjazz books, 12, 13; in daily press, 17-22; in Europe, 19-22; by educators, 21-22. See also Down Beat
Jazz Review, 141
Jefferson, Hilton, 229
Jenkins, Freddie, 199, 219
Jenkins, Gordon, 236
Jim Crowism, 255
Johnson, Bill, 156, 158, 159, 161, 162, 179
Johnson, Bunk, 57, 156
Johnson, Charlie, 179
Johnson, J. J., 280, 281
Jones, Isham, 227, 233
Jones, Jo, 241, 242
Jones, Quincy, 311, 312
Jones, Richard M., 57
Jones, Thad, 82

Index

Kansas City: activities in, 130, 241, 269; bands around, 195-96
Katz, Dick, 311
Kay, Connie, 286
Kenton, Stan, 128-29, 275-76
Kentucky Club Orchestra, 205
Keppard, Freddie, 139, 156, 157, 160, 164
Killian, Al, 242, 248
Kincaide, Dean, 236
Kirby, John, 197, 219
Kirk, Andy, 227, 240, 270
Klein, Manny, 195
Koenig, George, 230
Konitz, Lee, 276, 280, 285, 293-94, 311, 313
Krupa, Gene, 195, 230, 231, 238, 239, 254, 307

Laine, George "Papa," 156, 164
Lamond, Don, 311
Lang, Eddie, 194
Lannigan, Jim, 192
LaPorta, John, 277
LaRocca, Nick, 10, 156, 164, 165, 192
Leonard, Harvey, 310
Lesberg, Jack, 183
Levey, Stan, 273
Lewis, Ed, 242, 248
Lewis, John, 81, 262, 280, 285-86, 291-92. See also Modern Jazz Quartet
Lewis, Ted, 232
Livingston, Fud, 195, 236
Lopez, Vincent, 193
Lunceford, Jimmy, 140, 225, 227, 240

McEachern, Murray, 230, 231
Macero, Teo, 310
McGhee, Howard, 275
Machito, 272
McKenzie-Condon Chicagoans, 232
McKibbon, Al, 280
McKinney, William, 195
McPartland, Dick, 192
McPartland, Jimmy, 192
McPartland, Marian, 312
McShann, Jay, 267, 269
Magnolia Band, 156, 160
Mandel, Johnny, 311
Mann, Herbie, 287
Manne, Shelly, 276, 277
Marching bands, 149-52, 154-57, 176. See also Brass bands
Mares, Paul, 164, 192

Mariano, Charles, 312
Marmarosa, Dodo, 277
Marsh, Warne, 313
Marshall, Kaiser, 187, 197
Matthews, Mat, 287
Mehegan, John, 306, 310
Melody, 85, 112, 113. See also individual periods
Miley, Bubber, 199
Miller, Eddie, 229
Miller, Glenn, 195, 239
Millinder, Lucky, 261, 266
Mills, Irving, 198
Mingus, Charlie, 294, 313
Minor, Dan, 241, 242
Minton, Henry, 258
Minton's, 258-59, 261-62, 266, 269
Modal scales, 103, 121, 295, 321
Modern jazz. See Bop; Cool jazz
Modern Jazz Quartet, 42, 140, 286, 291, 292. See also Lewis, John
Mole, Miff, 195
Mondello, Toots, 229, 230, 231
Monk, Thelonious, 126, 140, 258, 259, 260, 261-62
Montrose, Jack, 312
Morton, Benny, 197, 242
Morton, Jelly Roll, 139, 144-45, 155, 164, 177
Moten, Bennie, 195, 241
Mulligan, Gerry, 140, 279, 280-82, 287
Mundy, Jimmy, 236, 238
Murphy, Spud, 236, 313
Murray, Kel, 223
Musso, Vido, 230, 231, 232

Nanton, Tricky Sam, 199, 200, 219, 221
Navarro, Fats, 275
Negro slavery: emergence from, 152-55
Nelson, Louis "Big Eye," 156
Newborn, Phineas, 81
New Orleans Feetwarmers, 182
New Orleans Rhythm Kings, 143, 164, 192, 193, 233
New Orleans style: instrumentation in, 150, 165-70; form in, 170-73, 180-82; melody in, 173-75; harmony of, 175; rhythm in, 177-78
Nichols, Red, 194-95, 232
Niehaus, Lennie, 312
Nonharmonic tones, 111-17
Noone, Jimmie, 179

Index

Norvo, Red, 252, 270
Notation: evolution of, 85-90; of special effects, 90, 91, 92; of chords, 111
Nunez, Alcide "Yellow," 164

Oliver, Joseph "King," 125, 139, 155, 156, 158-65, 179-84 *passim*, 186, 190, 191, 199. *See also* Creole Jazz Band
Oliver, Sy, 240
Olivier's Band, 156
Olsen, George, 225
Olympia Band, 150, 156, 160
Onward Brass Band, 155, 160
Original Creole Band, 156, 161
Original Dixieland Jazz Band, 10, 156, 164, 192, 209
Ory, Kid, 38, 160, 172
Overton, Hall, 312

Page, Walter, 241, 242
Paich, Marty, 312
Parker, Charlie, 73, 80, 126, 127, 140, 258, 260, 265, 266, 268-73, 274
Pasquall, Don, 197
Peerless Brass Band, 155
Peiffer, Bernard, 312
Pepper, Art, 276
Perez, Immanuel, 155, 157, 160, 163
Pettiford, Oscar, 274, 277
Peyton's Symphonic Syncopators, 183
Phillips, Flip, 270
Phonograph recordings, 163, 179, 194, 195
Pianists (modern), 285
Picou, Alphonse, 57, 150-51, 152, 155, 156
Piron, A. J., 188
Pitch, 92, 93
Pollack, Ben, 227, 232, 233, 239
Polyphony, 166-70
Popular music, 14, 15, 16, 210, 225-28, 256-57
Powell, Bud, 126, 258, 274
Powell, Mel, 262, 310
Powell, Specs, 270
Preswing: instrumentation of, 202-9; forms in, 209-11, 219-22; harmony in, 211-16; melody in, 212-13; rhythm in, 216-19
Previn, André, 312
Procope, Russell, 197

Progressive jazz, 129, 275-79
Progressives, 29, 74-76, 307

Quebec, Ike, 229

Raeburn, Boyd, 275, 277-78
Ragas, Henry, 164
Rags, 170, 171, 209
Ragtime, 156, 158, 177
Randolph, Popsie, 235
Rapollo, Leon, 233
Redman, Don, 187, 188, 189, 190, 194, 195, 202, 203, 204, 206, 214, 227
Reinhardt, Django, 263
Reliance Brass Band, 156
Rena, Kid, 151-52
Reuss, Allan, 230, 231
Rhythm, 85, 93, 94-98, 99, 101. *See also individual periods*
Rich, Buddy, 229
Riff, 40, 206, 207-8, 245, 288
Roach, Max, 260, 270, 272, 273, 280
Robechaux, John, 155
Roberts, Caughey, 248
Robertson, Zue, 160
Robinson, Ed, 152
Robinson, Eli, 248
Rodney, Red, 275
Rogers, Buddy, 232
Rogers, Shorty, 277, 283-84, 312
Rollini, Adrian, 195
Rollini, Art, 230, 231
Rugolo, Pete, 275
Rushing, Jimmy, 241
Russell, Curley, 270
Russell, George, 312
Russell, Luis, 199
Russell, Pee Wee, 43, 193
Russin, Babe, 229
Russo, Bill, 312

Safranski, Eddie, 276
St. Cyr, Johnny, 71
St. Joseph Brass Band, 155
Sampson, Edgar, 197, 229, 236
Sbarbaro, Tony, 164
Schertzer, Hymie, 229, 230, 231
Schoenberg, Arnold, 138, 145
Schuller, Gunther, 141, 280, 294-95
Schulman, Joe, 280
Schutt, Arthur, 194
Scott, Howard, 187
Scott, Robert, 248

Scott, Tony, 43, 137, 284
Shank, Bud, 287
Shaw, Artie, 225, 229, 239
Shields, Larry, 164, 165
Siegelstein, Sandy, 280
Sims, Zoot, 283
Sissle, Noble, 270
Smith, Bessie, 189
Smith, Jimmy, 287
Smith, Joe, 195
Smith, Russell, 197
Smith, Stuff, 71
Smith, Tab, 242
Snowden, Elmer, 198
Sousa, John Philip, 148-49, 150, 151
"Spasm" instruments, 159
Stacy, Jess, 230, 231, 232
Stark, Bobby, 197
Steele, Porter, 150
Stewart, Rex, 190, 195, 197
Stewart, Slam, 270
Stomps, 17, 209
Storyville, 156, 158, 160
Stravinsky, Igor, 307-9
Strayhorn, Billy, 200
Style: evolution of, 123; character-
 istics of, 123, 134-35; classifica-
 tions of, 125, 130-32; analysis of,
 137; criticism of, 141
Sullivan, Joe, 193
Superior Band, 150, 156
Sutton, Ralph, 183
Swing: definition of, 24, 27, 28, 29;
 form in, 244-45, 248-52; melody in,
 245; harmony of, 245-46; instru-
 mentation of, 243-44; rhythm in,
 246-47
Syncopation, 97, 98. *See also* Rhythm

Tate, Buddy, 242, 243, 248
Tate, Erskine, 192
Tatum, Art, 129, 140
Taylor, Billy, 312
Taylor, Cecil, 141
Teagarden, Jack, 72, 195
Teschemacher, Frank, 192
Tilton, Martha, 230
Tio, Lorenzo, 155, 157, 160, 199

Tio, Louis, 155
Tizol, Juan, 199, 219
Tjader, Cal, 312
Tone quality, 43, 44. *See also* Pitch
Tough, Dave, 193, 195, 229
Traditionalists, 29, 30, 74-76, 307
Tristano, Lennie, 81, 285, 313
Trumbauer, Frankie, 231
Tucker, Snakehips, 219

Vallee, Rudy, 203
Ventura, Charlie, 287
Venuti, Joe, 195

Waller, Fats, 195, 198
Wallington, George, 274
Ward, Helen, 230
Warren, Earl, 242, 248
Warrington, Johnny, 107
Washington, Jack, 242, 248
Washingtonians, 205
Waters, Ethel, 78, 189
Watkins, Julius, 311
Webb, Chick, 25, 199, 227, 240
Webster, Ben, 197, 229
Weiss, Sid, 252
Wells, Dickie, 197, 242, 248
Wess, Frank, 287
West Coast jazz, 281, 283, 306
Wettling, George, 183, 193, 229
Whetsel, Arthur, 198, 199, 219
Whiteman, Paul, 14, 16, 27, 193-94,
 209, 227
Wilber, Bob, 313
Wilkins, Ernie, 312
Williams, Claiborne, 155
Williams, Cootie, 27, 199, 219, 220,
 221, 270
Williams, Mary Lou, 262
Wilson, Teddy, 79, 238, 239, 252, 270
Winding, Kai, 276, 280, 281
Wolverines, 192, 193
Woods, Phil, 313

Young, Lester, 242, 243, 264, 282-83
Young, Trummy, 277

Zino, 160